PANCHAKA
IN
INDIAN MUSIC

Panchaka in Indian Music

Dr. P. V. Bose

Raj Publications
New Delhi - 110002 (INDIA)

Panchaka in Indian Music

₹ 950

2018

ISBN 978-81-86208-74-8

Published by : **Raj Publications**
108, 4855/24, Ansari Road,
Daryaganj, New Delhi - 110002
Tel. : 011- 23250939, 9811010939
E-mail- rajpublications@yahoo.co.in

Laser Typesetting : Sky Computers, Delhi-110 009

Printed at : G S Offset, Delhi

Contents

Preface

Treatises on Indian music on its exhibition have given various versions about the origin, development and greatness of music. As the *Sangita damodara* classifies in it about its concept of music by a sloka:

> "Vaidikam yāga kāryēshu prayōgāt mōkshadāyakam
> Lawkīkam raktimadhanat kēvalam lōka ranjakam
> Vaidīkam yadhi sangītam tammargamiti kathyate
> Loukīkam gīta makhyatam desiti bhwri gāyakaih"

('Vaidika' music is meant to be rendered during 'yagas' thus it leads man to salvation where as the 'loulika' music leads man only to the worldly pleasure)

Sarangadeva in his 'Sangita ratnakara' has given a different opinion about music as he says "gītam vādyam tatha Nriṭtam trayam sangīta muchyatē"

It gives us an idea that music is a combination of gitam (song), Vadyam (instrument) and Nrittam (Dance).

The Relevance of Panchaka in Music:

According to *sangita ratnakara*, there are five different stages through which the breath has to go before it is converted into a nada (musical sound). The breath starts its process through Nābhi (Navel), Hrudaya (Heart), Khanḍa (Throat), Murdhav (Head) and Asya (Nose). The sloka below establishes this fact.

> "Ātma vivakshā manōgam manah pracaryatemanah
>
> Dēhastham vāhni mahanti SA prerayati mārutam
>
> Brahma gandhi stithah sōtha kramadurdhava pathe charan
>
> Nābhi hruṭ khanta murdhasvēshva virbhavayati dvānim"
>
> (Sangita ratnakara)

It is believed according to Vedas "Tannada panchakam Sambhoh panchavaktra samud bhavam" i.e., the musical sound (Nada) that emerges from the five stages of the body is originated from the five faces of the Lord Siva. It is interesting to note that our great composers like Tyagaraja have mentioned about this, as it is evident from their compositions eg. Tyagaraja in his song 'Nāda tanumanisam' in the rag chittaranjini has described nada as 'Sadyo-jatadi pancha vaktraja sa ri ga ma pa dha ni Vara sapta swara'.

According to the Hindu belief, the Lord Siva has created five planets (grahas) from his five faces such as: Surya, chandra, Ankaraka, Guru and Sukra and that the five svaras have emerged from these five planets.

The nada is divided into five such as Sukshmam, Ati sukshmam, Vyaktam, Avyaktam and Kritrimam. The 'Sangita makarandam' further categorizes the Ahata nada into five:

> "Syo pyahatah pancha vidhō nāda stu pari kirtitah
>
> Nakha vayūja charniạmi lōha sarirajastatha
>
> Nakham vinadayah proktāh vamsyadya vāyu purakah
>
> Charmanicha miudamgadyāh lohastaladaya statha
>
> Deha nadena to yukta nadah pancha irdhah smrutah"

The Ahata nada is grouped under five such as Nakhajam, Vayujam, Chasmajam, Lohajam and sarirajam.

The pentatonic scale of Chinese music and the audava' are identical in character as the Chinese music also corresponds the five notes to the five natural agents:

1.	Kung (tonic)	=	Centre of the Earth
2.	Shang (Second)	=	Metal and autumn
3.	Kyo (major third)	=	Wood and spring
4.	Yu (Sixth)	=	Water & Winter
5.	Chi (fifth)	=	Five and summer.

This establishes that the origin of music is connected with the five elements.

It is amazing that the Panchaka in some form or the other has manifested in various branches of knowledge like, Philosophy, Mythology, Literature, Religion, Geography, Painting, and Dance etc.

The method adopted for collecting materials for this work was mainly based on the following:

1. A study of manuscripts on the subject found in various libraries and from personal collections.
2. Reference of lakshana grandhas (treatises) on music, Journals, Magazines and other books on the subject
3. Interviews with experts, artists, teachers and musicologists in the field.

In this book I have made an attempt to establish the significance of Panchaka in various fields and how it has manifested in different forms in the field of music and study the Ghana raga panchaka and their origin, development and manifestation in the Karnatic musical forms.

The Ghana Raga Panchaka

The Ghana ragas have a history of behind them. The five ragas are known as the 'Ghana raga panchakam' in the Vina sampradaya and it has been the practice for player on the Vina to play tanam in these ragas in the given order viz. Nata, Gaula, Arabhi, Varali and Sri. Various reasons are found in musical treatises for these five ragas being called 'Ghana' ragas. For instance, some of the subtle srutis of Karnatic music figure in them. The raga Nata contains the Shatsruti Rishabha and Dhaivata; Gaula contains the Eka Sruti Rishabha (which is lower than the Suddha Rishabha). Arabhi contains the *alpa prayogas* of Gandhara and Nishada and Varali contains the Suddha Gandhara and a particularly sharp Madhyama known as the "Varali Mahyama". Ragas like Nata and Arabhi are ancient ragas, which figure among the panns of Tamil Nadu in which Tevaram and the Divyaprabandha were being sung. Later, the Vina players developed tanam in these ragas to a remarkable degree of excellence and elaboration. Sri Raga is an auspicious raga and has a soothing effect especially after the shrill notes of the preceding Varali.

—— **Dr. P. V. Bose**

1

The Magical "Five"

The greatness of the number five is very significant in various fields like dance, literature, painting, theatre, mythology, geography, philosophy, theology, etc.

The performing arts in India are preserved mostly by transmitting them directly to the pupil from the teacher. Although we have a rich data concerning performing arts that existed in temples, it is difficult to assess the definite character and form of the theatre of those times. We come across terms like *Akamarga*, (way of *akam*), *Kutuvilakku* (Pot lamp) in the *Sangam* literature.

A literary base of various traditions of performing arts of Chola period can be traced in texts like *Pancha marabhu** . The *Pancha marabhu* dates from the end of ninth century A.D. categorizes performing arts into five namely: 1. *Isai.* (music), 2. *Vachiya* (Words) 3. *Nrutta* (dance), 4. *Abhinaya* (Mime). 5. *Tala marabhu* (Rhythm). The third among the five divisions, *nritta* is subdivided into 1. *Nritta vagai* (types of dances), 2. *Tandava* (masculine dance). 3. *Akamarga porul* (Subject matter of the

---

*'**Pancha Marabu** 'by Arivanaar-which was also written in 500 B.C almost the same time as Tholkaapiyam – describes in detail about music and dance. It talks about various hand gestures, *abhinaya, kooththu, naatyam.* It also describes the letters to be used for *jathis- tha,thi,tho,ki,ki*.

way of akam). 4. *Alankara porul* (rhythmic phrases), 5. *Venpa* (Metre). 6. *Kuttila karam* (Script for drama).

Panchaka and Dance

The *Pancha murthy kavuthvam*

There existed various rituals in connection with the development of culture and performing arts. One example for an important ritual that is shared by both the village and the temple is the custom of propitiating evil spirits and forces that are believed to be presiding or roaming about there. This must be done before the commencement of the festival and it is also performed symbolically as part of the daily worship. This is called *balidanam* i.e., gift of sacrifice to the *bali pita.* It comprised of the offering of rice with *kumkum* and fluid milk accompanied by suitable mantra. Beating of the drum and sometimes other instruments and dancing comprised of compositions relating to the God who is to be propitiated, the dance pieces are known as *Kavuthuvams* They were practiced by the *devadasis* of the nineteenth century. The custom became obsolete by the end of the first half of the twentieth century.

The important two sets of *kavuthuvums** are the *navasandhi kavuthuvums* (phrases for nine cardinal points), and *pancha murthy kavuthuvum* (phrases of five manifestations). In ancient ritual- magic compositions, which are performed together with *pancha murthy kavuthuvum* followed by classical, devotional and literary compositions are found in the performances of olden temples.

Panchaka and Mythology

The Concept of *Pancha Devata*

To the common man, however with the plan of life chalked out for his life, the

*ILango AdigaL in his *Silappathigaaram* (500 B.C) describes the **Kavuththuvum**-an item that is performed in the beginning to ward off evil forces-and then the 11 different dances called as **'Pathinoru aadal'**.

clash between tradition and innovation did not matter much. The *puranas* were the guiding spirit to him and the code of conduct for him was based on these *puranas.* In the earlier period, the God head in its three fold manifestation of Brahma, Vishnu, and Shiva had its other forms called *Panchadevata* namely *Shiva, Shakti, Vishnu, Skanda* and *Karthikeya)* were the major deities with varying shades of importance.

The old hymns, especially in their classical forms and varieties, formed the manual of religious worship praising the *Panchadevata* as it is liberally used in treatises like the *Pancharatra**

Pancha Chuda*:

Bhisma once told *Dharmaputra* that women were fickle minded and were the cause of all evils. To explain his statement he pointed out to the conversation between *Narada* and *Panchachuda*. *Narada* once conducted a world tour during the course of which he met *Pancachuda* and asked her the characteristics of women. She replied thus: "Even beautiful, venerable and noble ladies would stoop to folly. It is not the habit of women to leave away charming men of wealth if they get them conveniently. Any woman can be tamed if you please her in the proper way. If women remain faithful to their husbands it is because they are afraid of scandal. They will enjoy men without looking into their age or figure. The desire for men in women can be compared to that of *Antaka* (God of death) for the lives of men. This is the secret of womanhood.

Pancha Pranas

The five *pranas* (life breaths) of any living being are *Prāna, Apāna, Vyāna, Samāna and Udāna.* There is a story in *'Devi Bhagavata'* regarding the origin of the *Pancapranas*.

---

*Based on the Purusha Sukta (Rig Veda 10.90) the Pañcaratra Agamas teach that God (Narayana or Vasudeva) manifests Himself in five-fold forms: Para, Vyûha, Vibhava, Antaryamin, and Archa. These five aspects are how the absolute, formless Transcendent One (Para Brahman) is brought into living and loving touch with the mundane world so that living beings can interact with the divine. Modern Vaisnavism evolved from the Pancharatra and its theories.

A Name of *Rambha

Once *Sri Krishna* met *Radhadevi* at *Rasamandala* and in seclusion they spent in sexual sport the period of one day of Brahma. Then *Krishna* selecting an auspicious time dropped his vital fluid into her womb at the end of the sexual sport. Tired by the prolonged carnal sport and shaken by the impact of the hot semen *Radhadevi* perspired profusely and the exhaustion produced deep and long breaths. The whole universe was covered with her sweat and her sighs became the goddess of the life-giving breaths of all created animals. From the left side of her was born *Vayupatni* and to her right were born the *Pancapranas*. Besides these, another five younger *pranas* were also born. From the sweat of the *Devi* was born *Varuna* and from the left side of *Varuna* was born *Varunani*.

Mandukyopanisad gives the following details regarding the working of the Pranas in the body:- Prana was first used in the sense of breath. Later it got the meaning of life. Life is in fact breath to all living beings. Only when a man is awake his mind and sense organs are active. But *Prana* is active always in both the state of life. It may be said that when a man is asleep his senses merge with his mind and his mind with the prana. The five factors of *Prana* are the *Panchapranas.* The first of the five is called *Prana* itself. It is called Mukhya *prana.* Just as a king appoints his ministers at different places to do specified jobs the chief *Prana* posts the other *pranas* at different parts in the body with specific purposes of their own, *Prana* is seated in the heart and does the work of breathing. *Apana* is seated in anus and directs the organs of excretion of the body. *Vyana* is spread throughout the body and it is this life-wind, which keeps one alive even when breathing is stopped for some time.

When an archer stands in deep concentration with his bent bow without breathing he lives with the help of *Vyana*. *Samana* controls the breathing-in and breathing-out to a specified rhythm. *Samana* (equalizer) is so called because it balances the force of the in-coming and out-going breaths. There is school of thought that *Prana* is not seated in the heart but spread over the ears, eyes between the seats of *Prana* and *Apana*. This is also a reason why life-wind got that name. This breath does the work of prompting digestion. The four *pranas, Prana, Apana, Samana* and *Vyana* sustain life. The fifth one, *Udana*, takes the soul of the being out of the body when it dies.

Panchaapsaras

A lake of distinction - During exile of *Sri Rama* in the forests, *Agastya* showed *Sri Rama* this lake and described its origin thus: "In times of old a sage named *Mandakarni* built this lake. This sage living on air alone stood in the waters of this lake and practiced severe austerities for ten thousand years. Devas were frightened by the rigorous penance of *Mandakarni* and they sent five *devakanyakas* (celestial damsels) to the earth to entice the sage and stop his penance. The divine beauty of the girls attracted the sage and he lived with them in a grand building constructed within the lake itself. Even after the passing away of the sage and the damsels people used to hear dance and music from inside the lake. Because five *apsaras* lived in that lake it became known as *Panchaapsaras.*

The Five *Brahminical Hindu* Cults

The *Vishnava, Shiva, Shakti , Soura,* and *Ganapathi* were the five Hindu *Brahminical* cults in India. These Brahminical Hindu cults did not receive any approval of the orthodox *vedism* in beginning, for all of them did not approve of the *vedic* sacrificial in greater or lesser degree. But in process of growth of Hinduism during the epic age orthodox *vedism* had to make some compromises with these five types of Hindu cults and two non *brahminical* ones such as *Budha* and *Zanic* cults.

The best exponents of the *Brahminical* cults from the literary point of view were the *puranas*. The two epics especially the bigger ones were often interpreted by the intellectuals belonging to one or the other of these major cults in the interest of their own creeds. The five cults – deities are: 1. *Vishnu* (a composite god made up of *Vasudeva, Vishnu* and *Narayana.* 2. *Shiva* (also an amalgam of the *vedic rudra, pre-vedic proto shiva*, and *puranic shiva*) 3. *Sakti* (having constituent elements the pre-*vedic* and *vedic* mother Goddess, the object of worship of *vedic* sage – clans like the *katyas* and the *kusikas*, and the epic and puranic *Durga, - Parvathi – Vindhyavasin*) and the fourth and fifth cults *Suriya* and *Ganapathi* – formed the well known sects, dharma *sampradaya* of these five kinds *Vaishnava, Shiva , Saktha, Soura* and *Ganapathaya.*

Panchaka and Philosophy

Panchatatva

Panchatatva is an esoteric ritualism prescribed in *sakta* tantra . The general body of ideas, believes, and practices will on examination, be found to be permeated through and by the cult of *tantra.* The double framework of *vidika* and *tantrika* has ceased to be double in course of time. In the case of *Vamachara* (which means the practices of left), the *sadhaka* (aspirant) has to make use of certain kind of ritualism called *panchatathva.* Apart from the fact a full blooded counterpart of the essentials of the *panchatathva* worship in their gross and proxy forms can be traced down to all the *vedic shastras.*

Pancha Makaras

The five *pancha makaras* are the five articles that have different meanings in the material life such as; 1. Wine, 2. Meat, 3. Fish, 4. Cereals and 5. Sexual union. The aspirant who partakes of the five *tatvas* to please the deity within him incurs no demerit. Such a man looks upon wine and meat as Shakti and Shiva respectively, and is fully alive to the fact that the wine of which he is about to partake will make manifest the bliss that is the *Brahman* within him.

Pancha Samskara

According to the tenets of *Bhagavatism*, a true *vaishnava* has to follow the five ways of life that are called as *Pancha samskara*. These include *tapas* or *acharyas* initiating the student into the sacred fire by branding the latter's shoulders with symbols of Vishnu or initiating into wearing the symbols of the Lords foot by giving a spiritual name like *Narayana dasa, Govinda dasa* etc., which follows imparting the *mantra traya* consisting of the *ashta akshara*, the *dvaya,* and the *charana slokam* and handing over a *Saligrama* or other concrete objects for daily worship.

The *Pancha samskara and* the *Pancha kala* life are in theory means to secure the devotee's entry into the blissful world of *Vishnu.*

Panchaka and Religion

The Pancha jana

It is believed that there was no caste system in the early *Vedic* period. In the *"purusha suktham"* of the *Rig veda,* mentions about the five castes existed there as there is a word *Pancha jana* appearing in the *Rig Veda.* According to the traditional Indian interpretation, the *Pancha Jana* means, only a five fold nation, divided into five castes. It is beyond doubt that there was a gradation among the citizens according to the castes but it seems that caste system was not so rigid in the early *Vedic* period.

There is no any literature available of that time where one can find the rules and regulations adopted during the time. But, a division of the nation into different gradations according to the capacity and aptitudes of the individuals is seen in Iranian literature and also in the literature of other Indo- European nations. The *Pancha jana* referred in Rig veda was a division of five castes into Brahmin, Kshatriya, Vysya , Sudra and Nishadas.

The *Pancha kala* and *Pancha kalyana in Jainism*

The *Tirthankara,* who is omniscient and is immersed in infinite bliss is worshiped with thousand and eight times as *Sarveswara, Sarvahita, Mahadeava, Mahavishnu, Arhadeva,* etc.,. Such Tirthankaras appear in the world in different cosmic periods, which according to *Jain* philosophy insists of an age evolution and growth and an age of dissolution and decay. The former is called *Utsarpini* and the latter *Avasarpini*, the two represent the complete cosmic cycle of time. The period avasarpini is divided as per the fifth time- period called *Panchama kala.*

Further, the *Tirthankara* is associated with five kinds of festivals known as *Pancha kalyanam* in which all *devas* take part The pancha kalyanas are 1. Swargavatharana, a descent of the deva to become a tirthankara. 2. Mandarabhisheka, or janma-bhisheka, rejoicing at the birth of the tirthankara by performing an abhisheka. (Ablution) at the summit of Mandharagiri. 3. Dhiksha, when the theerthakara renounces the kingdom and the worldly treasure in order to become a Yogin. 4. Kevalolpathi, which represents the appearance of omniscient knowledge as a result of tapas and the destruction of karma.

5. Parinirvana, representing the complete destruction of all karmas and the attainment of salvation or the realization of Paramarthaswarupa.

In Jainism, further there are five "Paramesthins" called "Pancha paramesthins"- The great souls who do not have any definite function either of authority or instruction. There are five kinds of persons worshiped by the Jains as representing the ideal of life at different stages of realization.

Pancha Mahayajana

According to our *Puranas,* for a *Gruhasthasrami* (house-holder) the following five apparatuses are unavoidable: A sifter, a grinding stone, a broom, a wooden mortar and a water-pot. It is believed that a sin is committed when each of these is used and to remove the sins thus committed, the ancient sages have prescribed five *yajnas* and these five *yajnas* are called the *Pancha-mahayajnas.* They are the *Brahma-yajna,Pitruyajna, Devayajna, Bhutayajna* and *the Manusayajna.* Reciting of *Vedas* is *Brahmayajna.* Pleasing the manes by offering rice or libations of water is called *Pitruyajna.* Giving offerings to the demy-gods in the sacrificial fire is called *Devayajna* and a religious offering of rice to the crows is called *Bhutayajna.* Giving food for the guests is *Manusayajna.* One who does not do the *Panchamahayajnas* is no better than dead. Some scholars have classified the *Pancamahayajnas* as *Huta, Prahuta, Brahmyahuta, Prasita and Ahuta:*

Jāpō hutō hutō hōmah
Prahutō bhautitō bālih //
Brahmyāmi hutam dvijagnyarcca
Prasitam pitrutarpanam//

Ahuta is *Brahmayajna, huta* is *devayajna, Prahuta* is *bhutayajna, brahmyahuta* is *manusikayajna* and *prasita* is *pitruyajna*. Even if at times one finds it not possible to do *manusikayajna* one must perform daily *brahmayajna* and *daivayajna.* It is believed that the offerings given to Gods in the sacrificial fire go to the sun. The sun sends rains to the earth, which in turn make the plants, flourish. Vedas say that thus living beings increase. Just as all animals and objects depend on life breath for living, a *Brahmachari,* a *Vanaprastha* and *Sannyasi* depend upon a *gruhastha* for sustenance. Therefore, the *grhasthasrama* is the best of all *ashramas.*

Panchaasthikaya

Metaphysics forms an important portion of *Jain* literature. Every real object embodies in it self is an affirmative and a negative aspect synthesized and held together by its own complex nature. It maintains its identity and permanence only through the continued process of change consisting of origin and decay. Such ultimate reels are five in number such as *Jiva, Putgala, Dharma, Adharma* and *Akasha.*

These are primary constituent elements of cosmos, and are called *Panchaa-sthikaya,* the five *asthikayas*. *Asthi* means existence and *Kaya,* volume. *Asthikaya* there fore means a category, which is capable of having spatial relation. These five *asthikayas* relate to life or *athma* or souls. It comes under the *Chetana* (conscious category), the other four being under *Achetana* (unconscious-ness) category.

Pancha Karani

The *Buddhist* logicians adopt the five -step method of observation in order to attain knowledge of the inference, which is derived from the knowledge of an invariable relation between a sign and some thing bearing that sign. For example, one can easily relate smoke to its origin, fire. The invariable relation is established by the five step method of observation called *panchakarani* namely 1. Cause is not perceived, effect is also not perceived. 2. Cause is perceived 3. Effect is also perceived 4. Cause disappears. 5. Effect also disappears.

It is possible to have invariable connection of the casual as well as non- casual type that is called as *Vyapi*, e.g., by observing a many cases that wherever there is fire, there is smoke, and this kind of observation is called *vyatireka.* But in some exceptional cases we may have to depend on the single method of agreement in presence only, *Kevalanvaya.* In other exceptional cases of an opposite type, we may have to depend only on agreement in absence, *Kevala Vyatreka* e.g., when we have to analyze the five elements (the *pancha bhuta*) or to establish a proposition like the five elements, whichever is different from the other four elements (for example ether , air, fire, and water have no smell as earth is only element having smell).

The *Pancha Kanchuka* and *Panchaclesa*

Kala is the instrument where by the darkness that covers souls is removed in part. It evolves into two main states such as Vidya (Knowledge) and the Raga (attachment).

These two terms Vidya and Raga are often mistaken for jnana and avairagya, which are disposition of intellect. The later are purely material in order that they may attach to the soul. Jnana has a disposition of the intellect would account for individual cognition. This process would not be possible unless the cognitive faculty of man's brain is made manifest and this is done only through knowledge (Vidya). Similarly attachment appears in the intellect only as control by emotive faculty, which needs an instrument like the raga. These five – Kala, Niyathi, Kala, Vidya and Raga are called the five sheaths (Pancha kanchuka) which is related to the five hindrances called Pancha clesa. Avidya (ignorance) Asmita (egoism), Raga (attachment), Dvesha (aversion), and Abhinivesa (clinging to life).

The *Pancha Yatana Puja*

Attempts for reconciliation and rapprochement between the rival creeds were being made even from a very early period, when many of them were getting systematized. Approved smriti words like some of the dharma sastras of pre-Christian and post-Christian era; Manu and yajnavalkya smritis did not advocate the cause of any particular cult. Some epic passages like those in the Gita (chapter 7, 21, chapter 9, 23) though extolling the greatness of Vasudava Krishna helped bring out liberal and tolerant attitude among the sets.

Thus the orthodox Brahmins, known usually as smartas, evolved a kind of worship according to the approved *smritis* known as *panchayatanapuja* in which all principal deities of the five approved brahminical cults were the objects of veneration. The chief cult objects in it are conic which contained the emblem, one each, of the respective cults deities. It is difficult to trace the period in which the practice came into vogue among the *smartas.* But the archeological evidence proves the practice was introduced long before the mediaeval period.

It is interesting to note the characterization of this form of religious ceremonies: Five stones or symbols believed to be permeated by the essences of the five chief deities are: 1. The black stone that represents *Vishnu* 2. White stone that represents *Shiva's* essence 3. The red stone that represents the *Ganesha* 4. The small piece of metallic ore, which represents the *Parvati* wife of Shiva 5. The piece of crystal that represents the sun. All five symbols are placed on a round metal dish, called *Pancha yatana*, and are arranged in five different methods according to the preference given to any one of the five deities at the time of worship.

It is worth mentioning that placing in the centre, the symbol of any particular deity and thus giving special importance to the particular deity with the other four forming the four corners of a square, would indicate the particular cult – affiliation of the smarta worshipper.

The Five *Vrishni* Heroes

The Mora inscription (about twelve kilometres west of *Mathura*) of the first century A.D. speaks of *"Bhagavatam Vrishninam Panchamanam Pratimah*", the images of the group of five divine heroes of *Vrishni* family. The *Vayu purana* also mentions the five *vamsas* of *vrishni* and they were 1. Sankarshana, 2. Vasudeva 3. Pradyumna 4. Samba 5. Anirudha. There can hardly be any doubt that five vrishni heroes worshiped the title Bhagavata in the Mathura region about the beginning of chrisitan era.

*In the Vishnu Dharmothra, a work mentiond by Alberuni (A.D. 1030). and probably used by Brahmagupta (A.D. 628) recommended rules for construction of images of various divinities related to Bhagavata cult. These include the five *vrishni* heroes mentioned above.

The Five Great Prophets

It is believed that the five great prophets, namely; Revna-radhya, Marularadhya, Ekoromaradhya, Panditaradhya and Vishvaradhya, founded Vaishavism very long ago. According to another school of thought, these five prophets rose out of five great sthavaralingas of Bellari (Karnataka), Ujjni, (Karnataka), Kedara (Himachalpradesh), Srishilamalligarjuna (Tamil Nadu) and Banares, Uttrapradesh under different names in different ages. According to Sidhanta-Dipika by Dr. Ramana Shastri such opinions as the five great prophets founding the faith in each successive age should be taken only in figurative sense and not in a literal sense.

Panchaachara

Panchaachara are the five codes of conduct that lay down the rules of behavior for the individual members of the lingayata community. They are; 1, Lingachara 2. Sadachari 3. Sivachara 4. Bhrityachara and 5. Ganachara. The lingachara emphasizes on daily worship of linga, the representation of the divine and instructs the aspirant to be monotheistic. The Sadachari requires that a lingayata should follow of profession and strictly lead a moral and virtuous life. He should earn money through an honest path and utilize his savings for the betterment of others. By Sivachara the members are required to make no difference between one lingayata and another, as they are all devotees of Shiva. Shivachara therefore demands that a lingayata should dine and marry freely with other members of the same community even if they follow the different vocations. Bhrityachara is a devotee's attitude of complete facility towards Shiva and His other devotees. It enjoys up on the devotee to behave humbly and modestly towards man and woman and kindly to all animals. The Ganachara represents the spirit of vindication. The lingayata should not tolerate the adverse remarks on the Godhead and ill treatment against human beings and animals by any one and as the member of the community should strive for his betterment and uplift.

Pancharatra

By second century A.D. Bhagavathisim came to be generally known as

Pancharatra agama, the meaning of which is uncertain. It is perhaps derived from the fact that the original adherents of the cult probably sacrificed five times a year or observed some vows according to five ratras or seasons. According to the brahmanas, the pancharatra was a sacrifice performed by the purusha or Narayana over a period of five ratris (nights). However, etymo-logical meaning of the term pancharatra was that, it came to be regarded by the bhagavatas as superior to the vedas.

Panchaka and Geography

The *Pancha Bhuta*

The *prakruti* or nature is sub divided in to two parts, the Para and the Apara the formal denoting the spiritual or life factor (*Jivabhuta*) and the latter the material (Jata) universe with its eight elements. Of the eight elements the *apara prakruti* the first five are the states of existence of matter or the Pancha Bhuta as the last three being *Manas* (mind, the faculty of perception), *Budhi* (the intellect) and *Ahankara* (egoism)

None of the three is possible without the material body, which establishes the *Pancha bhutas* as the five fundamental elements.

The knowledge of what the *Panchabhutas* is as they are represented icono-graphicaly does desirable for a better under-standing about the *Pancha bhutas*. *Bhuta* means, state of existence, the word being derived from the root, to be.

In *Vaishesika darsana**, references can be seen about five states of existence or *Panchabhuta* such as *Prithvi, Aap, Tejas, Vayu* and *Akasha* that stand for Solidity, Liquidity, radiation, Gaseousness, and Ethereality respectively. In iconography, *Prithvi* or solidity is represented by a square or a cube: aap or liquidity by a circle, water or waterborne plants and animals: Tejas or radiation by light, satellite figures as of interlacing triangles, bright objects etc. *Vayu* or gaseousness by smoke; smoke colour, a globe flying bodies etc., and *akasha* or ether by empty ness (*sunya),* heavenly bodies as the

---

*A later division of the *nyaya school* of philosophy, also known as vaisesika-darsana. It was founded by Kanada Rishi and differs from the nyaya system of Gautama

sun, moon, etc.,

The various types of *Vigrahas* (icons with forms and diagrammatic representations.) are determined by conventions of these five types of manifestations of the *Pancha bhuta.*

Prithvi(earth) *Aap* (water) *Tejas* (fire) *Vayu* (air) and *Akasha* (sky) are the elements on which the world is composed. This is called the *Pancha bhutika Siddhantha* (doctrine of five elements). Besides the se five *Dravyas* elementary substances, people in India have reckoned Time, Space, Soul, and Mind also as *Patharthas* or categories. *Dravya,* one of the seven categories according to the *Nyaya Vyasisika sutras*, as nine *Svabhavas* (inherent properties). The seven *Patharthas* of *Vyasasika are Dravya, Guna, Karma, Samanya, Vishesha, Samvaya,* and *Abhava.*

The word *Pathartha* has got a very wide meaning. The literal meaning of which is a "matter". The vyasisikas of a later period included Ababa also and raised the number of art to seven. Gowtama, the Nyaya Sutrakara and Vatsyayana the Nyaya Bhashya kara and all their followers accepted the number of Arthas as seven.

All that can be perceived by the senses are included in the seven Patharthas according to the systems of Nyaya and Vyasyasika. According to Nyaya, Vyasyasika sutras there are seven Patharthas and they comprise nine kinds of materials, which correspond to the Pancha bhudas (five elements), Kala, (time) Dik (space) Athma (soul) and Manas (mind). They are described below:

1. **Prithvi** (earth): The characteristic of this Pathartha is smell. Prithvi is of two kinds, Nitya (eternal) and Anitya (perishable). Nitya is in the form of an atom (Paramanu) and Anitya is in the form of a material, Karya. They are classified into body, sense organs and objects.

2. **Jala** (water): Jala has a cold touch. It is of two kinds Nitya and Anitya. Nitya is in the form of Paramananda and Anitya in the form of karya.

3. **Agni** (fire): It generates heat. It is of two kinds Nitya and Anitya. Nitya is in the form of Paramanu and Anitya is in the form of Karya. There are four kinds of agnis (fire) such as fire of earth, fire of sky, fire of the stomach, and the fire commonly used.

4. **Vayu** (air): It is without form but with the sense of touch. It is also of two kinds Nitya and Anitya. Nitya is in the form of paramanu and anitya is in the form of Karya.

5. **Akasha** (sky): This is the carrier of sound. It is single and eternal.

Panchavati

The sacred place where Sri Rama built an ashram and lived for some time with Sita and Laksmana during their exile in the forests. There is a story about Pancavati in the Kamba Ramayana.

Pancavati is on the southern bank of the Godavari. Five Vatavrksas (banyan trees) stand here in a circle and therefore, the place got the name Pancavati. There is a legend about these banyan trees. Once five Gandharva youths encircled the sage Agastya in the forest as a sport and prevented him from moving towards any direction. The enraged sage cursed them to stand in the same position as banyan trees. Thus by obstructing the movements of a divine man they were forced to remain without movement as trees. Before they took the form of trees they begged the sage for deliverance from the curse. Agastya said, "One day Sri Rama with his wife and brother will come and stay in an ashram built in your midst. Their holy presence will give you salvation from my curse."

Sri Rama and Laksmana when they came to that forest decided to build an ashram in the centre of the circle formed by the five banyan trees. Laksmana started to build the hermitage. At first he cut down one of the trees standing tall and straight and to the surprise and astonishment of all the fallen trunk of the tree disappeared and there in its place lay the dead body of a demon youth. It was the body of Sambhukumara, son of Surpanakha. He was doing penance there when Sri Rama came there with Sita and becoming lustful at the sight of Sita he stood there as a tree. It was he who was cut down by Laksmana.

Sri Rama understood the thing that happened. He then explained to Sita and Laksmana many things about the frauds and deceits of the demons. After that they build their hermitage there and dwelt there for a long time.

Panchaka and Literature

The Panchatantra stands as a great example for the mani-festation of panchaka in the field of literature.

Panchatantra.

General information. An ancient book of distinction written by the scholar Visnusarma. The book is in the form of stories for the use of children to give them an idea of the different aspects of life.

Origin: There is a statement in the preface itself regarding the composition of this book: "Three sons were born to an emperor named Amarasakti. All the three were dull-witted. The emperor was very sorry for them but found no way to improve them. Greatly disappointed the King called the royal council and told them about his sons. Then one of the members of the council, a man named Sumati, stood up and said "Oh best of Kings, let us not try to teach your children the astras one by one. It will not only be an unpleasant study but would also take a long time to complete. If we can mix all the sastras cleverly and make it palatable like sweetmeats the children would take it easily. There is a suitable man also for this work in out state. He is Visnusarma, a kind-hearted scholar who is not only well versed in all the sastras but also an adept in the art of the up bringing of children. I am sure he would make your children wise and learned." When the emperor heard this he sent for Visnusarma and told him everything. After understanding well the nature of his would-be disciples and the ambition of their father, Visnusarma took charge of his wards and within six months he taught the sons of the emperor the science of government. The stories, which he used to teach them the science of administration, were all compiled into a volume called "Panchatantra".

A general idea of the book: The book contains five divisions each division illustrating one tantra (tact, diplomacy) by several stories. It contains prose and verse. The first tantra is called Mitrabheda. Stories under this head explain the philosophy of "Divide and rule" in politics. The main characters in these stories are two foxes named Karataka and Damanaka. Stories under Mitrabheda relate to how these sly foxes enjoy themselves in breaking the intimacy between a lion and an ox using slander against each other. 'Mirtralabha' is the theme of the next tantra.

It is an advice that you should select your friends with care selecting them only after studying them in detail properly. The author has selected as characters in his stories for this purpose a tortoise, a deer, a crow and a rat. The third tantra is called Kakolukiya. This deals with the evils behind an intimacy between born enemies. The main characters in the stories relating to this are a crow and an owl. The fourth tantra is called Labdhapranasa. It describes how a man loses what has come into his possession by his foolishness. A monkey and a crocodile are the characters in this story. The fifth tantra is Apariksitakaraka. It deals with the bad side of not looking into all the possible aspects of what your hear. Several stories are there to illustrate this point.

Popularity of the book. Though no correct records are there in history in support of the belief, it is believed that Amarasakti was the ruler of Mahilaropya in Deccan and that Pancatantra must have originated from there. But Panchatantra received a global publicity and popularity and was translated from Sanskrit into much other language during the period 531-575 A.D. That translation is not available at present. In the year 570 A.D. a poet named Bud translated it into the Syrian language. A scholar named Abdullah Ibaal Mogaffa in the year 750 A.D. translated it into the Arabic language. It was from this Arabic translation that it was translated into many European languages. The Greek translation appeared in the year 1080 A.D., Hebrew in 1100A.D., Latin in 1270 A.D., German in 1480 A.D., Italian in 1582 A.D. and French in 1678 A.D. Next to the Bible this is the book, which has received the greatest publicity and popularity. The great linguist Hertel says that Pancatantra has appeared in about 200 translations in fifty different languages.

Period of composition. Because the translation into the Syrian language appeared in the year 570 A.D. it must have been composed earlier than that date. Again, since it takes at least two centuries for a work to get popular enough to be translated into a foreign language, the composition must have been done early in the fourth century A.D. Some believe that the work was done in Kashmir. While others assert that it was written in Magadha. The original title of the book is believed to be 'Karataka and Damanaka' by a few.

Two editions. The different editions of the book are new found. One edition popular in Kashmir is known as Tantrakhyayika. The other is in the form found in Kathasaritsagara and Brhat-kathamanjari. The original Sanskrit work is very rarely found. There are several editions of this in Daksina Bharata. Changes in the stories according to the change of times are also noted. (History of Classical Sanskrit Literature).

B. Contents (Stories).

In the contents section of panchatantra there are five divisions such as: Suhurt labha (gaining friends), Mitrabheda (realizing friends), Sandivigraha (peace and war), Labha nasa (losing what you got), and Asampresyakrita (mis conceived action) that explain and teach the children the different experiences of life and their results.

Panchaka and Architecture

The Vastu principles are based on the unique science of 'space' (one of the Panchabhuta) and it establishes its origin from the primordial energy called "Brahman". It is said in the 'Taittiriya Upanishad', that Brahman evolved the space (Vyoma) first and from the space came forth the other forms of the Panchabhuta, air, fire, water, and earth.

The pronominal energy, according the technical tradition, is called 'Vastu' and elemental substances that issued forth are called manifest energy. The word 'Vastu' is derived from the word 'vas' (to dwell or exist); Vastu is a common term denoting both gross and subtle substances. It is significant that the energy dwells in each of the Panchabhuta and the 'vastus' cannot function with out the help of the 'Panchabhuta'.

It is definite that any thing in the universe, movable or immovable consists of the Panchabhuta, Earth, and Water etc. In short, what obtains in a molecule obtains in the universe too.

The following five reasons will help establish the above statement:

The Vastu-purusa is said to be lying with his face and stomach touching the ground.

His head is at the North-East (Aisanya) and legs at South-West (nairrtya). The pressure point, i.e., the Muladhara Cakra in our body is at the bottom. The Muladhara Chakra denotes earth (Prthvi) element. The base (Adhisthana) for the Muladhara cakra should be stable. As per the position in the plan of Vastu Purusa the direction is South-West (Nairrta). Accordingly, it has been prescribed that the South - West portion of a building should be built in such a way as to be able to bear heavier weight. Even according to atmospheric circle, South-West (Nairrtya), portion receives more heat. Accordingly, it has been suggested that the walls in that direction should be made thicker.

The Svadhistana Cakra in the body is in lower stomach, near two kidneys. It is connected with water (aape) element. According to *Vastu-purusa-Mandala*, the position of this Cakra is to the South and West. Therefore, it has been prescribed that wet areas, like bathroom, etc., should be constructed in that direction. It is for sewerage (utsarjana).

The *Manipura Cakra* is at the navel. This Cakra is related to energy/fire (tejas). While in the womb of the mother, the fetus is fed with the essence of food and energy through umbilical cord connected with its naval. The vastu Purusa Mandala shows Brahma at the place of navel. The Lotus is the base (asana or adhistana) of Brahma. Thus, it is the navel that connects Brahman with Jiva or Pinda or life. It has, therefore, been prescribed to keep this particular place unoccupied or vacant. Therefore, the central square within a building is to be kept open to the skies. It is believed that Vastu Purusa breathes through this open area.

Anahata Cakra is near the heart. It is related to atmosphere or air (Vayu). Lungs in the body regulate the air.

Visuddha Cakra is said to be in the throat. The hollowness in a throat denotes the ether (akasa) element. The word 'Om' is uttered through throat. The echo of an utterance exists in the hollow of the bone-box of head and the space in brain. The head of Vastu Purusa is at the North-East (aisanya). This direction is related to space (akasa). Atmospherically, this portion is cooler. It has, therefore, been suggested to construct a Puja room (devagraha) in this direction.

The limbs, other than the above, of Vastu Purusa are also connected with construction of a building. Liver is an important organ for digestion. Liver is towards the South-West in the body. The Sthapatis, therefore, suggest to place cooking room or kitchen towards that direction, because it is related to Agni. Rays of the Sun first reaches this direction. Pollution generated during the night is swept away by rays of the Sun. It is, therefore, possible that the suggestion of locating kitchen towards the South-East is due to this aspect.

The North-West is said to be the field presided by air (vayu). Organs like stomach, spleen and rectum of the Vastu Purusa fall on that portion. The store-room has been suggested towards that direction. A spleen, according to the science of medicine, does the work of storing and restoring blood in the body. Herbs of medicine are recommended to be planted towards the North-West. The suggestion through this recommendation appears to be that a dweller should get the fragrance of herbs through the air.

According to the Matsya Purana, the Vastu Purusa Mandala has particular deities of Vastu Purusa in respective places. The North-East (aisanya) is said to be occupied by Mercury (budha) and Vishnu. Accordingly, the chamber for worship in a house is to be situated in that direction.

The South-East (agneyi) is said to be occupied by the Moon and Parvati. The Moon is said to be the controller of mind and Parvati is the symbol of mother of mind. Frailty is the nature of mind. If these rules are followed, Parvati becomes the possessor of the house hold and it is suggested that cooking room be made in the South-East direction.

The North-East (Aisanya) is said to be occupied by Ketu and Citragupta. So it is recommended that treasury accounts and store lockers should be on that side.

The South-West (nairrtya) is said to be controlled by Rahu and Kama. So a bedroom should be situated in that direction. Rahu is said to be incomplete. Therefore, in order to bring completeness to life, this side must have been chosen for the bedroom.

As stated before, the Vastu Purusa lies with his back up. The concept may be that the burden is carried on the back. Accordingly the pillars are not to be raised on the sensitive points of Vastu Purusa. The sensitive points according to the science of physics are inlets and outlets. The sensitive points exist also on the foals of the arms and legs. Pillars, if erected on those points would not find enough base and support. Therefore, those points are to be avoided for pillars.

As stated before the South-West (nairrtya) should be heavier and the North-East (aisanya) should no be so. Aisanya is a place of akasa-tattva and, therefore, a place of deities. It is in consistence with Nature that the base should be heavier and the head should not be burdened. The hills and mountains and the trees too indicate so. Nature has given us five organs.

The main organs are the eyes for vision, the ears for hearing, the nose to smell and the mouth to taste. They all are, geographically speaking, in the head portion of a body. The head of the Vastu purusa as at the Aisanya. The head should be secure. It appears, therefore, that the North-East is to be kept from heavy structures like pillars, etc.

As our health is maintained, if we follow the rules of diet consistent with the rules of Nature, the heath of a building or Vastu can be maintained if the construction is made giving due regard to the principles of Nature The limbs in a body should invariably be in their proper places. So much so, the rooms in a house should be designed in their proper places. That will keep the house healthy and thereby the inmates too happy. As it would be abnormal if one's eyes were placed at the shoulder, the building too would look abnormal.

The Five Shapes of a Town

The Vastu shastra recommends five shapes for towns: 1. Chathura (square) 2. Agatara (rectangle) 3. Vrtta (circle); 4. Kritta Vrtta (elliptical); and 5. Gola vrtta (full circle).

According to vastu sastra, a town resembling Vajra-Suci or a diamond (octagonal) should be regarded as inauspicious. If the front part of the town is in the shape of a bow, it is considered as very good and auspicious.

For a town, the site should be selected at the bank of a river, seashore or lake. Milky trees, full of fruits and flowers, should surround the site.

The Eastern side of the town should be lowered to get sun rays on the door fronts. The site should not be selected on the Western side of a mountain. The capital of the state should be selected at the center of a town, classified as:

1. Stanza	-	Center of 800 villages
2. Dronamukha	-	Centre of 400 villages
3. Kharvitika	-	Centre of 200 villages
4. Samgrahana	-	Centre of 10 villages

The Agni-purana recommends highly the semi-lunar shape of the town. The holy city of Banaras is situated on the convex side of the Gangetic belt and presents a semi lunar phase. Nanjangud town near Mysore also is situated on the convex side of the river Kapila. The Matsya-Purana says that the semi lunar shape of a town is not auspicious. The development of industrial factories at Nanjangud brings the shape of the town to a semi lunar aspect. The factories may become sick.

India is situated to the North of the equator and north is the quarter of light, i.e., the area of the Devas, the shining ones. The South is the quarter of Yama or the God of death. The monsoon wind and rain in India are from South and West. Therefore country like India, if the ground is sloped towards that direction, the houses there will be dangerously open to every storm.

The engineer should consider the weather records of the area for the past ten years in designing any building. From the weather records obtained from the meteorological centre of the region, we can understand the influence of the site affected by the weather. In the consideration of the weather data, such as wind velocity and its direction. rainfall, evaporation, humidity of the area, sunlight and maximum and minimum temperature, etc., if we design the building, it will satisfy most of the specifications of Vastu.

The concepts of 'Vastu' are based on the Panchabhuta and that they have tremendous interactive influence on the human beings, whose physical exposition is made of these five divisions.

According to the technical concept, the technically called natya raga and the set of entertainment (inachjapayoga) are closely comparable to the Vedic sacrifices.

The growth and development of Mandapa is in the directions vertical and horizontal. They are human as urdhvavarma and Tunjale Karma. The details regarding ancient structures inevitably lost and few available features are scattered. The text Ajitagama explains Panchavarga sabhas.

Samarangana-Sutradhara, however is descriptive about a sabha. However the structure is seen beside Raval pahadi cave at Aihole has the five Vargas of mandapa, like Adhishtana, Bhitti, Prastara, Kantha, and sikhara.

Panchaka and Painting

In the *Manasollasa,* very interesting details are given on portrait painting, which is dependent in the first place on the three principal lines, called the plumb lines here named as the Brahma sutra and the two Paksasutras. The Brahmasutra is the line, which begins from the Kesanta (forehead where the line of hair begins) and passes through the middle of the two feet. This line, therefore, marks the centre of the body from head to foot.

The two Paksasutras are usually six angulas away from the Brahma sutra on either side. They start from the Karnanta (the top of the ear) and pass through the chin, the middle part of the knees, the outside skin and the second finger near the toe to the ground.

The Five Attitudes

With the variation of the distance between the central and side lines five different positions of the subject are obtained, in the same manner as the front, profile and three quarter positions are obtained in Western Art. The five positions are named in the Manasollasa as Raj, Ardharju, Saci, Ardhaksi and Bhittika. Rajusthana is the front position in which the distance between the Central plumb line (Brahma sutra) and the two Paksasutra, i.e., sidelines is six angulas on both the sides. Ardharjukasthana is that in, which the distance from the Brahmasutra to one Paksasutras is eight angulas on one side and four angulas on the other. The Sacisthaua is that in, which the distance from the Brahma sutra to one Paksasutra is ten angulas on one side and two angulas on the other. The Ardhaksikasthana is that in, which the distance from the Brahma sutra to one Paksasutra is eleven angulas on one side and one anguala on the other. Bhittikasthana is that in which only the Paksasutras are seen while the Brahma sutra disappears.

Vertical Measurements: - Next come the details of vertical measurements: -

First is the Mastaka-sutra, i.e., the line of the crown.

Four angulas below is the Kesanta (end of the front hair) sutra. This goes round the head three angulas above the Karnagra.

Two angulas below is the Tapanoddesa-sutra. This goes through the Sankhamadhya, one angula above the Karnagra and one angula above the occipital.

One angula below in the Kacotsanga-sutra, which goes from near the eyebrows, the upper end of the ear to the Sirsakurma (occiput).

One angula below is the Kaninika-sutra, which goes by the Apanga, the upper end of the Pippali and above the pit of the back of the head.

Two angulas below is the Nasamadhya-sutra. It goes through the high portion of the cheeks to the middle of the ear.

Two angulas below is the Nasagrasutra. It goes through the cheeks, the root of the ear, the Kesotpatti-pradesa and the back.

Half an angula below is the Vaktramadhya-sutra. It goes by the Sprkka or Krkatika.

Half an angula below is the Adhorostha-sutra. It goest by the joint of the chin to the back of the neck.

Two angulas below is the Hanvagra-sutra. It goest by the neck to the joint of the shoulder.

Four angulas below is the Hikka-sutra, It goes from below the shoulders and the tops of the hands.

Seven angulas below is the Vaksahsthala-sutra, It goes by the red part of the nipples and the armpit joints to the backbone.

Five angulas below is the Vibhramasanga-sutra. It goes below the nipples, the part between the breast and the backbone, the upper-part of the below joint to the middle of the back.

Six angulas below is the Nabhi-sutra. It goes by the end of the biceps to the back.

Six angulas below is the Babhi-sutra. It goes by the lions to the top of the Kakundaras (buttocks).

Four angulas below is the Pakvasayasutra. It goes by the middle of the Nitamba(hips) above the Sphiks i.e., fleshy part of the buttocks.

With the varieties of the brushes and their use in the delineation of the details of the pictorial art.

Plasters and ointments really should have been taken up, with the backgrounds as it is for their preparation that plasters and ointments were used in ancient India.

Brick Plaster: - brick-plaster is preferred to Clay plaster of the S.S. (to be taken notice of, ahead). "Brick powder of three kinds has to be mixed with clay, one third-part (in amount of the brick powder). Having mixed saffron with oil (one) should mix (lit place) (with it) gum resin, bees' wax, liquorices, molasses and mudga preparation in equal parts. One-third part of burnt yellow-myrobalan should be added therein. Finally the astringent made of the Bell-tree (Foronica elephantum), destructive (of all injurious agents) mixed in proportion of two to one should be added by an intelligent artist and also a portion of sand, proportionate to the amount of the whole. Then the artist should drench (this mixture) with moist split pulse dissolved in water. The whole of this moist preparation has to be kept in a safe place for one month only. After the moisture has evaporated within a month, a skilful artist should put this dried(yet still damp) plaster on the wall, having carefully considered everything. It should be plain, even, well distributed, without ridges or holes, neither too thick nor too thin. Should it (look) ill done after having become (quite) dry (due to shrinkage), then it ought to be carefully smoothed by coatings of plaster made of that clay (as mentioned before mixed with resin of the Salvatore (Shore robust) and with oil. (It is further made) smooth by (repeated) anointing, constant sprinkling with water and by careful polish."

The Clay Plaster:- The clay for the purpose of ointment and plaster should be procured from the auspicious places like vapid, kappa, adage, lotus beds, dashikis, the roots of the trees, the banks of the rivers, thickets, etc. These are the sources from which this clay ought to be procured. These various clays are of different colors and are declared auspicious for the respective castes. This clay should be free from gravels and the liquids obtained from the trees like Salmali, Masa, Kakubha, Madhuka, Triphala, etc,. and they should then be mixed with the clay along with also a good quantity of sand too in it. Then afterwards, the hair of the horses or the hair of the bullocks and also the skin of the coconut, i.e. fibres, also husks of the grain, form a constituent of the compound. The quantity of the sand and the clay should be in equal measure. All these compounded into a levitated powder (Kalka) should be distilled into some suitable cloth I.e., what we call (Kapadachana). Other details are difficult to be obtained as the text (9 to 11vs.) are corrupt. My surmise, however, is that this compound is directed to be boiled in order to make it a fast ointment.

This Lepya, in its various compounds, a typical technique of which has just been hinted at, to all intents and purpose, was the substitute for the modern paints of various colours. Mixture of liquids of different varieties of soils along with other ingredients stood good for the paints of old and they were more durable and faster than what we have these days. Mention of the Vajra-lepa (cf. Manasollasa) in connection with the inconoplastic art had already been made. All these lepas, vajra and otherwise really belonged to the one and same category.

Five Colours and Brushes

Colours

Let us now proceed with colours. Our text does not give any detailed information about colours. Visnudharmottara, the most representative treatise on painting, gives two sets of colour-varieties. The first

Set consists of five primary colours – red, white, yellow, black and green and the second one white, yellow, black, blue and colour of the myrobalan. Bharata-Natyasastra's classification of five primary colours tallies with the former set of Visnudharmottara. Silparatna, a latter treatise of great repute, mentions, white. Red, yellow, soot and syama (dark, blue and black) as primary colours "The Abhilasitartha-cintamani (cf. Manasollasa) knows as pure colours, white made of conch shell, red (prepared from red lead or from alaktaka juice, i.e., black or from red chalk – gairika, green-brown (Haritala)' i.e. sulphurated arsenic, and black from kajjala (soot, used eye-black).

"The mixing of these colours is left to the ingenuity of the artist. He may coat them with lack and resin. Colouring substance are gold, silver, copper, mica, deep coloured brass, red lead, vermilion, tin, yellow, orpiment,. Yellow myrobalan, lac, indigo and some kind of iron oxide" Visnudharmottara, Part III, Chapter 40. In Silparatnam(cf. Ch. 46 vs. 119-130) prescriptions for the preparation of these vegetable and mineral colours are given.

> "Red chalk for instance ought to be ground on stone and left covered with water for a day, red lead also ought to be ground and covered with water for half a day, red, arsenic, however, should be made into powder but it should not be covered with water. Then the colours should be ground one more and again put into water for five days. Afterwards, they should be mixed with the exudation of the Nimba tree, then at last they are ready to be applied on walls and pictures."

The Pancha Varna

Primary Colours

According to the Vishnudharmotara, as already referred before, there are only five primary colours and Abhilashidarta-chintamani, however mentions only four. Indian texts on painting generally give only four colours as primary ones exceeding the Western list by the addition of white. It may however be pointed out here that blue and black are different. Black is well known. What is the nature of blue? Ab.C. gives it:

"This colour is, therefore, different from kajjala(for Krishna) and is absolutely essential for preparing secondary colours. These five colours are kept in separate cups so that they might be used as pure colours or mixed to produce secondary colour-tints".

The Aparajitapracha, also recognizes only four colours, but it has an innovation. Here colours are related to the different styles like Nagara and Dravida, etc.

"The texts on painting like the Chitrasutra in the Vishnu-dharmottara, the chapters on painting in the Abhilasitarthacintamani and the Sivatatvaratnakara and the Citralaksana chapter of the Silparatna, etc. give a list of the various tints got by mixing primary colors. It is remarkable that Bana has set at naught the limited color variety of these texts and given out in his catalogue of innumerable tints that deep and close study of nature which had enabled him to grasp the extreme subtlety of difference between tint and tint. In spite of the limited number of colors stated the texts on painting are not unacquainted with subtle differences in the same color. The *Silparatna* gives three gradations of red- Sindura for light red, Gairika (mountain-born) red (mineral chalks) for a middle tint and Laksha (lac) juice for a deep colour. The Abhilasitarthacintamani and the Sivatattvaratnakara tell us that vermilion is for reddish brown, and red lac or sap, red sanders and mountain born chalks are for crimson tint. They echo Bana's statements. White and black give the grey of smoke' blue and white the colour of the pigeon similar to the Rajavara and the hemp flower. Red mountain chalk and conch powder give a peculiar pale red (Dhumracchaya). Darada (Vermilion) mixed with white gives the pale red of the red – lily while Alaktaka (red lac or sap) combined with white gives the colour of the sun's horses. The difference is very slight here. Pure indigo (Nili) of the colour of the blue lily gives a green tint when mixed with yellow pigment. Red lac with lamp-black guves a dark brown and with blue, the colour of the Jambu fruit."

The tints got by mixing primary colours – like smoke grey, pigeon colour, the different varieties of red, brown, green and the colour of the Jambu fruit are clearly given by Bana. The variegated hue to which he refers is given by the Silparatna as a convenient colour for artist; but according to Srikumara it is got by mixing red, black and yellow in equal proportions. Red and yellow give the colour of Bakula flowers which Bana describes as Dhusara (Tawny). This is the same as flame colour. There are also other varieties of red given in the Silparatna. The green of the parrot's wing described by Bana as not dissimilar from that of the plantain leaf is got by a mixture of Hnritala (yellow) and blue, and the purple of the Jambu fruit so cleverly described by the parrot in the Kadambart is the result of the union of red lack and blue. The yellowish white of the inner petals of the Ketaki flower noted by Bana is the type of white got by mixing Haritala and conch-powder as laid down in the Abhilasitarthacintamani. The rosy colour of the pigeon's leg in the Kadambari is the 'Gaura' type of rosy white in the Silparatna, which is the same as the Saurasvasadrsaprabha (colour of the sun's horses) of the Abhilasitarthacintamani and the Sivatattvaratnakara, through the 'Gaura' of these books is slightly different from that of the Silparatna being got by mixing red and yellow instead of red and white. The pingala type of yellow, that Bana states as the colour of honey, is not the result of a mixture of white and yellow in the proportion of one is to two that the Silparatna gives. It is a tawny colour-more red than yellow-something like Pinjara type of reddish brown as the colour of ripe paddy fields a really true observation; and this colour is lighter than that of honey which has a greater proportion of red. This might be the same as the Atirakta of the Silparatna with yellow and red in the proportion of one is to two.

The variegated colour of deer, tigers, peacocks, tittiries, etc as given by Bana is quite in accordance with the rule of the Abhila-sitarthacintamani and the Sivatattvaratrakara that holds the use of different colours for the effect of the animals absolutely necessary. It might be two colours or three or more."

Colour - Substances :- As described in the V.D. are manifold - a workable list, however, is Kanaka (gold), rajata (silver), tamra (copper), abhraka (mica), rajavanta (an inferior diamond of Virata country what is called 'Lajawar' in eastern districts like Gorakhpur), sindura, trapu, haritala, sudha, laksa, hingulaka, and nila, Loha is also mentioned as a colour substance.

We can divide colours into two broad classes-natural and artificial. Dr. Motichand observes: 'The natural pigments comprised of certain elements, compound minerals and vegetable extracts; and the artificial, all manufactured salts or the pigments owing their colours to vegetable or insect dye-stuff'-(Mughal Painting p.18).

Now leaving aside the order of the colour-substances as tabulated above, let us say a few words on some of the more important colour-substances.

Sudha- The Vishnudharmothara. III: 40-2 enjoins the use of lime (Sudha) for white.

Sindura- In the preparation of red pigments many substances, such as red stones and red clays, red ocher (geru) hiraunji, etc., are used and orange lead, i.e., sindura is also an important colouring material in it.

Hingula- also goes with sindura. It is vermilion or crude cinnabar or sulphide of mercury. It is called 'igur' in Hindi. That sometimes outline was drown in vermilion is referred to in the Mahavamsa.

Nila- Indigo and Rajavarta, the blue par-excellence, are prominent among blue-pigments.

Indigo (nila) – "This colour was manufactured in India in antiquity and largely exported to Greece and Roma. It is also mentioned in the Visnudharmottara, III, 40, 26, as one of the colouring materials. The colour is extracted from certain plant known in modern botany as indigo ferae. In the beginning it seem to have been largely used for dyeing cloth but later on, specially in the painting of the Akbar school, it was used as a colour.

Five Kinds of Brush

Brushes – The Samarangana-Sutradhara under Vilekha-laksana gives a variety of five fold brushes. They are technically called Kuraka, Hastakurcaka, Bhasakurcaka, collakurcana and Vartani. Each of them has been provided with a particular shape of their points and they are tabulated as follows-

Types		**Shapes**
1. Kurchaka Vatankurakara	-	points like those of the sprouts of Banyan tree.
2. Hastakurchaka Asvatthankurakara	-	an Asvattha tree
3. Bhasakurchaka Suchinibha	-	an Indian fig tree.
4. Callakurchana Udumbarakara	-	another variety of an Indian fig tree.
5. Vartani	-	—

2

Panchaka And Origin of Music

"SRINUPĀRVATI PURVAM ME SARVALOKA SUKHAYACA
SADYŌJATA MUKHAT PRITHVI GANDHARASCHA SWARŌBHAVAT
PRITHVI YASCARMA VĀDYANI JĀTANI TADANANTARAM
VĀMADĒVA MUKHA TAPAH DHYAVASCHA SWAROBHAVAT
ADBHYO JĀTANI SANKHĀDI VADYĀNI SUBHA GANANE
AKHŌRADANALAH SHADJAH RISHABHASCHA TATHA BHAVĀN
JATĀNI HYAGNITO LOKE KAMSYA VADYANI PARVATI TATHASTAT
PURUSHĀD VATRAD VATHA; PANCHAMA EVACHA TASMAD VATHAT
SAMUTHPANNAM VENUVADYAM RANDRA VADHYAKAM
ESANASYA NISHADASCHA MADHYAMASCHA SWARASTATHA
AKASO PI SAMUTHPANNAH TANTRIVADYAM TATHO BHAVAT"*

In Hindu mythology, it is believed that the evolution of music was connected to one of the trinity, Siva.

---

* *Sangita Kalpadrumam* of Muthaiyya Bhagavatar (Part I- Chapter I- *Upotghatam*) also refers to the *sloka* given in the *Sangita Makaranda* supporting the mythological origin of Indian Music.

According to the *puranas*, music had emerged from the five faces (Pancha mukha) of the Lord. The music that has emerged from the Pancha mukha of Siva was practiced and flourished by the Devas and Maharishis like Brahma, Parvati, Matanga, Kashyapa, and others. The music later on was divided into two primary categories such as the Laukika, ands the Vaidika.

According to Sangita ratnakaram, the creation of music was based on the Pancha bhuta, which is considered to be the body of the Virada purusha or the Prabrahma. The Pancha bhuta consists of Sky, Air, Water, Fire and Earth.

If we try to link up various stands of thoughts that we find in the early Upanisads, the five faces (Panchamukha) cum mouths of Shiva have been conceived as five flames i.e., blazing tongues of the sacrificial fire which has been considered as the sacred symbol of Shiva.The five faces of Shiva are also Mahadeva (Northern), Bhairava (southern), Nadi Vaktra (Western), Umavaktra (Eastern) and the fifth one, Sada Shiva on the top is known as lsana. Another vedic name for Shiva is Rudra, which corresponds to Agni or fire, one of the Panchabhutas. The treatises on music like Sangita ratnakara, mention fire and air in connection with the origin of musical sounds (Nada). It has been stated in Sangitha Ratnakara as;

> "Dehastham vahnimahanti sa preyati marutam
> Na-karena prana-namanam da-karanenamanalam viduh
> Jatah pranagni-samyogattena nade bidhiyate"

In the vedic time the rigs or stanzas with notes, were known as Samagana. The Samagana was sung before the presiding deities like Varuna, Mithra, Indra, Agni and others. The Gandharva type of music was considered as sacred music because; it evolved by the side of the holy Vedic. The Gandarva music was schemed on the basis of jati. As for the origin of ragas, it is stated that the five ragas evolved from the five mouths of Lord Shiva were the basic ragas. We notice that the Shiva-Shakti cult was predominant during the epic age. The practice of worship of Shiva and Shakthi is very ancient, as it is evidenced from the findings of the pre-historic Indus-Valley mounds.

In some of the *ancient rock-cut temples** Shiva has been depicted as the five-faced god. The names of the faces are: Sadyojata, Vamadeva, Aghora, Tatpurusa, and Isana, which are again the five aspects of the sun. The mythological interpretation of the origin of the of the ragas relates to the five mouths of Shiva, and the five ragas conceived correspond to these five mouth-cum-gods:

1. Sadyojata ... Sri
2. Vamadeva ... Vasanta
3. Aghora ... Bhairava
4. Tatpurusha ... Panchama
5. Isana ... Megha

The five faces of Shiva are represented as five main ragas, and these ragas are the icons of music. The five elements (Pancabhuta) like earth (Kshiti), water (ap), fire (tejas), air (marut) and ether (vyoma) have been considered as the symbols of the above mentioned ragas. Mono cryptic letters like lam, yam, ram vam, ham, signifies the five elements. In Tantra, these letters are known as chakras.

The chakras are possessed of different colours and presiding deities (Pancha varna and Panca devata). The five Tantric code-languages (vija-mantras), plexus (chakras) and colours have also been taken as the symbols of the five ragas. They are as follows:

Five face – cum-Mouth of Shiva	**Pancabhuta**	**Monographic Letters**	**Cakra**	**Raga**
Sadyojata	Earth	Lam	Muladhara	Sri
Vamdeva	Water	Yam	Svadhisthana	Vasanta
Aghora	Fire	Ram	Manipura	Bhairava
Tatpurusha	Air	Vam	Anahata	Panchama
Isana	Ether	Ham	Visuddha	Megha

*Chapter-9 of 'Exploring ancient skies: an encyclopedic survey of archaeo astronomy' By David H. Kelley, E. F. Milone.

In the Tantric literature of Buddhists, five dhyani-Buddhas or Tathagats have been mentioned as being conceived in accordance with the five skandas, designed after the Panca-bhuta. The five elements (Panca-bhuta) with the five sense organs,

Panchendriya evolved from the five potential elements were known as generic essences of the sound (sabda) touch (sparsa), co lour (rupa), taste (rasa) and smell (gandha). The five dhyani-Buddhas were considered as the five emanations (panchamukha) of Shiva.

The five dhyani-Buddhas and five kinds of consciousness (panchajana):

The five dhyani-Buddhas have been depicted as five kinds of consciousness such as: a) svisudha-dharma-dhatujana (Virochana), b) adarsa-jnana (akshobhya), C) pratyaveksana-jnana (Amitabha), d) somanta-jnana (Ratnasambhava), and e) krtyanusthana-jnana (Amoghasiddhi). The five dhyani-Buddhas may be mentioned according to the five faces of Shiva as:

Dhyani-Buddhas	Skanda	Direc-tions	Colours	Panca-bhuta	Pance-ndriya	Loca-tions
1. Amogha-siddhi	Samskara	North	Green	Kshiti	Gandha	Legs
2. Amitabha sambhava	Samijna	West	Red	Ape	Rasa	Mouth
3. Ratna	Vedana	South	Yellow	Tejas	Rupa	Navel
4. Akshobhya	Vijnana	East	Blue	Marut	Sparsa	Heart
5. Virochana	Rupa	Centre	White	Vyoma	Sabda	Head

It is established that the conception of primal emanations of the five ragas evolved purely on the basis mythico-philosophical ideas of man.

The subconscious mind is the storehouse of energy, and it has been conceived as the eternal blazing fire in an inverted triangular altar. It may be said the conceptual forms of the panchadevata may be composed in different ways.

Panchagunas* :

As per the Vedas the human body while in the womb of the mother or later takes different qualities (Panchagunas) from the Panchabhuta. They are 1) Akashaguna, 2) Vayuguna, 3) Tejoguna, 4) Jalaguna and 5) Prithviguna.

The Panchaka has manifested in all spheres and facets of Indian life, be it cultural political, social or religious.

The following is a list of Panchaka as manifested in different fields.

Panchaka

(As manifested in various musical and non -musical spheres)

Musical :

Panchamam	A janya raga derived from the 22-melakarta raga in the 72-melakarta scheme of karnatic music. Arohana : srdpns – sndpmgrs.
Panchamam	The fifth note in the saptak.
Panchama sruti	The interval between chathusruti rishabamand suddha madhyama with a frequency of 32/27.
Panchama nadam	A janya raga derived from the 45th melakarta raga Subhapantuvarali. Arohanam: srgmns- sndpmgrs
Ghana raga Kirtanamala	Nine songs composed in ganaragas, five of thee primary group of ganaraga panchaka Nattai, Gowla, Arabhi, Varalai and Sree and four of the secondary group Kedara, Ritigowla, saranganattai, and bowli by Swati tirunal.
Pancha nada	Five categories of nada according to Matanga muni such as

	Sushma, Atisushmam, Vyaktam, Avyaktam and krithrimam.
Pancha nada	Five categories of nada according to Narada such as Nakajam, Vayujam, Charmajam, Lohajam and Sarirajam.
Pancha rupi	A janya raga derived from 70th melakarta Nasikabhooshani. Arohanam: srmpds -sndpmgrs.
Panchalankara	Five alankaras mentioned in Sangita ratnakara Chakrakaram, Javam, Shangam, Padmanibham, Varidham.
Pancha jati	Five jatis or varieties of laghu namely Tisram , Chaturasram, Kandam , Misram and Sankirnam.
Pancha jati	Five varieties of prabhandas namely Madini, Anandini, Deepini, Bhavini and Taravali.
Pancha swara prastara	Combinations of five swaras in the swaraprastara prakaranam.
Pancharaga swarajati	Swarajati composed by Swati tirunal in the regas Kalyani, Begada, Atana, Surruti, and Todi set to triputa tala.
Pancharatnam	Five kritis composed in the ghanaragas namely Natta, Gowla, Arabhi, Varali and Sri.
Ghana raga Panchakam	Natta, Gowla, Arabhi, Varali and Sri.
Dvitiya Ghanaraga Panchakam	Narayanagowla., Ritigowla, Kedara gowla, Bowli and Saranga nattai.
Pancharatna Kritis of Tyagaraja	Ghanaraga pancharatnam, Kalahastisa Pancharatnam, Kovur pancharatnam, and Tiruvotriyur pancharatnam.
Five sruti jatis	Deepta, Ayata, Karuna, mridu and Madhya.
Panchasthayis	Five sthayis such as Anumandra, Mandra, Madhya, Tara amd Ati tara.
The Pancha Vadya	The five instruments comprising Madalam, Iddaka, Timila, Kombu and Ila talam.
The five branches of Manodharma sangita	Alapana, Tana, Pallavi, Niraval and Kalpana swara.

Pancha gati	The five gatis applicable to the laghu namely Tisragati, Chatusra gati, Kanda gati, Misragati and sankeerna gati.
The five rhythmical phrase	Ta thin gi na thom. Imposed of five syllables.
Pancha mukha vadyam	A five faced drum with plain drums.
Pancha taleswaram	A talamalika prabhandam in five talas set to five Margi talas.
Khanda chapu	A variety of chapu tala that consists of five akshara kala in an avarta.
Khanda gati	Refers to a rhythm where each aksharakala of the tala consists of five sub divisions .
Khanda laghu	A variety of laghu consisting five akshara kala.
Pancha linga sthala kritis	These are five songs in praise of five lingas namely Prithvi, Ap, teyu, Vayu and Akasha. Each contains the vaggeyakara mudra, raga mudra, sthalamudra and linga mudra.

Non-Musical:

Pancha Devi	Durga, Radha, Lakshmi Saraswati and Savitri, the five different forms of nature,
Pancha Danus	A king of the race of Puru.
Pancha Ganga	An ancient kingdaom of Uttara bharata during the time of Pandavas .
Pancha Ganga	A sacred place of Uttara bharata.
Panchagni	Rohini a daughter and soma a son were born to Nisha, the third wife Manu., an agni.Besides this, they had five sons in the form of agni . And these are called Panchagni. They are Vishvanara, Visvapati, Sanihita, Kapila and Agrani.
Panchajana	A mighty asura who lived inside a conch
Panchajana	A King who gave his daughter Panchajani in marriage to the Great Sage daksha.

Panchajana	The five castes Brahmins, Kshatriyas, Vysas , sudras and Nishadas.
Panchajani	The beautiful daughter of Visvarupa.
Panchajanya	The conch of Sri krishna.
Panchajanya	A forest near the mountain Raivataka.
Panchajanya	An agni it was so called as it was born of the parts of five sages.
Panchaka	One of the two soldiers presented to Subhramanya. By indra.
Panchakarna Vatsayanam	A vedic preceptor.
Panchakshara-mahatmi	Namasivaya composed of five letters.
Panchala	An ancient village of bharata.
Panchali	Wife of the five brothers of Pandavas .
Panchasiksha	A sage of ancient times who was a diciple of Asuri
Panchatantra	An ancient book of distinction written by the scholar Vishnu sarma in the form of stories.
	For the use of children.
Pancha bhuta masana	Prithvi (Earth), Ap (Water). Tejas (Fire), Vayu (Air) and Akasa (Ether).
Panchabrah-	This is a divine cot with brahma, vishnu , sivan, and eswara as its four legs and sadasiva as a couch.
Pancha Kanya	Five women who are said to have remained virgins even after their marriage. Namely Ahalya, Draupathi, Kunthi, Tara and Mandodari.
Pancha Dravya	Five materials, milk, ghee, curd, cowdung, and cow's urine.
Pancha Deva	Vishnu, Siva, Surya, Ganesh and Durga.

Pancha Pran	Five varieties of prana namely pran, apan, saman, vyan and udahan.
Pancha ratna	Neelam, Padmarag, Munga, Moti and Heera.
Panchavati	A place near godavari.
Panchavati	A group of five trees namely Peepal, Vata, Bhel, Harada and Ashoka.
Panchasheel	A five fundamental principles of buddhism such as Astheya, Ahimsa, Brahmacharya, Sathya and Detachment from material life.
Panchamritha	Milk, Honey, Curd, Ghee and a mixture of Jaggery.

3

Significance of Panchaka in Indian Music

Significance of the Term Panchaka in Music

Panchaka's manifestation in various branches of music can be seen from the time of Vedas. The following facts form interesting prelude to the study of the *Saman* scale and *Panchaka.*

The original sound first produced is duel- the octave of three notes, then the fifth- from which all other sounds came. Five principal sounds were selected from innumerable sounds that existed in the world which was adequate to represent the world we live in. Probably the *'audava'* the scale of 5 notes must have been created in this way which corresponds to the five directions and five elements. Later on two auxiliary notes were added to the five note scale and completed the scale of 7, which corresponded to the seven celestial planets. The corresponding note to the constant tonic note (shadja) in *Sama gana* was known as the '*ison*' in Byzantine music. It was also called as *chandovath sruti* in ancient Indian music.

The *Vedic* hymns can be considered as most authentic examples for world's ancient system of music.

The *Vedic* hymns are composed of *chandas* or *Vedic* metres. A hymn is chanted according to the need of occasion. It is a recitation of collective types. The rhythm of

Sama gana obeys the rule of *laya*, but does not employ any *tala,* a cycle of measures. Hence *Sama gana* is only a chant which employs 5 instead of 3 notes and controls the original rig of repeating the *sthobha* letters over and over again.

The five rules related to the wording of *Sama Veda* are:

1. The Uhagana - Obviously composed in view of a regular instruction of rite. It contains the main chants that are sung by the three chanters.

2. The Uhyagana- regular order is sometimes interrupted for Samans, the melodies of which are of such holiness that they must be practiced in the words and united in a separate collection, the Uhya-gana. i.e., a scholastic abbreviation of uha rahasya gana.

3. Uttarachika mainly contains the texts of uha and Uhya gana, namely, crossing each other, according to the order of rite.

4. Grama-geya-gana and Aranya-gana are prominently sacerdotal books. These two books contain each melody which is provided with a stanza only .*Grama geya gana* contains songs that are memorized in the house of the teacher and *Aranya gana* is studied outside the village.

5. *Poorvarchika* and *Aranyaka* samhita comprise the texts of the grama *geya gana* and *aranya-gana*. Texts that occur in *grama geya gana* and asume a new melody in the Aryanya gana are not maintained again in the *Aranya Samhitas.*

Although there are two established views that *saman* chant has 5 divisions out of 7 divisions by different schools, the view that holds that there are only 5 divisions seems to be correct. The five bhaktis are used only in Brahmayajna prasna where as the seven bhaktis are used in sacrifices.

Panchama Veda and Pancha Upavedas

When we analyze the term Pancaka in different facets of life, it is astounding that Panchaka in some form or the other has appeared in various fields like Dance, Literature,

Theatre, Mythology, Geography, etc.While probing into the detail and original background of the Panchaka in different fields, the greatness of this magical number 5 is really astonishing.

The Natyashastra of Bharata is considered to be the 'Pancha Veda' the fifth Veda, and it is the Veda of all art forms of India.

In the cultural domain of vedas there is another group of five disciplines called upavedas: 1. Natyaveda (Dance attached Atharva Veda) 2. Gandharva Veda (Music attached to Sama Veda) 3. Dhanur Veda (Archery attached to Yajur Veda) 4. Arya Veda (Medical science attached to the Atharva Veda) and 5. Sthapatya Veda (Art and Architecture attached to the Atharva Veda).

There seems to be another set of 5 Upa Vedas referred to by the architects and sculptors of South India such as 1. Sabda Veda (poetry) 2. Andhra Veda (Music) 3. Natya Veda (Dance) 4. Vastu Veda (Architecture) and 5. Silpa Veda (Sculpture). These five Upa Vedas fall under two distinct categories of universe, the former three under 'Sabda prapancha' (universe of articulated sound forms, ie. sound) and the other two under Artha Prapancha (the universe of meterial forms i.e., visual objects)

The Pancha Vidha Saman

Saman or *Sama gana* consisted of five parts, *parasthara, udgita, prathihara, upadrava* and *nidhana*. They were also called as *alapana, udgraha, melapaka or anudgraha, druvaka* and *abhog* in later days. Prasthara, the first kind was like a prelude sung by the *prasthola,* i.e. the convener or the organizer of the ceremonies. *Udgita* was the main theme of the song sung by the *udgatha*, the narratar. *Prathihara* was the first response or reply sung by the second priest. *Upadrava* was the second response sung by the narrator and the *Nidhana* was a closing song sung or a chorus sung by all the participants of the ceremonies.

The singer while singing the texts very often resorted to the use of sthobhas or sounds of particular meaning like *him, a, au, ho,vi, bha* etc. which are about a thousand in number. These were called as *phul* or *pushpa* (blossoms of flowers).

Though the number of notes used in this music varied according to various schools, *Gana* was mostly sung with five notes. The *saman* had a sacramental character and was closely connected with liturgy whose central theme was *soma* sacrifice. The extraction of juice from the soma plant for Gods was all a series of interrelated rituals.

Panchabhuta and Nada (Musical Sound)

Hindu metaphysics explains how the world is composed of the five elements which we perceive separately by five distinct senses. The senses that correspond to the five elements can perceive also the lower elements but not the higher one. For earth whose corresponding sense is smell, can be perceived by all senses; Water which corresponds to the sense of taste is perceived by all senses except smell; Fire which corresponds to the sense of sight can't be tasted or smelt; Air which corresponds touch cannot be visible; and finally, Ether can be perceived only through sounds*

Being unable to verify our hearing perceptions with the help of any other sense, it is impossible for us to justify the divisions of sound because we have not direct element of comparison. Sound can only be utilized through its reaction upon other elements, such as Air. For example, Air's sensible quality is touch. Therefore sound is a vibration of Air which by touching our ear forces the eardrum to vibrate.

Air can be considered further as the covering which prevents sound that is the vibration of the Ether. When the Air is allowed to vibrate it allows the sound to pass and it becomes the vehicle of sound. The speed of sound wave which is lower in Air than in most liquids and solids becomes slower as the temperature of the air goes down. That is when the speed of atoms decreases. So, at the absolute zero the speed of the sound wave in still air would be nil. As the ear cannot perceive the Air it is considered that airwaves and consequent sounds are not perceived by the ear as an air vibration. Still-air is opaque to the perception of the ideas. When the air is to make to vibrate then it is saved that sound (*Dwani*) which is the vehicle of the idea (Sphota) should be considered as a quality of the idea. That is an accessory phenomenon.

While the divisions of the light like blue, red, yellow, green etc., the divisions of

***Manusmruti , Chapter- I, Verse 20.**

sound are the subjects of constant extroversy. Hence it becomes difficult to fix the divisions of the sound as we do the divisions of light. Hearing as the sensitive organ of the Ether is at the limit of our perceptions. Thus the natural and real divisions of sound are not generally demonstrable. The realistic ratio between two sounds is however of different nature; it represents musical vibrations. The same ratio also represents the relative rank of the sound in the scale of harmonics; for example 25/24 is the interval between the 24th and 25th harmonics. The same ratio also represents the length ratio of pipes or strings etc., this ratios are considered as the expression of general law of sound.

Saman and the Early Church Music

A curious resemblance existed between the Saman hand and what is known as the Guidonian hand. The guidonian hand refers to the practice of using the human hand as an aid in memorizing the scale and its solemnization syllables, probably, instituted by guide of Arezzo (A.D. 980-1050). It is a sketch of a hand with the names of tunes inscribed in its various parts. It some how attained a supernatural significance, and has stood for a complete mastery of the mediaeval system of hexachord and mutation, as the epitome of the entire system of church modes.

It is interesting to note that this mode of using the hand was in both the systems, though they find no place in art music. While singing Saman, the singer intonates his musical tunes with the help of five fingers of the right hand as follows:

1st finger - the thumb stands to denote the first note to be sung.

2nd finger - next to the thumb, denotes the 2nd note lower than the first.

3rd finger-the middle finger denotes the third note lower than the second.

4th finger-denotes the fourth note of the saman.

The last finger denotes the 5th note of the saman.

In the procedure the thumb is made to move and touch the other fingers, and helps the Saman singer to sing the Saman tunes with proper intonation. The fingers serve as a musical staff in Sama gana. This tradition is still in current in Sama gana singing. This tradition of denoting notes by touching the finger must have been begun to enable the singer to intonate correctly, the tunes of Saman. Thus any number from 1-5 placed above the first letter of Saman becomes the fundamental tone of the saman.

The Pancha Nada

Matanga muni in '*Brihadesi'* divides the *nada* into five as he puts it:

"*Sushmo nado guhavasi brudaye chati sushmakah*

Kanta madhye sthito vyaktah avyakta staludesake

Kritimo mukha desetu joneyam panchavidho bndhaih"*

He categorizes *nada* into five such as *Sushmam, Atisushmam, Vyaktam, Avyaktam* and *Kritirimam.*

"Ati Sushmascha pushto pushtascha kritrimam"

When Sarangadeva and Parsvadeva name *Vyaktam and Avyaktam as Pushtam* and *Apushtam, Grandhas* like Brihadesi give the origin of these nadas eg. *Sushma* originates from naval, *Atisushma* from the head and *kritrima* from the face**.

Ahata nada is further divided into five namely: - 1. *Nakhajam, Vayujam, Charm jam, Loohajam* and *Sarirajam* according to the *Sangita makaranda****.

1. ***Nakhajam***

This nada emerges from the strings when they vibrate. E.g., Nada originates from stringed instruments like Veena, Sitar etc.

2. *Vayujam*

This kind of nada is produced due to the air blow. E.g., Nada originates from wind instruments like Flute, Nadaswara etc.

---

* Brihadesi- Section - II- 'Nada'

**Sangita Ratnakara- Section -II, 'Pintotpati Prakaranam'

*** Sangita Makaranda- Chapter IV- 'Swaradhyaya"

3. *Charmajam*

This kind of nada is produced when stimulated on the skinned instruments e.g., Nada emerges from skinned instruments like Mridanga, Chenda etc.

4. *Lohajam*

This nada is produced of metahi vibration e.g. Nada produced from instruments like Chengila, Jala etc.

5. *Sarirajam*

The throat of human beings produces this kind of nada. E.g., Nada produced vocally. E.g. Human voice

The Pancha Jaati Srutis

Sangita ratnakara mentions about the five jatis of sruti such as*, Dipta, Ayata, Karuna, Mrudu* and *Madhya*.*

The *Pancha Alankaras*

According to *Sangita parjata*, there are five kinds of *alankaras* to be used for *ragas.* The sloka given in the book is as follows:

> ***"Chakrakaro javoschaiva sankhah padmanibhah smritah***
> ***Varidaschedi tesham hi lakshnam chapi kathyate"****

These five kinds of alankaras mentioned here is 1. *Chakrakaram, 2. Javam, 3. Shankham, 4. Padmanitham, 5. Varidam.*

1. *Chakrakaram*

The usages of svaras as per this alankara, it starts from rishabha sung four times followed by shadja once and rishabha three times.

---

*Sangita Kalpadrumam- Section-I, Chapter III- 'Sruti Prakaranam'

E.g. r r r r   s   r r r
g g g g   r   g g g

2. *Javam*

The svaras goes in the ascending order and descending order and gradually reduces the length

E.g. S r g m p d n s n d p m g r s
S r g m p d n d p m g r s

3. *Sankham*

In this starting from the tara sthai shadja with janta prayoga of 4 aksharakala (2 each) followed by one nishada and dhaivata.

E.g. S S n d   N N d p

4. *Padmakaram*

It goes as follows:

S r   s s s   r g g
R r g   r r r   g m m

5. *Varidam*

Starting from shadja followed by the seventh note for three times, Varidam is sung as follows.

S n n n S d d d S p p p etc.

Pancha Taleswaram

"Alapach pragatalah syatpruthag dvih pada panchakam
Chachatputena tenaiva svarah padasthata param
Dvichachatputa manenapadaih padaha sambhavaih
Karoyontara Stataschapapudena padapanchakam
Tadvaitena svarah pada sthat dvimanena chauitarah

Hudukka padaistha dam shad pitaputrakena cha

Pruthak padamni pancha dvisknaiva svara padakam

Tad dvimanaschankhapadairantarah syata tastrust

Pragyat tatha swarah padah padam muraja sambhavaih

Antarah purva vatas mada bhoyaschavilambitah

Prabandha namna prangmanam metru samatha anangatam

Vakyamalapake nyasah pancha tālesvaro bhavēt

Viravatarah srungara tilakascheti sadvidha

Vira srungarayo stena priyante sarvadevatah"

This is a kind of Prabandha. It begins with a *ragalapana* and is set to five marga talas like Chachatputa, Chachaputa, Shadpitaputraka Sampakweshtaka and Utghata. There are five *padas* with different *dhatus*. All the padas are to be repeatedly rendered in all these five talas. As this kind of prabandha is set to the five marga latas, it came to be known as *Pancha taleswara.**

Panchaka – Its Relation to Notes and Scales

From the musical intervals, utilized in the different systems of music in the world, it is established that their number and the combination are limited in practice. The number of acoustics ratios has district significance in relation to one sound to another in a musical scale. By the permutation of the ratios between different notes, the number of sounds within one octave becomes 53. Further six secondary ones are added to the 53. In all the systems of music in the world be it Hindu, Arabic, Greek or Chinese, we came across the same number of divisions.

Audava:

In Indian music, the scale with five notes is called '*Audava*'. Bharata in his Natya sastra describes audava as:

'Pancha svara manda vitam vijnēyam'

The sangita ratnakara says:

"Vantiyantyudavō treti vyomōkta muduvambudheh
Panchanam tachabhirteshu pancha squkhya tadndbhava
Anduvi sastiyesham cha svarastetanduva matah
Te samjata yatra gite tadouduvitamuchyate
Tat sambandhadonduvam cha pancha svaramidam viduh"

'*Udu*' in Sanskrit means star. The sky is known as '*Uduvam*' as the sky is seen with galaxy of stars. *Akasa* (sky) is the fifth element of the five elements, the *Panchabhuta* thus corresponds number five. When five svaras form a scale it is called '*audava*' scale. Although *ether* the fifth element is mentioned in its substance, this image can be used to represent things, which are not with in the limits of the elements. In the world that is composed of five elements, probably no prime number higher than "5" can enter into the compositions of the substance from which a melodic or an harmonics relation of *nada* emerges naturally. With the introduction of the factor 5 gives us the harmonic scale of which the characteristic intervals are the harmonic major third (5/4), the minor third (6/5), the major half-tone (16/15), the minor halftone 25/24 etc.

There is a fundamental difference between the numerical substance from which the intervals are made and their posterior grouping according to certain numbers for symbolic representation.

The highest number utilized for harmonic intervals is '5' where a completely manifested scale has only seven sounds because in the scale of fifths, only three successive fifths remain with in the limits of the third power beyond which we go out of this worlds extension. But the role of fifths and fourths subsidiary times, these limits is pushed back by one more step. Thus appears the scale of nine sounds, the absolute basis of the structure of all music.

Where we build a series of four ascends and four descending fifths. We obtain a series of nine sounds, which constitutes the first of the universal harmonic scale.

E.g., The four ascending fifths are :

1. G (Pa) =3/2, 2. D (RI) = 9/8 3. A + (Dha+)=27/16 4. E+ (Ga+) = 81/64.

The five fifths are B+ (Ni+) = 342/128 = 278: 14 etc.

The cyclic scale is called scale of fifths because its basic interval happens to be the fifth successive note of the modern diatonic scale. In reality the interval of fifth corresponds to the number "3" its ratio being 3/2, and nowhere in the scale of fifths does the numerical element "5" appear. Musical intervals appear under two aspects: one mathematical, of numbers and logical ratio, the other symbolical and psychological, in which the relations of sounds and their harmony stimulates the musical ideas and philosophy in us.

The fifth is the third sound of harmonies, the first being the fundamental and second its octave. In Chinese music it is said that: "one has produced two, two has produced three, and three has produced all the numbers". It is understood that the third sound, the fifth by its revolutions, produces all other sounds.

Audava and the Chinese Penta tonic scale

The Chinese music and Indian music have certainly some common origin both these systems are based on the universal principles. Traces of this common origin can be found in all their respective technical expressions. There are many historical evidences that these two continuous share a common ancestral house of either but in course of time both these countries have taken two different ways in the developmental process of music of their countries. Fifteen to twenty centuries ago these two countries had a common plat form of music as it is evident in many old documents that there used to be exchanges of orchestra between these two countries.

It is interesting to note that even the Chinese system of music is also based on the five elements like Indians and Greeks, the Chinese recognize in music a perceptible representation of the relation by which the different elements of manifestation are connected. The Chinese thought goes on the two principles, Supplementary and concordant such as positive, spiritual, active, male and warm and second, negative material, passive female and cold. These two terms correspond to the Sanskrit words *Linga and Yoni*, which symbolize Siva and Shakti in other words, Purusha and Prakruti. Chinese system is probably the only system that emphasizes the importance of pentatonic scale. The priority was evidently given to the five first fifths which correspond to the five elements and which alone can be expressed by the integral number according to the traditional definitions. It has to be accepted that the idea that the 'primitive' spectrum had only five colours, which is obviously absurd.

From the history of music of China it becomes evident that the musicians like Chenkeyu (544.520 BC) have mentioned about the place of penta tonic scale in Chinese music and it also shows that there existed the seven-note scale from the very early period. Chenkeyu explained about seven degrees, which is otherwise called in Chinese seven 'lyn', and it indicates that, four or five centuries before the beginning of Christian era, these existed seven note scale. The seven notes were there called the seven beginnings, Chi-shi.

Taking any one of the notes of the first cycle as the tonic note a scale of five notes can be obtained which forms simple ratios with the tonic. The scale of fifth is, therefore in variable and does not allow the study of harmonic preparations and Chords.

"The five notes, ascending to Sen-ma Teshien, correspond to the five types: hevang-chang, thai-cheu, ku-syen, lin-chang and nan-lyu. The numerous given by the Chinese to correspond with the relative length of tubes in the pentatonic scale are: 81, 54, 72, 48 and 64. These numbers hold great cosmological significance in Chinese culture. The numbers 3 and 2 symbolize heaven and earth respectively. The five degrees of Chinese scale are as follows:

1. Kung (c) (Sa)	=	1	=	81/81.
2. Chi (G) (Pa)	=	3/2	=	81/54
3. Shang (D) (Ri)	=	9/8	=	81/72
4. Yu (A +) (Dha+)	=	27/16	=	81/48
5. Kyo (E+) (Ga+)	=	81/64		

If we follow the endless series of fifths, it will dead us to octave after octave, into different vibrating stages, perceived as sound, light, touch taste or smell, and finally, the structure of matter and of atom itself. The graphic representation of fifths will successively give us all important symbolic and geometrical constructions representing as the square, the pentagon, the dodecagon, the circle, the spiral, the babymith, the zigzag etc.

In Chinese concept, the five degrees of scales are assimilated to the prince, ministers, people, works, and the material somas. These degrees are arranged according to the hierarch of the group as:

The degree Kung (tonic) represents the Prince.

The degree Shang (second) represents the ministers

The degree keyo (third) represents the people

The degree Chi (fifth) represents public works

The degree yie (sixth) represents the products.

The five notes correspond to the five natural agents:

Kung (tonic)	-	Centre of the earth
Shang (second)	-	metal and autum
Kyo (major third)	-	wood and spring
Chi (fifth)	-	Fire and summer
Yu (sixth)	-	water and winter.

Panchaka and Tala

Structural pattern outlining a tala is fundamental to both Karnatic and Hindustani branches of Indian music. E.g., North Indian theental of 16 matras is based on the tali and khali. Same principles and the khali parts of the tala are indicated while playing Tabla by closing the bass sand of the bayan (left). This particular feature is predominent in Mridangam playing as well.

The Pancha jatis of a tala:

"Chaturasra statha trya srah Misrah khanta stathaivacha
Sankīrṇah panchadhajneyah jātayah kramatō budhaih"

(Sangitaratnakara)

(Jaatis are five such as Chaturasra, Tisra, Misra, Khanta and Sankirna, which consists of 4, 3, 7, 5, and 9 aksharakalas respectively.)

Chaturasra has four akshara kalas as the word suggests the meaning four. Tisra means 'of three', Misra means the mixture of Tisra and Chaturasra resulting seven aksharakalas, Khanta means 'part' thus khanta denotes the half part of Tisra, and Misra.and Sankirna is a mixture of the two jaatis, Khanta and Chaturasra.

Jaati is considered to be the seventh of the Taladasa pranas. Though there are 32 types of patterns for a sequence of five syllables for instance, one pattern cannot be suitable substitute for another. The tonal qualities of the different aksharas (sasabda) also play a predominent role in choosing a particular pattern. Basically the term jatis is related to the total number of syllabic instants in a sequence and hence the number of jatis can be considered as infinite. But it is conceived by an ancients scholars that a lengthy sequence could be reeknoned in terms of subsequences. All such sub-sequences, forming non overlapping segments of a sequence, were then classified into a smaller number of jaatis as it was necessary to make the quantam of classification compact. Thus five one-digit numbers were chosen to represent the sequences. The numbers are 4,3, 7, 5 and 9 designated with the names chaturana, Tisra, Misra, Khanta and Sankirna respectively accordingly to the aksharakalas they take.in terms of these jatis as any rhtymic sequence can belong to one of this jatis. These jaatis only affect the laghu of a tala where these 5 jatis are applied to the sapta talas they result in 35 talas. Further the five verities of gatis, Chaturasra, Tisram, Kharta, Misra, and Sankirna are applied to the 35 talas as the gatis are also applicable to all angas of a tala it results in 175 talas.

Panchanga Prasthara

Prasthara means splitting a tala anga by menas of mathematical permutation and combinations. There are some norms to avoid repetitions while splitting the Anga.

Panchanga Prasthara is one the three systems of Prastharas adopted namely, Chatuanga Prasthara, Panchanga Prasthara and Samyuklanga Prasthara.

In Panchanga prasthara only 5 tala angas such as Anudruta, Druta, Laghu Guru and Pluta are to be used while splitting the Anga. This is meant for splitting the angas dealing with the five jatis. The Panchanga Prasthara has 22 divisions as follows:

1. ***Prasthara:-*** This means the mode of splitting the Anga. This is of two kinds: 1. ***Nyaya Prasthara*** splitting the Anga as per rules with out any omissions of any tala anga. 2. ***Khanda prasthara**:-* This is divided again into two subdivisions they (1) ***Heena prasthara*:-** Splitting up of the Tala anga keeping the derived Prasthara tala devoid of a tala anga mentioned in particular (2). **Yukta Prasthara**: - Splitting prasthara tala with a particular number of a particular Tala anga mentioned in particular.

2. ***Sankhya**:-* The total number of the prasthara talas got by splitting an Anga.

3. ***Patala:-*** The total number of the occurance of the least angle of a particular system while splitting an Anga

4. ***Meha patala*: -** The total number of all the Angas occurs while splitting an Anga.

5. ***Nashta:* -** While splitting Angas we get innumerable Prasthara talas

6. ***Uddishta**:* - The short-cut method of answering a question about the serial number of a particular Prastara Tala bearing a particular seriatim of Tala Angas, among all the innumerable Prastara Talas, with the help of some sigures, is called Uddishta.

7. ***Anudruta Meru*** (table):- Detailed particulars of all the prastara Talas such as devoid of Anudruta, having one Anudruta, two Anudrutas, three Anudrutas and so on, of all the Anga Prastaras.

8. ***Anudruta Meru Nashta*: -** The short –cut method of answering a question about eh seritim of the Tala Angas of a particular Prastara Tala having a particular serial number, with the help of the figures mentioned in the Meru.

9. ***Anudruta Meru Uddishta**:* - The short-cut method of answering a question about eh serial number of a particular Prastara Tala having a particular seriatim of Tala Angas, with the help of figures mentioned in the Meru.

10. ***Druta Meru***:- Detailed particulars of all the Prastara Talas such as devoid of Druta, having one Durta, two Drutas, three Drutas and so on, of all the Anga Prastaras.

11. ***Druta Meru Nashta*****:** - See item No. 8

12. ***Druta Meru Uddishta*****: -** See item No.9.

13.***Laghu Meru:*** - Detailed particulars of all the Prastara Talas such as devoid of Laghu, having one Laghu, two Laghus, three Laghus and so on, of all the Anga Prastaras,

14. ***Laghu Meru Nashta***: - See item No. 8.

15. ***Laghu Meru Uddishta*****: -** See item No. 9.

16. ***Guru Meru*****: -** Detailed particulars of all the Prastara Talas such as devoid of Guru, having one Guru, two Gurus, and three Gurus and so on, of all the Anga Prastaras.

17. ***Guru Meru Nashta*****:** See item No.8.

18. ***Guru Meru Uddishta*****: -** See item No.9.

19. ***Pluta Meru*****: -** Detailed particulars of all the Prastara Talas such as devoid of Pluta, having one Pluta, two Plutas, three Plutas and so on, of all the Anga Prastaras.

20. ***Pluta Meru Nashta:*** - See item No.8.

21. ***Pluta Meru Uddishta***: - See item No.9.

22. ***Samyoga Meru**:* - a combination of all the Merus mentioned above.

Pancha Tala

References can be seen of Pancha tala in treatises like Sangita ratnakara. These five old talas are as follows:

Chachatputam – This tala consists of 8 matras and 32 aksharas

Chachputam – This consists of 6 matras and 24 aksharas.

Shadpitaputram – This consists of 12 matras and 48 aksharas

Sampakveshtam – This consists of 12 metras and 48 aksharas.

Udghatam – This consists of 6 matra and 24 aksharas.

Panchaka and Musical instruments

Pancha Mukha Vadya

Mythological background

To an Indian, music is a medium to express the religious sentiments of people. It helps transport musical expressions from society to society. The musical entertainment was an essential part of any festivals of yesteryears.

The author of *Basavapuranam** says - when Nandikesvara was born in the mortal world has Basavesvara, devotee of Lord Shiva, his birth was commemorated were the Panchamukha vadya, the great five faced musical instrument is played.

His birth was celebrated in a grand scale where each person was assigned to play on a particular instrument, such as Maddala, Valagrolu or Valakrolu a wind instrument, to sustain the harmony, more appropriately to keep the Sruti (Ottu), Kamsyatalam and Sittitalam.

This musical performance was followed by dance performance. A few musician devotees like Nadarasagnudu Nali Sankariya, who had sound knowledge of music with an expert dancer like Natyanamitandi Gallidevayya were said to have worshipped Lord Shiva through their performances to the accompaniment of the beat of the Damaru, and the Ghanta (Gong) and other musical instruments.

---

* Hindu religious reformer, teacher, theologian, and administrator of the royal treasury of the Calukya king Bijjala I (reigned 1156–67). Basava is the subject of the Basava-Purana, one of the sacred texts of the Hindu Lingayat sect. (Encyclopedia Britanica)

According to Sankar Pandurang Pandit it had been usual to accept to term as referring to the sounds of five musical instruments, the Panchamukha vadya. Following his idea, Walter Elliot quoted to passages from "Ferishtah". He attempted to find in the term Panchamukha vadya and institution of having music played five times a day at stipulated hours as in the "Naubat" the imperial band of Persia. He also ported from the Ninteenth book of Chand Prithviraj Raso** in which it is mentioned that music was played five times a day at the palace gate of Padamsingh, father of Padmavathi. It is pointed out that the passage Chand also refers to a sound of five kinds of music playing every day rather than to the royal band being played five times a day.

In the Ajanta caves 1 to 26, it is well depicted about the drums used dining Gupta period and at Ellora. There are caves depicting the Shiva dancing with the drums as accompaniment. The scenes there show that these drums were handled by a lady tied to her waist and some times hung on her left shoulder.

The cylindrical drums with five faces, the Pancha mukha vadya can be seen in the Nataraja temple at Chidambaram, which belongs to the 16th century A.D. and on the pillar of the mukha anandapa of Kasi Viswanatha temple at Thenkasi. The instrument had five independent resonators all in shape of a pot and the performer labeled as'Banugopan' had ten hands. The first drum is placed on the ground and played by the first and tenth hands. The second drum is played by the second hand of the player and placed on his right, the third instrument is held in the third have and played by the fourth hand, the fourth one is held in the eight hand and played by the seventh hand and the fifth drum is placed on the ground and on the left side and played by the ninth hand.

It can be seen from the Chidambaram temple's representation of Panchamukha vadya, the drum is a very huge one and has a common resonator with five different faces – four in four corners and one in the centre.

The Panchamukha vadya is still played at festivals at the Tyagaraja temple at Tiruvarur. It is interesting to note that the five faces of this drum are named after the

---

** One of the earliest Manuscripts dating 12th Century. Chand Prithviraj Raso was a poet in the Court of Prithviraj Chouhan. (Encyclopedia Britanica)

five faces of Shiva: Sadyojata, Isana, Tatpurusha, Aghara and Vamadeva. Due to its size it is mostly kept in position on a four-wheeled carriage. The diameter of the central face is slightly bigger than the other four. References about Panchamukha Vadya can be seen in the Tamil literary works like Kalladam by Arunagirinathar. The drum is called as Kudamazha and Kuda Panchamukhi.

The cylindrical drum has been in existence from the begining of Christian era. It is first evidenced in the sculptures of Sanchi. This kind of drum is mostly played in processions. The drum is horizontally held across the body of the player tied up with leather strap. It is played by two thick sticks held in the hands of the player. This drum with a netted strap is held horizontally as it is evidenced in the Ajantha cave paintings. The vertical posture of the drum can be seen in the chola frescoes at Thanjavur. But the size of the drum is smaller than the drum seen in Sanchi.

The Structure of *Panchamukha Vadya*

Four pieces of goat-skin are stretched over the four faces on the sides and for the central face there is an outer ring of skin in addition to that of playing face as in the case of mridangam. The skin of milch cow is also used for the purpose. The skin is tied to the instrument by ropes tied to a metallic ring which goes a round the mouth of the resonator. The instrument is played as solo or in conjunction with the sudhamadhalam.

Panchamukha Vadya is probably the heaviest instrument of all the drums. The skin of the faces on the North and South is thin, while the skin of the faces on the Eastern and Western sides is slightly thick. The skin on the Central face, giving the lowest note is very thick. The figures seen in sculptures and paintings give us a mythological idea that the performance of the Panchamukha Vadya was a Deva (celestial) who was subjected to a curse and was told that he would attain freedom from the curse when he performed on this five-faced instrument during the dance of Nataraja.

The *Pancha Maha Sabda*

The Pancha maha sabda or five great sounds comprised of five instruments:

Tivari, Datta, Kahamdikka, Jayaghanta and Kale. The victorious and gallant warriors were given the honour of going in the streets preceded by the band of five instruments. The Pancha maha sabda occurs in the inscriptions denotes titles describing donors of land and other beneficiaries. The prince is said to be the 'Samadhigata Panchamaha sabdha literally meaning, he who has attained the five great sounds or words. References of these can be seen in Kannada inscriptions, sirur inscription and charwar inscription of Vikrama samvat.

In the record of Kanker plates* (A.D. 1213-1214) the epithet is mentioned in connection with Mahamandalika Pamparajadeva who is said to have received the boon from Katyayini Devi. There are inscriptions ranging from A.D. 913 TO 1159 A.D., referring to Mahamandalika panparaja deva. As there are different versions about the Pancha maha sabda, it is commonly interpreted as 'five big drums' as the term Pancha maha sabda refers only to five sounds.*

PANCHA VADYA

The Pancha vadya that comprises of five percussion instruments played in the temples of Kerala is considered to be divine in nature. Hence it is also called as 'Deva vadyam'. The performance of Pancha vadya gives scope for each player to show his talent as each performer is given opportunity to perform indirectly during the performance. Pancha vadyas are mainly of two varieties viz., Anushtana Vadya and Sudha Vadya, depending on the occasions on which it is used.

The term 'Pancha vadya' refers to a group of five instruments played together. It is interesting to trace the evolution of Pancha vadya. The basic Anushtana vadyas are originally classified under the head, Pancha vadya. The following sloka establishes the kinds of instruments used for pancha vadya:

"Dhakka cha kamsya vādyam cha

Bhēri shankhas cha maddhala:

* Inscriptions of Orissa: Circa 5th- 8th Century A.D by Sangita Tripathi, Indian Council for Historical Research (Page No.151)

Pancha vadya miti pralm

Raga Martha visarada:

According to the sloka Pancha vadya is referred to as a group of instruments consisting of Idakka (dhakka), Ilattalam or Chengila (Kamsya vadya), Chenta (Bheri), Shankham and Maddhalam. But today's Pancha vadya is different from the above mentioned in respect of its presentation, the instruments grouped under etc.The present Pancha vadya has a wind instrument called 'Kompu' in its group instead of Shankha. There was Bheri or Chenda in the old group which is now replaced by Timila.

The '*Vadya visesham'* is the instrumental performance that takes place during 'Kudiyattam' performance on the occasion of 'Satvika bhava'. This is also referred to as 'Pancha Vadya'. Here the group of five that consists of the instruments, Milavu, Itakka, Sankhu, Kuli talam and Kurum kuzhal.

This also differs from present Pancha Vadya because the present pancha vadya does not take Milavu, Kurumkuzhal and Kuli talam in its group.

Rudra Anushtana vadya is played in connection with the 'velakkinezhunnellikal' in the temples of Kerala, during the Idakka Pradakshinam. This is performed at night during the festivals. After the completion of Idakka pradakshinam, a brief 'Koti padi seva' is performed which is a performance of songs along with instruments in praise of the deities. After the Koti padiseva is over a conch is blown thrice which the performers follow on Timila and Madhalam. The Maddhalam is used to keep the rhythm. The Maddhalam and conch are played at the beginning and end of the performances which is known as 'Kuttittal' (The group performance of all the instruments simultaneously.) This performance is also known as 'Pancha vadya'.

The style of performance of this kind of Pancha vadya resembles a lot of the present day Pancha vadya both are based on Triputa tala of 7 akshara kala. The conch is blown at the commence-ment. The instruments used are also common, except for Kurum kuzhal, which is not found in the present Pancha vadya. Both follow certain rules in common as seen in the description of Pancha maha sabda. The verities of vadyas viz., Tatam [Stringed instruments], Avanadham (Instruments covered by skin like drums), Ghanam (Made of metal like gong and cymbals) and Sushiram (Wind instruments played with 'Jaya Jaya Gosham' (slogans like, 'Hail to the Lord'}. Thus the Idakka pradakshina pancha vadya has so much in common to the variety of Pancha vadya mentioned to in the Grandhas.

The Idakka pradakshina Pancha vadya that has been is vogue in most of the temples till 50 years ago was performed according to the rules relating to the 'Anushtana Panchavadya'. It is based on Triputa tala of 7 aksharakala. In the beginning as an introductory avarta or rhythmic cycle consists of 56 akshara kala is performed in a very slow tempo is (7x8= 56). This is equal to seven-chempata vattam (One chempata vattam consists of 8 akshara kalas). The Ilatalam that keeps the tempo follows the chempta vattam.

The sacred stage in the performance comes to of 28 Aksharakalas (half of 56). Only three "avarthas', rhythmic cycles are played at this stage and these three avartas are played at three degrees of speed viz., Vilambam (slow), Madhyam (middle) and Drutam (fast). When the vadyas are played in three speeds it is called 'Kalasa'. After this stage there is three more stages with avartas of 14 aksharakalas, 7 aksharakalas and 3 ½ aksharakalas respectively played as kootikottu and it comes to Eka tala at the end. This is then followed by an item called 'Timila idachil', where the Timila players show their ability. This pattern of performance is similar to that of today's Pancha vadya Performance.

The Pancha Vadya of today is an improved version of the Pancha vadya mentioned above. The tala akshara kala for the first stage has been increased to 896 and 1792 in present system. The first stage consists of an avarta of 1792 akshara kalas, the next stage is of 896 aksharakalas and the following stages are of 448, 224, 112 and 52 aksharakalas respectively. Except for these changes in the number of aksharakalas, the Pancha vadya of today does not vary much from the Anushtana Pancha Vadyam of olden days.

The instruments forming the group of five in the present Pancha vadyam are: Timila, Sudha Maddhalam, Idakka, kompu and Ilatalam. The shankhu is blown thrice at the commencement of the performance. The procedure of the performance is the same as described before.

It is only 60 to 70 years since Pancha vadya is elevated to the present artistic status. The two personalities who contributed immensly for the development of the vadya are Venkata chala Iyer popularly known as Vankitachalam Swamy of Tiruvilluvamala and Madhava Vaniyar.

Pancha vadya is mainly used during temple procession after the deeparadhana at sunset. Here instead of Sudha madhalam, Toppi Maddhalam is usually used. This practice is still found in some of the temples in Kerala like the one at Chottanikkara in the Ernakulam district.

The full band of Pancha vadya consists of 7 Timilas, 6 Maddhalam, 9 Itaykas, 7 Kompus, 1 Ilatalam and 1 Shankhu. Another of version of 11 Timilas, 5 Maddhalam, 11 Ilatalam and 9 Kompus are also used in the present Pancha vadya. Some of the best performances can be witnessed during the 'Pooram' festival at Trichur, Kerala. Though the Pancha vadya has become popular through festivals, but the Pancha vadya played as a part of the temple rituals is slowly becoming obsolete.

It is important to analyze few instruments that form a Pancha vadya from account to the present Pancha vadya. Timia, Itayka, Madhalam, Sudhamadhalam, Toppi Maddhalam, Shankhu, Kombu, Kuzhal etc.

Timila

Timila is yet another instrument, which is indispensable in temples having daily Sivelis, for on ordinary days, the pani before the commencement of Siveli, is usually played on the Timila. It also has an important place in the popular pancha vadya performance. It has been specifically referred to even in the tantric works like 'Isanasivagurudeva paddhati'. As an example one sloka is given below.

Sangitanrtta vaditraihi sankha kahala Gomukhaihi
Timilanaka Bheryadyairnadadbhiranaratam"

In the above-mentioned sloka, the sounding of instruments including Timila, Bheri and so on along with vocal music and dance, during the abhishekam done with the water contained in the Madhya ghata (the pot kept at the centre among the group of pots) is refered to. Timila is referred to in many Tiruppukal hymns also. Two instances are given below.

"Kalaikkai vatta timilai parai kotta

Kanakamayilvitta katir pongu kotukal"

"Ituparai ciru paraikal

Timilayotu tavilarai"

The tullal songs of Kunjan Nambiar as said in the case of Centre contain many references to the temple instruments of Kerala. The two examples cited in the case of Chenta can be quoted here for they contain references to Timila also. Another example from "anayuddham" is given below.*

"Tittiyutukkum *timilakal*

Ottum maddalametra tarattil"

Here many instruments including Titti, Utukku, Timila, Ottu, and Maddalam are said to have been sounded as Krishna sets out for the battle field to win over Bana.

A sculptural representation of a similar hour-glass shaped drum suspended from the left shoulder is found in the Aurangabad cave sculpture. In Sanchi, Bhehrut, Amaravati sculptures it is named as Ankhyamrdanga. The resemblance is only in shape. It is depicted as held in a horizontal position. It is shown as being played with palm as in the case of Timila.

There is an interesting mythological story relating to the origin of this instrument Timila. The Asura Surapadma was fascinated by the Damaru held in one of the hands of Lord Siva and he wanted it. But Lord did not want to give it to the Asura. So the Lord asked Surapadma to make a similar instrument. Accordingly Surapadma made one hourglass shaped drum, but slightly longer. When it was sounded, it was felt that there

---

Varma, A.R. Rajaraja (2005). Keralapanineeyam, Kottayam: D C Books, 301-302. ISBN 81-713-0672-1

was something lacking in its tonal effect. Then the Lord made a hole at the centre of shell i.e., near its narrowed waist, by piercing the same with his little finger. After this when the drum was sounded, it was found that its tonal quality was good. This drum was called Tamil.

Structure

The Timila is an hour-glass shaped drum. The shell is made of Jackwood. The size of the wood as per the Sastras is measured according to the 'viral' [finger]

Length	- 24 ½ viral
Diameter at the mouth of the shell	- 6 viral
The diameter at the waist	- 2 ½ viral
The thickness of the shell	- ¾ viral

But now the most commonly found measurements are

Length	- 18 3/4viral
Diameter at the mouths of the shell	- 5 ¾ viral
Circumference at the waist	- 10 7/8 viral
Thickness of the shell	- 3/8 viral

Usually length of the Kutti or shell and the circumference of the mouth will be almost equal.

The shell is hollowed out of a single block of Jack wood and both the outer and inner surfaces of the shell are rubbed so well till the whole shell becomes smooth surfaced. Any projection or irregularity inside the shell will affect the tonal quality of the instrument adversely. A hole is made at the waist. The wood chosen for the shell also must be free from damage. A wild creeper called Vannamkuti or nala in Malayalam is cut, bent and joined to make the frames called 'Valayam' or 'Valayal' in Malayalam. The inner diameter of these frames will be slightly more than the outer diameter of the shell mouths. A gum made of raw-rice is used to glue the skin on these frames. This pasting of the skin to the round frame is a job to be done properly, the tonal quality of Timila is bound to be poor. Calf-skin is usually used for this purpose of making the drum-heads. After making the Vattams or the drum-heads, 6 equally distanced holes are made on the skin very close to the frames. The leather from old cows or bullocks is used to make the long leather brace which is passed through these six holes and pulled closer to hold the drum heads in their position, i.e., on the either side of the shell. This leather brace or strap is only ½ an inch in width. The two leather drum heads with the long leather brace passing though the holes, without the shell is called 'Pota' in Malayalam. The 'pota' is formed at first, the shell is inserted in between, and then the leather strap is pulled and tightened so that the drum-heads get fixed at the two sides or mouths of the shell. After this, the remaining length of the strap is tied round the narrow waist of the drum. The tension of the drum-heads can be altered by pulling or loosening this leather strap. As in the case of Chenta this drum is also suspended from the left shoulder with the help of the 'Katcca' or the long cloth attached to the leather strapes. The drum will be hanging in a slightly slanting position. The one drum-head which is above, alone is used for playing and it is played with both the hands (palms) i.e., giving alternate strokes with each hand.

Only two tones are produced 'ta' and 'tom' and so all the Jatis have to be produced by the quick beats with the palm. There is no place for fingering in the playing technique of this drum. Both the hands have the same function. The proficiency in playing this instrument is achieved by the rigorous practice of the exercise, meant for the easy and quick movement of the hands, in giving these alternate strokes.

The basic lessons are:

Ta kita (3 syllables)

Ta ka ta kita (5 syllables)

Ta ka ta ka ta ki ta (7 syllables)

Ta kkita ta ka (4 syllables)

Timila is used not only for pani playing and Siveli, but also for panchavadyam. There is even a special item called Timila idacchil towards the end of the pancha vadyam performance.

Itaykka

Itaykka is one of the main instruments from the point of view of the temple rituals. Temples with just Sankhu vili(the sounding of the conch) and Pujakottu, to temples with three Sivelis, need Itaykka. The drum might have got its name, from the way it is held while playing. The term 'ita' has two meanings – one is'the left' and the other is 'in the middle'. Both are applicable in this context. Because the drum is held at the middle of its shell with the left hand and played. There are references to this instrument in the Tevaram. For instances

"Kattirikai tuttiri karangu
Tuti takkaiyotitakkai pataham
Ettanai pulappil karuvi ttiralalampa
Vimaiyorkal parasa"

The Tiruppukal hymns of Arunagiri Natar also refer to Itaykka.

Tiruppugal 5 Dimita Dimi Dim..................
Itakkai

Tiruppugal 100 Tara rara ri ri ri ri ri......
Itakkaiyum Utukkaiyum Atira

*The Malayalam work 'Chandrotsavam' by Payyur Bhattatirippad the date of which is roughly estimated as 15th century A.D. makes mention of this instrument, in the context of describing the Chandrotsavam (Lunar festivals).

"Itayilitayil Venllikkahalam
It pataha mitayakka maddalam baddha talam
Virutu kulal Visesha Vadakanam prayogam
Palavayumulavayi hanta candrotsavadau"

The Tullal songs of Kunjan Nambiar refer to Itaykka among the other temple instruments. An instrument resembling this instrument hung from the shoulders and manipulation of the strings done at the centre with the left hand and played with the right hand is represented in the temple sculpture. In konark sun temple also we find the representation of this instrument. In the Adi Kesavaperumal temple at Tiruvattar (the former or original family temple of the Travancore Royal family), now in Tamilnadu near Nagercoil, sculptural representation of this instrument is found.

Itaykka [also called Etakka] is an hour-glass shaped drum not as long as the Timila. The shell is hollowed out of a single block of wood taken from Jack tree (Artocarpus), Red sandal wood tree Santalinus), black wood or black Cassia fistula. The shell is about 7 inches in length and has a diameter of 4 ½ inches at the mouths. The shell is narrower at the centre than at the edges. On both the sides, small nails are fixed near the mouths and thin threads made of palm fibre or horse hair are fastened to these nails in such a way, that they pass across the two mouths. It is the vibration of these strings along with the membranes of the drum heads that give the characteristic tone to the instrument. This phenomenon is referred to in Malayalam as 'Sabdattinu tari Undakkuka'.

Each end or mouth of the shell is covered with a thin membrane taken from the intestine of a cow. Some say that the membrane is the inner skin of the body of the cow itself called Ulluri in Malayalam. Whatever it is, the membrane is very thin. The membranes are mounted on circular wooden frames having a diameter of 8 inches and a thickness of one inch. These frames are made of Jack wood or Anjili wood and covered with the thin membrane. Six holes are made on the frame for inserting the cotton thread or cord. The two drum heads thus made are held in position on either side of the shell by interlacing the cotton thread in between them and tying another cord around the waist of the drum. The tension of the cord connecting the drum heads to the shell is just enough to keep the skin in form contact with each mouth. Hence, though the skin extends beyond the mouth of the shell, for an annular space, about three inces wide, it remains erect and does not slant down there. Four rounded sticks of wood called Jivakkol about four inches in length and about one inch in thickness are attached to the shell near the drum-heads. Eight small balls made of cotton are suspended from either end of the Jivakkol, so that 16 balls will be hanging from each of the Jivakkols. So total number of balls hanging from the four Jivakkols will be 64. These four Jivakkols are said to represent the four

Vedas, the 64 balls and the 64 arts. The six holes through which the cotton thread pass, holding the drum heads in their position, are said to represent the six Sastras.

The Itaykka is suspended from the left shoulder by means of a cotton cord called Kaccha attached to the threads passing above the shell in such a way that the drum hangs in front of the performer in more or less a horizontal position. It will be slightly slanting to one side, the side on which it is played being on the higher level. The shell of the drum is held by the left hand at the centre or the waist and the drum is played with the thin stick held in the right hand. This stick is made of Konna wood (Cassia Fistuea) and it has a length of 15 to 20 c.m. with a thickness of about 5 c.m. It has a slight curvature towards that end which comes into contact with the drum-head, while playing. While the right hand is used to make strokes with the stick, the left hand is used to make tonal variations by moving the shell up and down against the drum-heads in a rubbing fashion. In the books on musical instruments including that of S. Krishnaswami it is said that the tonal variations are produced by manipulating the strings on the cord wound round the waist with the left hand. But what the player actually does is that he moves the shell up and down against the skin-covered drum-heads with his left hand. While he does this, the tension of the string holding the drum heads is altered thus resulting in tonal variation. At the initial stage the student of Itaykka practices the basic lessons not on the Itaykka but on a device called 'Kaimetta'. The strokes are made not with the thin skin, but with a hammer shaped stick made of Tamarind wood (Tamarindu lndica). Kaimetta is a flat piece of wood having a length of four inces and a thickness of 1½ inches, covered at the back with leather and stuffed with coconut fibre, and also provided with a leather hand above. The kaimetta is held in the left hand, the cushioned portion resting against the palm and the fingers inserted through the leather handle holding the Kaimetta in position. The hammer like stick is held in the right hand and the basic lessons are practised on the Kaimetta. The basic lessons are:

(1) *Ta - kku - kkum*
(2) *Ta - kku - kku - kkum*
(3) *Ki - ta - ta*

Of these Jatis, *'ta'* is played as a straight stroke called *'Nerukol'*. As mentioned in the case of Centa, here also *'ki'* and *'ta'* are played by moving the wrist inward and outward respectively. In addition to these separate syllables for these separate movements, there is one more syllable *'kku'* which is played by making both these movements, i.e., moving the wrist inward and outward.

Maddalam

Maddhalam is a drum of great antiquity because; even the Puranas speak of Nandikesvara's performance on the Maddalam during Lord Siva's dance. The original Sanskrit name for this instrument seems to be 'Maddhala' and the derivation of this word is given as 'Marda lati iti Mardalaha' – that which receives blows. Due to the association of Maddala with the cosmic dance of Siva, it is called a Deva Vadya. This association of divinity particularly of Siva is expressed in the 'Sangita Makaranda'.

> "*Dakahinange Sthito Rudra Uma Vama Bhage Pratishthitah*
> Siva sakti mayo Nado Mardale Parikirtitah"

(*Siva* is present on the right head and Uma on the left head of the *Mardala* and the sound from the *Mardala* is *Sivasaktimaya*.)

In Tamil the instrument is known as *Mattalam* and reference to this durm is found in Tamil Literature.

> "*Mattalam Mulanga Variccangam Ninruta"*
> "Mattalam mudaliya Layangu palliyam"
> *"Takita tta kita .... Tani mattalam mulanga varuvone*"

In Malayalam it is referred to as *Maddalam.* Some old manu-scripts mention this instrument as mattalam or Mattali. The work 'Candrotsavam' ascribed to Payyur *Bhattatirippad* seems to be the earliest work in Malayalam to mention this drum, Maddalam. The lines quoted in the case of Itaykka on can be quoted here also. Similarly the verses quoted from 'Syamantakam' and 'Banayuddham' of Kunjan Nambiar quoted in the case of Timila and Itaykka can be cited as example in the case of Maddalam also.

In music literature, Sangitaratnakara' of Sarangadeva (13th centruy) seems to be the earliest to mention this instrument. Several verses are devoted to its specifications, construction and the ceremonies for playing it, beginning as

> "*Atha Mardalam lakshyati*
> *Nirdosha bija vrkshotthah*"

The first portion of this may be summarised as follows: Wood of a good tree bearing fruits has to be used for the barrel shaped shell. Thickness of the shell is to be ½ finger (Angulam), length – 21 angulams and right face – 13 angulams. The middle of the body or shell should be thicker by a finger or angulam. Circular thick hides are to be fixed on either side: 14 holes are to be made at the rim of the leather, and fastned by hide-straps interlocked in zigzag manner. Rings are to be fixed on either end. Through these rings a silk or attractive cloth band has to be passed and tied to the waist for playing. Such an instrument is called Maddhala, Mrdanga or Muraja. Suitable minerals have to be mixed with rice-paste and applied to the left head in a thick layer and slightly smeared on the other head. The instrument produces thunderous sounds. The jatis used are ta, di, te tem hen, nam da etc.

The '*Sangita Makaranda*' of Narada also gives more or less the same description in the lines

> "*Mardala khadira sreshtho*
> *Hinaha syadanya darujah*"

and so on. Here it is mentioned that Khadira wood (Acrecacatechu) is the best for the manufacture of Maddalam, others are inferior.

Sculptural representation of an instrument resembling Maddalam is found in the Konarak temple (12th-13th century A.D.). Maddhalam is depicted in one of the pillars of the Pradakshina Vali in the Adikesava perumal temple at Tiruvattar near Nagercoil.

Even during the period, known as the Golden age of Karnatic Music, we hear of Tambi Appa attached to Tiruvarur temple, who was a disciple of Muttuswami Dikshitar and who was also an expert in playing Sudha Maddalam. While its use in Tamilnadu has become rare, it is widely used in Kerala during temple rituals and temple festivals.

The shape of the Maddhalam of Kerala is similar to the Mridangam, though there are a few important differences in the structure and playing technique. The Maddalam is tied round the waist in such a way that the instrument will be in front of the player in a horizontal position. Of the three varieties of instruments mentioned in the Natya Shastra, viz. Ankhya (that which is kept on the lap), Alingya (that which is kept in an embracing position) and Urdhvaka (that which is kept in an upright position), Maddalam belongs to the second variety, viz. Aalingya Maddalam is mainly of two kinds.

(1) *Suddha maddalam* and

(2) *Toppi maddalam.*

Suddha Maddala

The instrument is about 28 inches long and the diameter at the two ends is about 11 and 10 inches respectively. A ridge ¾" x 1" called Ulikappuram protrudes outside, round the middle portion of the barrel or the wooden shell. The shell is known as Kutti in Malayalam. Normally jackwood is used to make the barrel-shapped shell. But Konna (Cassia Listula) and Venga (Peterocarpus marsupium) are also used. It is reported that formerly the straps as well as the drum-heads were made of ox hide. These leather straps or braces called 'Vary' in Malayalam, passing over Ulikappuram hold tightly the drum-heads to the shell. A paste made fin carbon obtained by burning are coconut palm founds and Purana Katta (iron slag) and cooked raw-rice is applied in a thick circular layer on the left-head and the juice of the raw betel nut is rubbed on to make the paste adhere better. On the right head nothing is applied. The leather drum-heads are attached to the leather hoops called Mudra Varu, woven with the leather braces, as in the case of the Mridangam. Mostly there will be 16 holes in the hoops, through which the leather straps, connecting the two heads to the shell pass. The holes are called Kannu in Malayalam. The straps are tightened to fix the heads on either side of the shell. Handle like structures called Katu varu made by winding thin leather straps on a thread, are attached, to the leather straps passing over the shell, near each of the heads. It is these Katu Varu found on either side (left as well as right) that the two ends of the Kacca are fastened. Kacca is the long cloth used to tie the instrument around the waist. Two metal hooks will be threaded in the Kacca on either side. Kacca is usually kept tied to the straps. When the instrument is to be played, the player inserts himself or gets into the gap between the drum and the kacca in such a way that the Maddalam will be in front of his waist and the Kacca at the back. Then the metal hooks are connected to the leather straps passing horizontally over the shell, thus keeping the drum in its position suitable for playing.

Toppi Maddalam

In size and construction it is similar to the Mrdanga. It does not have the Mittu leather as in the Mridanga and the bulge on the middle portion of the shell. No flour paste is applied to the left head. Toppi Maddalam does not have the pleasing and the characteristic sound as the Suddha Maddalam. Toppi Maddalam is normally meant for rituals inside the temple. It is also used for art forms like Ottam, Tullal and Krshnattam. It is now being replaced by Mridanga.

In addition to these two varieties, there seems to be one more variety, viz. Vira Maddalam. The details about its structure are not available, but the occasions, on which it is used, we can assume that it is z large version of the Sudha Maddalam.

As its very name suggests it is obviously intended for Vira rasa and is associated with royality eg. In every ritual and function connected with the Maharajas of Cochin, the Vira Maddalam is played. It is a king size instrument. It was used during the military marches and campaigns and during 'Atta Chamayam' procession of the Maharaja of Cochin – this procession being a commemoration of a victory of their dynasty. For the elephant procession of Triprayar Tevar (Sri Rama) for the famous Arattupula Puram Viramaddalam is used, the idea being that Sri Rama is received with royal honours.

We find that these three maddalams differ mainly in size though most of the other details including the posture in which they are held and played are the same. All these are tied to the waist and played with both the hands.

It is not possible to adjust the Sruti in the middle of the performances as done in the case of Mridangam. But once the Sruti is set, it does not alter easily. Fingering is also less, when compared to the Mridangam technique. Fingers particularly of the right hand are covered with fumed cloth, rings and caps for protection and also four louder sounds, as in the case of the Tavil players. Another important difference between Maddalam and Mridangam is that the Mittu leather is not found in the Maddalam it is played with the left hand. Because of the bigger size of the instrument and its use in the open air, the force of the beats is much more and justifies the Sanskrit name 'Mardala' fully. Since the instrument is very heavy, the strain that is involved is not only in playing for hours together with the instrument tied to the waist but also walking with it in procession.

Maddalam is played during temple rituals, in temple festivals and elephant procession, in Kathakali, in Krishnattam and in some folk arts in Kerala. It is one among the five instruments constituting the Pancha vadya group. The special item played on this instrument during Vilakkacaram in a temple is called Maddalappattu and in connection with a Kathakali performances, Maddhala kkeli.

The student does not commence with their learning on the Maddalam itself. Instead they use a dummy instrument called Sravanappalaka literally a plank for hearing. This consists of two circular planks held in vertical position and fixed on either side of wooden reapers running horizontally.

Sankhu

Sankhu is of great antiquity and is referred to even in the Puranas. According to Hindu Mythology, it is one among the four attributes of Lord Vishnu – Chakra, Gatha and Padma (Conch, Discuss, Club and Lotus). In the Mahabharata the names for the conches of Lord Krishna, Arjuna and Bhima are given as Panchajanyam, Devadattam, and Paundram. Conch was blown to declare war and also for welcoming importance guests.

Sankhu is represented in the famous Ajanta paintings, Shankhu attached to a metal piece is also found in the Amaravati sculpture (I and II century A.D.). It is also represented in the sculpture found in the Balikkalpura of Adikesavapperumal temple.

When we take consideration the technical aspects and artistic skill, Shankhu stands only next to other wind instruments. But the auspicious sound of the conch which reminds one of the Pranava i.e. Omakara nada is inevitable for all the rituals or Anushthana karmas. We can even say that no other Anushthana Vadya possesses this much divinity and sanctity.

Structure

Shankhu or Conch is actually the strong outer shell of a Mollusk of the ocean. There are two varieties – Itampuri and Valampuri. Valampuri is a rare one while Itampuri is very common. Coil-like structure circling round and round resembling the tops of some vessels having grooves, are found inside the conch. Depending on the clock-wise or ante clock-wise direction of these grooves, the Shankhu is called Itampuri (spiral to the left) and Valampuri (spiral to the right). Valampuri Shankhu is something very special. Valampuri Sankhu sometimes becomes an object of worship instead of being an object for worship.

Technique

There is a saying that Shankhu should be played as 'Shankhu' meaning that the pictorial representation of the sound of the Shankhu must resemble the shape of the Shankhu i.e. narrow at both the ends and wide in the middle. This can be achieved by sounding the Shankhu in such a way that in the beginning the sound will be feeble, and then it gradually increases in Volume and pitch reaching the highest peak and then gradually fades out and merges in the thin air. One who blows the Shankhu should control his breadth as long as he can, so that the Sankhu nada can be heard for a longer duration. The blowing must be incessant also. Sounding the Shankhu with breaks in between is considered inauspicious and is believed to bring on evil effects. There is a saying conveying this view 'Muri Sankhu mutikkum'

The primary and the most common instrumental performance connected with the daily Pujas of the temple are Shankhu Vili or blowing of the Conch and Puja Kottu or sounding of the drums during Pujas. The temple authorities and devotees see to it that at least these two items are done without fail. If that is also not possible, they try to maintain at least the Shankhu Vili. The Omkara nada emanating from the Shankhu spreads far and wide in a calm atmosphere. Wherever the Shankhu nada from the temple reaches, the blessings of the God are also supposed to reach…

Though one, who blows the Shankhu, must have good practice to produce the proper sound from the Vadya, there are no special exercises meant for this. He learns to blow the conch, by listening to his seniors blowing it and imitating the same.

During most of the rituals blowing Shankhu is an indispensable into thick cords is inserted through these holes and tield in such a way that they serve as handles, to hold and play the instrument. By holding these handles in each of the hands, the two circular pieces are struck together and then the tip of one piece is slid over the other and this gives a prolonged jingling sound. This is done especially when playing in slow tempo. This shuffling action is the peculiarity in its playing.

The normal sized Ilattalam will have a diameter of 13 ½ c.m. Bigger Ilattalams are also there.

In ancient granthas it is referred to as Brahma talam. Sculptural representation of the same is found in the Konark temple. In the Adikesava temple at Tiruvattar (now in Tamilnadu) also this is represented in the sculptures.

In 'Unni nilisandesam' (14th century – author is unknown) a similar instrument is referred to in the line

"Talam pole pulari vanitaykkagataucandrasuryau"

Here the rising sun and the setting moon are compared to the two discs constituting the 'talam' while in action. It seems as though the sun and moon constituted the 'talam' to be played by the Lady viz. Dawn. Kunjan Nambiar has mentioned Ilattalam also in his Tullal stories along with other instruments. For example in 'Balyutbhavam' he refers to the instrument in the lines quoted below:

"Melattinokkunna cengilayu mila
Ttalavum tittiyum tamburu vinayum".

Itattalam is used to keep rhythm during Chenta melam, Pancha vadyam and Tayambaka. They actually add melakkoluppu or live ness to these performances. No special exercises are taught. The knowledge of different talas and experience gained through listening and practice is enough. This instrument is used in Kathakali also. The assistant singer called 'Sinkiti' is the one who plays this instrument, while singing. The jingling sound of Ilattalam gives more beauty to any performance, in which it is used.

The Kurum Kuzhal

The Kurum-Kuzhal, also called Kuzhal, is one of the musical instruments traditionally used in temple-worship in Kerala. It belongs to the class of "Sushira Vadyas" or Wind instruments. It is a double reed pipe-a diminutive Nagaswaram- and is almost the same as the Shehanai of the North and the Mukha-Veena of the South.

The instrument may be 12 to 18 inches long. It consists of a conical wooden pipe (called Olavu) with a metal bell bottom attachment called Kizh Anasu. At the top end the reed (Narukku) is fixed to a small metal top attachment called Mel-Anasu. In some instruments there will not be a top attachment since that portion will also be turned out of the same piece of wood as the tube. The bottom attachment may also be of wood. The reed is made by a detailed process from a reed plant growing wild in marshy places. This is fixed to a small tube called Nelli, which is inserted, at the top of the pipe to fit properly. Formerly a circular metal or horn or mother of pearl is called Kavulidikki used to be fixed at the end of the reed. This disc is rarely seen nowadays. This disc is said to help-quite correctly. I should think-even toothless artists play properly. Spare reeds, a horn or ivory bedekin (to clear the reeds) are hung from a string connecting the top and bottom attachments. It has seven holes in one line and there is one more hole at the top on the lower side, which is closed by the left thumb while playing.

The word Kuzhal (Kulal) means a tube both in Malayalam and Tamil. In musical parlance Kuzhal means a musical instrument. To differentiate instruments, names like Oda Kuzhal (flute), Kurum Kuzhal (short pipe) etc. are given. Kuzhal is mentioned even in one of the earliest Malayalam works, the Ramakathapattu of the 14th century. Kunchan Nambiar in his Tulla Works mentions the name Kurum Kuzhal itself along with other instruments including Nagaswaram.

The expression "Kottum Kuzhalum" and "Kombum Kuzhalum" are often seen in literature as well as spoken language. Kuzhal is also mentioned in Silappadikaram, the famous Tamil epic.

This type of double reed pipes is found all over the world, but, when a Keralite considers the process of its development, he gets nostalgic memories of the toy "peepee" made from coconut palm leaf by children. A one inch bit of coconut palm leaf is folded length-wise. The two halves are manipulated to take slightly curved shape so that the ends would be elliptical. This would serve as a toy reed and when long bits of palm-leaf are wound round this, to make a conical tube, the child gets a good toy whistle. Fixing the leaf reed to the tubular leaf stem of a papaya plant further develops this toy. Some holes are also made on the tubular stem to produce different notes!

We see the next development in the Kuzhal used by the Paraya community in Kerala. The reed is made of four bits of Palm-leaf (Palmyrah). In the instruments normally available in Trichur District the stem is a conical tube made of any jungle wood and is about 6" long and 1" diameter at the bottom. A thin bell-metal bell attached to this is about 4" long and has a diameter of 4 ¼" at the end. The bottom most hole is 2" from the end of the wooden tube. There are 4 more holes and the distance between each is being gradually reduced. There is a coconut shell disc lip-guard between the top hole and the reed called Kavilaati. The bell is called Kuzhal Talam. There is not top attachment but the reed is fixed to small metal tube (Nelli) and fixed to the top with strings in a crude way.

The play this pipe for their social functions like the attainment of puberty of girls, death ceremonies, for festivals like buffalo race, 'Dance with a Headgear' (Mudiyattam), the Oracle (Velichapad), dance in Devi Temples etc. They have some songs, which they sing in a peculiar mode appropriate to the occasion and the notes produced in their Kuzhal correspond to these chants. A trained ear can easily distinguish the different modes of these chants. The following svaras are heard: Sa Ga Ma Pa Ga Ma Pa Dha Pa Ma Pa Ma Pa Ga. While they produced only some 3 or 4 notes on their Kuzhal it has a weird, eerie or haunting effect, especially when one hears it at night. The 5 holes in this primitive instrument remind one of the pentatonic scales in the development of music.

There is another folk instrument known as 'Eazhava Vadyam' which is seen in the Tenmalappuram area of Palghat District, where there is a good deal of Tamilian influence. As the name suggests the Eazhava community plays the instrument and it is used for some social functions and for rituals and festivals in Kali Temples. A normal instrument has a conical wooden tube about 13 inches long, with bottom diameter about ¾ inch. The bell metal bottom attachment is called Kalam (corruption for Kahalam), which is about 4" long with its bottom diameter also about 4 inches. The top metal attachment is called Melani and is about 2 ½ inches long. There are seven playing holes plus four more vent holes at the bottom. Mandara Wood (Bauhinia purpures) is claimed to be the best. Black wood and Palmyrah wood are also seen. The reed used to be made of palm leaf but now only Nagaswaram reeds are used. The tube of Timiri Nagaswaram is sometimes used now since the demand for a new instrument is almost nil and no one seems to know how to make it. Their practice lessons are called Charali but they do not identify the svaras as SA RI GA MA etc. The students learn from observation of the demonstration of the Guru. After learning the Charali in which there are some 12 lessons they learn to play some pieces, which they call Chindu. Normally half tones are at produced, but of late they have started rendering film songs. The drum accompaniment is called Thavil (which is a bit different from the normal thavil of Tamil Nadu). They do not use Ottu or Sruti. A team consists of 2 or 3 pipers, one drummer and one Elathalam player.

The Nair community in Kerala normally plays the Kurum Kuzhal. Some families have been pipers for generations at some of the temples and many of them have the honorific title of Panicker-which is normally the equivalent of an Army Sergeant or drillmaster. Some references are seen about the use of the Kuzhal during the marching of the Army. The fact that the Nair Community, which is noted for its military traditions, is playing it and that the players are called Panicker goes to show its martial tradition.

In Kerala there are a few special castes known as Ambalavasis or temple servants, like the Marar, the Pisharoti, Warrier etc. The Marars are the traditional drummers and musicians in the temple and for some of the most important rituals they play the instruments like Sankhu, Chengila, Paani Maram, Edakka, Chenda and Thimila. There is no place for instruments like Kuzhal or Kombu during these rituals like Sri Bhutta Bali etc. As such one is led to be conclusion that the Kuzhal and Kombu were in fact "foreign" instruments, which later got absorbed into the temple service in Kerala. The Kuzhal is used now in some of the temples- for Palli Unarthal, for Seva three times a day, for Seeveli or circumam-bulation with the Utsava Vigraha (called Thedambu), for Chenda Melam during elephant procession, during festivals and also for Kootiyattam-the traditional Sanskrit Stage of Kerala.

An instrument called Madhukari is described in the Sangita Ratnakara of Sarngadeva.

This may be translated as follows:

A good Madhukari is 18 'angulas' long (one angula is a little more than one inch) and may be made of horn or wood and is shaped like Kahala (conical tube). The opening at the blowing end is the size of Tuvar (Dal) seed. Four inches off the mouth, 7 holes are to be made as in flute and another hole is made on the lower side between the mouth and the first hole. For getting a sweet sound a 4-inch copper tube of the diameter of barley seed is fixed to the mouth and on top of that a circular disc of ivory or mother of pearl is to be fixed. In the hole of the tube a reed having the shape of a partially opened Jasmine bud made from Deva Nala (a reed plant) and made soft by cooking in milk is to be fixed. The Madhukari is to be played like a Vamsa (flute). The hole in the lower side is to be closed by the left thumb.

When one compares the specifications given for Madhukari with that of Kurum Kuzhal we see they are almost identical.

The instrument used to be made in Kerala in several places like Trippunithura near Cochin and Panamana Village in Palghat District, Tiruvilwamala in Trichur Dist. etc. Due to decline in temple finances, the temple arts also declined and the demand for the instrument became negligible. Hence it is no longer made in Kerala. It is usually obtained from manufacturers of Nagaswaram in Tamil Nadu, from places like Narasingampettai in Tanjore District. Old broken Nagaswarams are also cut to make

Kurum Kuzhal now.

Training

Traditionally the young boy goes to help his relatives who play in the temple. He keeps the cymbals for Talam. Then he starts playing the Sruti (Ottu) and learns to breathe and blow at the same time. This is called Swasam Marikkuka. For this a bamboo tube is taken and blowing is practiced on it. Saptasvarams are learnt-first vocally, then on the instrument. Teaching goes on as in the case of traditionally Carnatic Music, with saptasvaram, Varisai, Alankaram, Gitam, Varnam and Kirtanam. Then the student graduates to the playing of Ragas and Parru. Parru is similar to the rendering of a Pallavi. It is described later.

With the decline in the patronage for the temple arts the income of the artists also went down very much; so much so, all Kuzhal artists have taken to the playing of Nagaswaram, since it is in greater demand, especially for marriages etc. They have neglected the kuzhal and this has led to a great deterioration in the standard of playing, and one can rarely come across a Kurum-Kuzhal artist who can play it really well.

The holes in the Kurum-Kuzhal are made to correspond to the Harikambhoji scale. Sharper or flatter notes are rendered not only by opening or closing the holes partially but also are the adjustment of the reed in the lips, pulling it out or pushing it inside the mouth and thus effectively altering the length of the air column in the tube. The last hole (in the bottom end) is taken as the shadja, the solitary hole in the lower side closed by the thumb is the nishada and the first hole (at the top end) is the upper shadja. So the player is handicapped when he has to play the notes below the basic shadja. By closing the last hole near the bell-bottom, with the little finger he can get Nishada and by pulling the reed out the can produce Dhaivata and even Panchama.

We may now compare the Kurum-Kuzhal with other similar instruments. As already mentioned this type of wind instrument is found in many places. We considered earlier the details of Madhukari as given in the Sangita Ratnakara. This name exists in its Prakrit or slang form in the Mohuri of Orissa. It is used in temple rituals and in folk dances in Orissa. This name is again further corrupted in the Mori of Mysore.

The Nagaswaram is a development of Madhukari. The name Nagaswaram is not mentioned in literature before the 14th century. There is no hole in the Nagaswaram in the lower side to be closed by the thumb. There are also 5 holes at the bottom in Nagaswaram, which are for the control of air exit. The shadja is kept on the third hole from the top and this enables the player to render the lower notes up to Gendarme even. So, what is shadja in the Nagaswaram will be Panchama in Kurum-Kuzhal. As the length of the Nagaswaram is much greater, the pitch is lower.

The Shane is almost like the Kurum-kasha in size and appearance, but it does not have a thumbhole on the lower side.

Mukha Veena

This instrument was once popular in Tamil Nadu and it is still in use in some temples. It used to be part of the Bharata Natyam orchestra (Cinna Melam). In the description of this instrument got from one source the size of a normal instrument is given as 11 inches. It has 8 holes but no 'thumb' hole on the lower side. The last but one hole is kept as the Shadja. But, in the description got from another source it is mentioned that in olden days Mukha Veena used to be about 14 inches long and that it had seven holes plus a 'thumb' hole in the lower side and the lowest hole is taken as the Shadja.

From these we can conclude that the older Mukha veena is identical with the Kurum Kuzhal. Mukha-Veena is mentioned in Malayalam literature also and it is probably in areas Like Trivandrum where Tamil influence is more, that the instrument was known by both the names Mukha Veena and Kuruam Kuzhal. Traditionally the wood to be used for the tube is Karungali (Sanskrit Khadira, Acacia Sundra, and Tamil Karungali. Ebony and Dark Rosewood were also used.

The reed used to be made a plant known as Amma growing in marshy places. This Amma (called Sara in Sanskrit) is also used for some Vedic sacrificial purposes in Kerala. The reed is collected during the summer before the advent of the rains. It is dried in the shade and kept aside for a year. It is then cooked by inserting it in par-boiling paddy. It is again dried and then it is cooked with some meat. It is then washed and dried. Bits are cut to size and cylindrical piece of wood is inserted inside and rubbed with a strong string or a piece of gut. It is then put in a press to give it the proper shape. Nowadays no one attempts to make it in Kerala. They get it from manufacturers in Tamil Nadu. However the proper size required for Kurum Kuzhal is smaller than that required for the Nagaswaram and what they get in Tamil Nadu is the one normally required for Nagaswaram. With the ill-fitting reed the quality of the performance declines.

All instruments made from the cut tubes of old Nagaswarams do necessarily have the top and also the bottom attachments. These are made of good bell metal. The artists always keep these metal attachments well polished which makes the attachments glitter in the Sun during elephant processions. Formerly the bell-shaped attachment used to be plain in shape but now the shape is more artistic with ridges and rings around it.

The Use of *Kurum-Kuzhal* in Temple service in Kerala

It is used for Pallid Unarthal, early morning between 3 and 5 a.m. It is also used for 'seva' morning, noon, evening and night, for Deeparadhana etc. Though the instrument is mostly replaced by Nagaswaram it can still be seen in some of the temples. The following Ragas are normally played according to the time of the day.

3 to 5 a.m.	Bhoopalam
6 a.m.	Desakshi and Bilahari
10 a.m.	Saveri, Dhanyasi, Bhairavi
3 to 4 p.m.	Purvi Kalyani
6 p.m	Kalyani, Sankarabharanam, Nettai
8 p.m.	Thodi, Kambhonji, Yedukulakambhoji, Neelambari Mukhari, Ananda Bhairavi, Kanakkurunji

Seeveli. In many temples the portable deity (Utsava Vigraha) is taken to circumambulate the temple three times at morning, noon and night. This is done to the accompaniment of many instruments like Chenda, Kambu, and Kuzhal etc. In some temples like Tiruvilwamala (Trichur Dist.) special importance is given to the Kuzhal and the playing of several Ragas can be heard according to the time of the day.

In some temples during Pujas: (done with the doors of the sanctum closed)-Nata

Atachu Puja- the Kuzhal is played. This is replaced by Nagaswaram in many places.

During temple festivals there are some special occasions when Kurum Kuzhal is to be played. The ritual is known as Vilakku Aacharam.

The deity is brought out from the Sanctum and kept in a convenient spot. Then several instruments are played individually. This is an occasion for the artists to demonstrate their talents. First a Thayambaka is played on the Chenda. Then a Keli or Parru is played on the Maddalam, then a Parru is rendered on the Kombu and finally a Parru is played on the Kuzhal. Normally only one person plays. He is accompanied by Sruti (drone), a Chenda and one Elathalam (big size cymbals). The playing is started with a few snatches of Natta Raga. Then the main Raga is elaborated. Usually Kamboji, Kalyani, Sankarabharanam, Bhairavi, Ananda Bhairavi, Neelambari, Mukharim Devagandhari etc. are played. Then the rendering of the Parru proper starts. This is akin to the rendering of a Pallavi. The rhythm-keepers join only at this stage, unlike the Nagaswaram where the Thavil is played even during the short intervals of the playing of the Ragam. First it is rendered in Vilamba Kalam. Then it is rendered in faster tempo when usually another Ragam will be played. The Tala used is normally only Chempata (Adi Tala). After rendering in the faster tempo a Nadai is played, usually tisram. This is called Kooru Vayikkal. Then Suruti Ragam is played in a Tala of 4 matras (three bears and a wave). Then a Kalasam (muthayippu) is played in Eka Tala and Madhyamavati Raga. For this sometimes only one cymbal is used by beating it with a stick (a miniature Chengila or Chembakalam). If times permits some Kirtanas are rendered before doing the final Muthayippu in Eka Tala. For this the Kuzhal is accompanied on Toppi Maddalam and not by the Chenda.

It is a pity that a real top-class Patru is no longer available to be enjoyed. The Patru-playing in Tripunithura temple in its hey-day used to take about 4 hours on Valiavilakku Festival day. This should give an idea of the importance given to Kuzhal.

The next function in the festival is known as the Edakka pradakshinam. The deity is taken round the temple to the accompaniment of instruments like Edakka, Toppi Maddalam, Kombu, Thimila, and Kuzhal during this procession. First Nata Ragam is played. Some Rakti Ragas are rendered, set normally to Triputa (or Misra Chapu) talam. The Ragas heard normally are Yedukulakamboji, Paadi, Ananda Bhairavi, Kanakkurunji etc. Some Padams are also played. One such is Mathada bara deno. Some of the Sringara Padams of Kathakali may also be used. In areas surrounding the Thiruvilwamala temple a Pad am heard is Kamini Mani. On probing into the matter I was delighted to find that this is a Mani. On probing into the matter I was delighted to find that this is a Mani Pravala Pada of Swati Tirunal. The full text is given below. The subject matter of the same is a conversation between a Nayika and her Sakhi. The Nayika asks, "why is perspiration seen on your face, why are your eyes red, why is your hair disheveled" etc. The Sakhi gives evasive replies and finally the Nayika concludes that they are proof that her maid through whom she had sent a message to her Lord had herself had a union with Lord Padmanabha.

It may be mentioned here that some of the court musicians of Trivandrum were natives of Tiruvilwamala and the last remnants of the original Mohini Attam survived at the same place. Thanks to poet Vallathol this was revived at The Kerala Kalamandalm. The song Kamini Mani was one of the songs used for Mohini Attam long ago. The original Ragam seen for this song is a strange one-Poorva Kamodari (or Purvikambhoji). It is now rendered as a Ragamalika, usually in the following Ragas, Paadi (Kathakali type). Kanakkurunji, Punnagavarali, Gopikavasantham. The use of Tisrajati Triputa, the use of Rakti Ragas and the use of some of the Sringara Padas during Edakka Pradakshinam would go to show that at one time there might have been the dancing of women preceding the deity.

After Edakka Pradakshinam Chenda Melam for the Elephant procession starts. The procession is a slow one and they stay at some sports for a long time to complete one of the stages in Chenda-playing. A Chenda Melam consists of a number of Chendas, Etam Talams, Kombus and Kuzhals. A few Chenda will be rendering the vinyasams (complicated rhythms) while the rest of the Chendas will be 'beating' the time. There may be as many Kombus and Kuzhals as the number of Uruttu Chendas (vinyasam-players). The Kuzhal artists will be facing these Chnda players and they effectively control the pace and Tala of the Chenda Melam. The chief of the Kuzhal players will be showing signals by drawing circles in the air with his instrument (called Kuzhal Minnikkuka) to regulate the play and to show where the Kalasams (Muthayippu) are to be played. During the interval between periodic Etta Kalasms the Kuzhal may be playing some melody.

For example, for Panchari Melam in Chenda the Tala is Rupaka of 6 Matras. The first phase is done in an extremely slow tempo of 16 Kala Chowkam or 96 Matras. The Eta Kalasam will start at the 80th Matra, from when on, the Kuzhal also will play the Jatis and continue it till the 16th Matra of the next Tala Vatta. By his signs the Kuzhal player will indicate the number of Matras played.

There used to be some conventions as to the Ragas to be played by the Kuzhal artists for various Melams (i.e. for the Chenda melam rendered in different Talams. For Pandi Melam Bhairavi is usually rendered in different Talams and for Panchari Melam Sankarabharanam, Arabhi for Chempata and Saveri for Chempa etc.

Unfortunately however at the present day not two Kuzhals will have the Sruti and now two players will be rendering in the same way with the result that it will be a veritable cacophony, but during the Kalasams they will be playing the Jatis of the Talam and it would add to the over-all grandeur of the Chenda melam. Thus during some stage of the Chenda melam the Kurum Kuzhal has the function of only a Tala Vadya.

Kurum Kuzhal is one of the instruments used in Koodiyattam, the traditional Sanskrit stage of Kerala. This theatre form as it exists to-day is considered to be more than a 1000 years old, its present form being shaped by the a Chera King Kulasekara Varma. The Chakyars who do Abhinaya in Koodiyattam are said to be the same community as the Chakkaiyan mentioned in Silappatikaram. Kuzhal also is mentioned in Silappatikaram as being used for the dances. So this tradition of using the Kuzhal in dance forms is nearly 200 years old.

Unfortunately however at present there is no proper function for the Kuzhal in Koodiyattam. The Sanskrit verse are only chanted and not sung. The kuzhal player renders whatever raga he feels suitable for the occasion.

KOMBU VADYA OF KERALA

Kombu Vadya one of the pancha vadyas of Kerala belongs to the class of Sushira Vadyas or wind instruments. Unlike other wind instruments this is not used for melody but only as a Laya or Tala instrument.

The word Kombu (in Malayalam and Tamil) literally means an horn. It is well known that horns of animals (esoecuakkt cattle) were used as a primitive musical instrument in early times. In course of time animal horn was replaced by metal and the shape also underwent and changes. The Sanskrit word for Kombu is Sringa and the instrument is mentioned with that name in the Puranas.

The earliest reference to an instrument made of horn seems to be in the Mahabharata where it is referred to as Govinshanika (made out of the horn of cow).

The reference in Bhagavata is more appropriate to our subject. The divine cow-herd Krishna is said to be having a Sringa Vadya with him always in addition to the flute. One epithet of His is 'Sringapriya'. Once when he wanted to set out for Vanabhojana (a picnic in the forest) he roused his cow-herd friends early morning by blowing his Sringa.

In the Tamil classic Silappatikaram though the instrument is not mentioned in the text, the commentator Adiyarkunallar mentions that Kombu Vadya was popular at that time.

The great Malayalam poet Thunchathu Ezhuthachan (13th century A.D.) in his Kilippattu mentions Sringa along with several other instruments as being used in the war. Musical instruments made from animal horns are still used by tribal folks in India. The instruments are known as Singha, Singhi, Kohuk etc. in North India. The Todas and Kotas of Nilgiris use musical instruments made out of buffalo horn in their rituals. Buffalo horn instruments are used during worship in a Durga Temple in Kasaragode (Kerala) and it is used even in Dussera processions in Mysore. Instruments similar to the Kombu of Kerala are found in other parts of India also. The Jodkom of Andhra is similar in shape and size. Narasingha of Himachal Pradesh is an S- shaped instrument and bigger in size.

The instrument Sringa is referred to in several Sanskrit texts on Music. Sangita Makaranda of Narada refers to it.

Sringam cha kahalas ceti sushiradi prakirtitah.

In Sangita Ratnakara the instrument is first referred to as

"Vamsikah Pavikah Pavahkahalah Sankhavadakah
Muhari-Sringavadyadyah"

Sangita Ratnakara also gives details about the instrument:

"A flawless horn of a buffalo with an opening having the shape of a she elephant's face (oval shaped) is to be polished and oiled or waxed and made properly fit. An 8inch piece of a bullock's horn shaped as a Dhattura flower should be fitted for increasing the sound. The end (evidently of the buffalo horn) should be cut by two or three inches and a hole made for blowing. By blowing 'Thu', 'Dhu' two different sounds are made and this big sound from it is apt for the dance of cowherds".

It is significant that Sarngadeva in his Sangita Ratnakara has mentioned that the Sringa is used by cowherds and the Bhagavata also mentions Krishna, the King of cowherds as using it.

As already pointed out the Kombu of Kerala is a semi-circular or c-shaped instrument. It is made of good bell-metal. The tablature is conical and it is in three pieces. The instruments are normally in two sizes –Thimiri or smaller one and Bari, the bigger one. Occasionally, an intermediate size known as Eta Bari is also seen. In the Thimiri instrument the curvature at the outer end is slightly turned inside. The Bari is slightly more in curvature than a semi-circle. In the smaller instrument the pieces are fixed together by inserting one end of a piece into one end of the next piece, the tightness being effected by jamming a bit of cloth while inserting, In the bigger instrument the joint is effected by a locking arrangement, the stud at one end getting locked inside a groove in the next piece at the correct position. One string is tied from one end to the other diametrically; the piece of string is held by the hand while playing. It is mainly a protection against the pieces falling apart due to some sudden jerk in the crowds during elephant processions.

At the blowing end the tube is flared to about ¾ inch diameter to the shape of a cup. The lips are pressed against this and blown hard-as with a bugle. Production of different tones is controlled by the lips, tongue and the force of blowing. The outer end is flared to a bell mouth to a diameter of 3 inces. This outer end piece is called 'Ummathu

Muri' (literally a piece resembling Dhattura flower). It is singnificant that the Sangita Ratnakara also describes the shape as that of a Dhattura flower.

The three pieces of the instrument are made by casting bell metal in clay moulds by the process usually known as "Lost wax process". Each piece of the Bari instrument is about 19 inches long. The diameter (if the circle were to be completed) would be about 27 inches. After casting, the pieces are properly filed and polished. As the artisans use comparatively crude methods, some variations in pitch (Sruti) between instruments will be found. In order to adjust the pitch, sections of the tube are either shortened (by cutting away a piece and brazing) or lengthened by increasing the length by casting in situ. The blowing orifice is widened by filling, if necessary. If it be too wide, the size is reduced by pushing in, tight and flush, metal tubing. The Sruti of a Bari instrument will be about 4 or 5 'Kattai' (middle F or G.). The weight of a Bari instrument is about 3 lbs. Each piece of a Thimiri instrument will be about 15 inces and its Sruti will be about 7 or 8 "kattai" (middle B or higher C).

Formerly only the Thimiri instruments were being used temples. The Bari instrument is comparatively of recent origin. It came into prominence with the development and refinement of Pancha Vadya by Venkichan Swamy. Of late Bari instrument is mainly used, the Thimiri is found more with Harijans who use it for their folk festivals.

In central Kerala area (former Cochin State and adjacent areas only the Nair community plays this instrument in temples, whereas drums like Thimila and Chenda were the almost exclusive preserves of the Marar community. Notable exceptions are some Nambudiri and Tamil Brahmins who became famous in playing some of these instruments. In all old and important temples Kombu is an essential instrument for daily Pooja, Seeveli etc. During Utsavas this instrument is sued in all the temples. It is used as part of the ensemble for Sri Bhuta Bali, Velakkacharam, Kombu Pattu, Chenda Melam, Edakka Pradakshinam and Pancha Vadyam. In folk religious festivals like 'Vettakkorumakan Pattu', 'Paana', 'Theyyam', 'Mudiyettu' etc. this instrument is sued. Even the Harijans use this instrument for some of their festivals and dance. The Syrian Christians of Kerala use this instrument for some of their processions but the playing isdone by Harijans usually. Kombu was one of the instruments used during the marching of armies in Kerala. Its martial tradition is still maintained in its use in the Atha Chamayam Procession in Tripunithura near Cochin. Atha Chamayam Procession was started in commemorations of a victory of the Maharajas of Cochin. Though the Maharajas have become commoners, the procession continues as a 'People's' procession.

Unlike other 'Sushira Vadyas' there are no holes or stops for producing various notes in this instrument. It is used as a 'Laya Vadya' in Kerala. The Keralite has a special aptitude for Laya and he has raised this instrument from its primitive levels to that of a classical instrument for Laya. Much of the attraction for Pancha Vadya and Chenda Melam is due to the use of this instrument. It is essentially an out-door instrument and its sound can be heard for miles around, especially in the villages.

Methods of Teaching

First the student is taught to make proper sounds with the Kombu. The lips have to be rounded and the blowing proper. Normal blowing will give the basic note (Sa) and harder blowing will give its higher octave. By controlled blowing it is possible to get Pa and even its octave (Tara Panchama) but it requires much practice and strength of blow, else it is likely to produce discordant notes. Normal playing is therefore confined to the basic note and its higher octave. The strenght of blow can vary the basic note by about a Sruti (and naturally the higher octave also and tonal variations are possible.

The student is then taught to play graded Jatis in Chempata Tala (Jhompata or Adi Tala). This Tala of 8 matras is 'marked time' by 3 beats 1 wave and again 3 beats and 2 waves.

The mnemonics for the first lesion are 'They, Tha tha, Thai, Tha tha, They, Tha tha, Thai, Dhey Dhey'.

Nine different variations of this pattern are taught.

The second lesson is the playing of different Jatis for 4 Tala Vattoms. Third lession is the Kalasam (Muthayipu or Mora).

After these preliminary lessons the student is initiated into the playing of Kombu for Chenda Melam.

Chenda Melam is an ensemble of a large of Chenda (Durms). The other instruments, which join the Melam, are Ela Talam (Brahma Talam), Kuzhal (similar to Thimiri Nagaswaram) and Kombu. Among the Chenda artists a good number will beat out the Tala on the booming (Valam Tala) side of the Chenda.

There will be a number of Kombus. They play together for every kalasam which is played at the end of every few Tala Vatoms. Before the start of the Kalasam all the Kombus will get ready by blowing the lower note. The people on top of the elephants holding the Alavattom (peacock-feather fan) and Venchamaram (Yak tail Swish) will take their cue and stand up holding their fan and swish ready. When the Kalasam is played the swish is waved. This is one of the most picturesque sights of the elephant procession in Kerala.

The Kombu will play for one more Tala Vattom after the Kalasam.

For Chenda Melam, different Talas are used. The Kombu artist has to be proficient in all these talas. Normally Chenda Melam is played in Panchari (Rupakam), Pandi (Tisrajati Triputa) and Chempata (Aadi).

The following Talas are also used:

Atanta (Khanda jati Ata)

Champa (Misra jati Jhampa)

Dhruva (Caturasra Jati Dhruva)

Anchatanta Tala (a Tala of 16 Matras)

For Atanta Tala the time is kept by showing 4 beats 1 wave, 4 beats 1 wave, one beat one wave, and one beat one wave. (Total 14 matras).

The name Anchatanta Tala is probably derived because instead of our beats of Atanta Tala, 5 beats are made for Anchatanta (Anchu means five). This Tala does not fit in the Sapta Tala scheme or 108 Talas scheme in Carnatic music.

Laya Vinyasa on the Kombu is known as Kombu Pattu. During temple festivals before the idol (Utsava Vigraha) is taken round temple on elephants (Pradakshina) the idol in brought to the outer courtyards of the temple and kept on view. Individual instruments like Kombu, Kuzhal, Maddalam etc, are brought in front of the idol and they are played one after another. Such demonstrations on the instruments are called 'Pattu Vayikkuka'.

The duration of the playing of Kombu may be up to an hour depending on the ability of the artist and the time available. Pattu is usually played in Chempata, Atanta, Anchantanta, Chempa or Tala Thericha Chempa. 'Tala Theresa Chempa' is a picturesque colloquial name given by these artists for Khandajati Triputa Tala of nine matras. Since it is one matra short of Chempada Tala of 10 matras, they call it Chempa with its end cut off (Tala Thericha-end cut off).

Kombu is one of the main instruments in Pachna Vadyam of Kerala. Here also as in Chenda Melam, the Kombu is played mainly during the Kalasams of the Pancha Vadyam. At this jucture Alavattom and Venchamaram will be exhibited on top of the elephants.

The artist here Sri Kandangi Appu Nair of Machat is attached to the Bhagavathi temple Thiruvanikkavu of Machat near Vadakkancherry in Trichur District. In this temple some extra importance is given to Kombu Vadyam. During the annula Para ceremony, paddy offerings are collected from lpeople miles around. Only one Kuzhal and four Kombus are used. No drums are played. As a lot of distance and houses have to be covered, the temple servants have to run literally –the Konbu players as well.

At the temple at Maruvathoor near Guruvayoor a very big-sized Kombu is used but of late only the last piece of it is used just to sound it like a Conch during Deeparadhana.

4

Panchaka and *Ragas* in Various Treatises on Music

The *Ghana Ragas* and Their Definitions

The origin and development of *Ghana ragas* are to be studied in order to know their significance and place in the sphere of music from early age.

The literature on Indian music and its scales originate from the most remote antiquity. There were many treatises on *Gandharva* Veda even before the time of *Bharata.* Though they are not available today, the writers on Indian music have often taken references from those *Granthas*. The first complete work on the subject is probably the '*Natya Shastra'* of *Bharata* though it is not a work primarily on music. Another work of authority on music is *Matanga's Brihadesi,* which is relevant even today. The *Sangita ratnakara* of *Sarangadeva* appeared five centuries later, which became a great source of music for the writers that came later. "*Sangita sudha*" though fragmentary is useful in its description about *ragas* as given by *Vidyaranya* in his book '*Sangita Sara'* is yet to be discovered. *Tulajendra*'s '*Sangita Saramruta'* can be considered as the latest work on *ragas* of Indian music. In the *ragas* described by him, *Sancharis* are given and authority of *Thaya, Gita, Prabandha* or *Suladi* is cited. The description of ragas as given in '*Sangita Saramuruta'* perhaps represents the way they were employed in the era immediately preceding that of the musical Trinity of Carnatic Music. Though the

'*Saramuruta*' treats of *Sruti, Svaras, Gitas* and other topics, the chapter on *raga* is very interesting to study as it gives one a very clear idea about how the *ragas* have existed in olden days and what was the nature of a *raga.*

Similarly, the names of some *ragas* prevailing today are given in *Sarangadeva*'s *Sangita ratnakara*. *Tulajendra* begins the *raga* chapters with a brief description of the nature of *raga* on the authority of *Bharata* and *Matanga*. *Ragas* are of many kinds, they are derived out of scales and their purpose is to create pleasurable moments through their melody to the minds of the audience. The traditional descriptions of a *raga* are given as a musical rendering beautified by sounds of difficult pitches giving pleasure to the minds of the listener. In short, *raga* in music is a combination of musical notes producing a pleasing effect.

The Classificaiton of *Ragas* in General

The origin and development of *ragas* and their definitions explained in various old treatises on music are with various versions, which sometimes are contradicting to each other. *Matanga Muni* in "*Brihaddesi*" says:

"Svara varna visishtēna dvani Bhēdena Va punah
*Ranjyate yēna kathitah saragah sammatah satam"**

(One which is decorated by *svaras* and *varnas* and also pleasing to the ears of the people is called a raga)

Sangita Darpana gives another version about the origin of ragas as follows:

"Siva sakti samayogād rāgānam sambhavo matah
Panchasyat pancha rāganam shāstasya girima mukhat
Sadyojatathu Srīrago Vāma dēvad Vasantakah
Aghōrad bhairavo bhutatpurushat panchamō bhavat
Isanakhyanmēgha rāgah Nātyarambhe Sivadabhut
*Girijaya Mukhallyasye Natanarayano bhavat"**

(Ragas have emerged from the celestial union of *Siva and Parvati*. Five ragas have emerged from the five faces of Siva. (The five faces of Siva are *Sadyojata, Vāmadeva, Aghōra, Tatpurusha* and *Īsana*) such as *sri* raga from *sadyōjata, Vasanta* raga from *Vamadeva*, *Bhairava* raga from *Aghora*, *Panchama* raga from *Tatpurusha* and *Megha* raga from *Isana.* And from *Parvati's lasya nrutta* produced the raga *Natanarayana.)*

Similarly, *Bharata* puts it in a different way as he gives it in the sloka:

> "*Gōpi bhirgita marabdame kaikam krishna sannidhou*
>
> Tenajatani ragānam sahasrāni tu shodasa
>
> Rāgēshu tēshu shadtrimsād rāga jagati visrutāh
>
> *Kala knamena tatrapi hrasa eva tu drusyate*"*

(The *Gōpis* around *Sri Krishna* sang one *rāga* each thus came into being sixteen thousand *rāgas.* Thirty six among these only have become popular in the world....)

The ragas are further classified by different authors to *Raganga* ragas, *Upanga-bhashanga* ragas, *Ghana* ragas, *Rakti* rags, *Desi* ragas etc.

Ragas according to the traditional classifications fall into ten divisions. The first six divisions from *Grama* ragas to *Antara Bhasha* have long ago become obsolete. The rest four divisions beginning from *raganga* existed from long ago. The *ragangas* are those derived from the *gramas*. The ragas, which concieve the characters of old *'Bhashas'* are called *'Bhashangas'*. *Kriyangas* are those which produce emotional appeals to the minds like *Karuna, Utsaha, and Soka* etc. These terms like *Raganga, Kriyanga, Upanga, Bhashanga* etc. have a very different meaning when compared to the ragas mentioned in the "*Sampradaya Pradarshini*" or other books. According to *Tulajendra* there never existed the *Gandhara grama*. He comes to the conclusion that all the *ragas* in practice have emerged only from the *Shadja grama*. The *Gramas* were the means of obtaining *murchanas* with different intervals. A set of seven notes

---

*** Sangita Kalpadrumam of Muthaiya Bhagavatar- Section-II, Chapter 12, 'Raga Prakaranam' (Pages- 1 & 2)**

emerging from a *grama* yielded different order of intervals which gave raise to more than 7 *jatis* if another jati of seven notes could be formed into a new grama. It would be possible to have seven more different orders of intervals, resulting in seven more jatis. The gamut of twelve semi tones comprehends and includes within itself all the scales that were based on the different *gramas*.

Venkatamahi had a difference of opinion when he did not agree to the view of *Sarangadava* that there were twelve *vikrita svaras* in addition to seven *sudha svaras.* His seventy two Melakarta scheme is based on the gamut of twelve notes. Though there are numerous ragas after the establishment of the 72 *melakarta,* the musicians paid more attention to the traditionally handled down *ragas* that are employed in *Gita, Thaya, Prabandha* and *Alapa*. But there seems to be a change in the trend during the period of the Trinity- Tyagaraja, Muthu swami Dishitar and Syama shastri.

The twelve notes only represent the twelve *svarasthanas* and the *srutis* in a *svarasthana* are not to be rendered successively but relatively according to the usage. Whatever is the number of srutis, whether 22 or more, they can be grouped so as to form the 12 *svarasthanas* and these *svarasthanas* alone can be considered as the derivations of *melas*.

The statement that the number of *srutis* was 22 when the value of the *saptaka* was given as four *srutis* each for s*a, ma* and *pa*, two *srutis* each for *ga* and *ni* and three *srutis* each for *ri* and *dha* can be considered relatively authentic. These *srutis* were used as measurements of the magnitude of intervals. When other notes than classical ones came into being, these were considered as *vikrita svaras* with intervals different from their classical counter parts. The 22 *srutis* were not considered to be notes. The *srutis* were regarded as units of measurements. The interval between *ma* and *pa* was best understood and regarded the best of all. Probably the ancient scale was formed only by means of measurements with *chatursruti* interval. When the *rishabha* and *dhaivata* underwent slight changes according to their tonal values and slightly flattering their intervals, being less than four *srutis*, they were valued at *trisruti*. The intervals of *gandhara* and *nishada*, which were found to be even less were named *dvisruti*. The *trisruti* does not mean an interval exactly ¾ of a *chatursruti* nor do any three successive *srutis* in the gamut form always a *trisruti*. The 22 micro tones are the subtle variation of notes that account for variation in *ragas* even in those cases where identical scales are employed.

The scales are formed only on the basis of semi tonal interval. The most remarkable change had taken place during the time of *Matanga*, and perhaps the rudiments of it might be traced back to the time of *Bharatha.* According to *Tulajendra* the *madhyama grama* is the foundation stone on which the *ragas* are built up. Gradually the *gramas* have become obsolete and the *ragas* existed.

Tulajendra describes the ten *lakshanas* of ragas though the old *jatis* had thirteen *lakshanas.* The ten *lakshanas* of *ragas* described are mostly based on the *lakshanas* of *jatis*. The concept of the fundamental notes as the supreme basis of a raga has rendered most of these *lakshanas* obsolete. *Graha svaras* and *Nyasa svaras* are now identified with shadja. In certain popular *ragas*, the *amsa svaras* do exist apart from *shadja.* E.g., In *Arabhi*, one of the *ghanaragas*, the *rishabha* is considered to be *amsasvara* as well as *jiva svara*. He mentions that the 72 *melas* were formulated as a matter of *prastara* and considers *Sri raga* as the formost and auspicious among all *ragas*. The raga, *Sri* has not only a mythological origin but also regarded as the oldest of all scales. Sri raga, one of the present *ghana ragas* is said to have derived as the first offspring of *shadja grama,* which was itself, the scale of *samagana.* The other ragas are *Sudhanati, Malavagaula, Velavarali, Varali, Ramakriya, Sankarabharanam, Kamboji, Bhairavi, Mukhari, Vagavahini, Sindhuramakriya, Hejujji, Samavarali, Vasantabhairavi, Bhinnashadja, Deshakshi, Chayanata* and *kalyani. Sri* raga is described as an ancient one and also called variously as *grama raga* or *raganga raga* and as prince of all ragas capable of yielding prosperity. It is mentioned as a *sampurna raga* with *shadja* as *graha*, *amsa* and *nyasa svaras*. The notes it took are *sudha shadja, sudha madhyama, sudha panchama, Pancha sruti dhaivata, Pancha sruti rishabha, sadharana gandhara and kaisiki nishada*. The *Panchasruti* is to be understood relevantly today as *chatursruti.* The character of the scale relates to the present day *Kharaharapriya* scale. The derivatives of *Sri raga mela* in addition to the present sri raga are stated as *Kannadagaula, Devagandhari, Salaga bhairavi, Sudha desi, Madhava manohari, Saindhavi, kapi and Huseni (*all *sampurana ragas); Sri* *ranjani, Malavasri, Devamanohari, Jayantasena and Manirangu (*all *shadavas)* and *Madhyamavati and Suddha dhanyasi (audavas).*

According Tulajendra the *dhaivata* in *Sri raga* is *alpa svara.* He mentions the permissible and non-permissible *sancharas* in *Sri raga* in accordance with *Gita, Prabandha, Thaya, Alapa and Suladi. Shadja* is mentioned as *Graha, Amsa* and *Nyasa.*

The Shad Rāgas

Sri raga is considered to be one of the shad ragas (six ragas) mentioned in the old treatises. These *shad ragas* are considered to be *purusha ragas* from which 36 sthree *ragas* (female ragas) were derived. The 6 *purusha ragas* are: *Malavam, Mallaram, Sri raga, Vasantham, Hindolam* and *Karnatam.*

Ahobala in '*Sangita parijata*' mentions about 11340 ragas, which is a probable number of *melas* that can derive from the *Sudha* and *Vikruta* svaras. He further classifies them into five such as *Sudha, Bhinna, Vesara, Gaudi* and *Sadharani.* He also mentions about the *lakshanas* of 122 ragas.

There is also a reference of Ghana ragas. The list of 8 ragas mentioned as Ghana ragas is given below.

1. Nata,2. Gaula, 3. Varali, 4. Bauli, 5. Sri, 6. Arabhi, 7. Malavasri, 8. Ritigaula.

The two sets of *Ghana ragas* in practice such as 1. *Nata, Gaula, Varali, Arabhi* and *Sri* and II. *Kadara, Riti gaula, Narayana gaula, Saranga Nata,* and *Bauli* are defined in various treatises. ***A few select references* on Ghana ragas by various authors are given below:***

1. NĀTA

1. *Nata Raga Dhyanam*:

(a) "*Dhanaksharo hinam kripan kheta dharinam*

Dhanushsharagrahalstham druta pratapamugra sekhara

Yudhi pracharinam kabhandha samvirittam dayaparam
Sadha bhajani nata raga chandramouli sekharam"

(*Raga Sagara*)

(b) "*Shadjamsaka grahanyasa sampurnascha samaswara*
Tatha thracha mandracha yara gandhara panchaniou
Bhashaya manjari tasya angam natabhidhiyate" (*Jaga deva*)

(c) "*Bhahirsa dhenu girisajasa mudhya pancha*
Kakalyamalpa hari reva matha varohe
Gandhara varja mapi rajani nata rage
Sampurna shadava gane ganitastu purnai
Sama pah sanidhah rih shadja sruti
Ga sadharanah alpa dhaivatah kakalinih"

(*Parameswarah*)

(d) "Nado nisi suchou vire
Shadjamsascha madhatkatah" (*Narayanah)*

(e) *"Ristu tivra taro yasmin*
Gandharastivra samjnakah
Dhastu tivra tarah prokto
Nishadastivra namakah
Avarohe dha gou nasto
Nadari swara murchana
Sayam geyah " (Ahobala)

Nāta Raga

Tulajendra considers *Nata raga as a mela.* He further says that of the notes of this *mela*, *sa, ma* and *pa* are *suddha*, *ri* and *dha* are *shatsruti, ga* is *antara* and *ni* is *kakali*. Of this *mela* the principal raga is *Suddha nati*. It is *sampurna* and *bhashanga,* not indeed, in the modern sense. It omits *dhaivata* and *gandhara* in *avaroha*. It is sung in the evening. Its *svaragati* both in the *aroha* and the *avaroha* is straight. The *Udgraha prayoga* is: *sa sa sa ni pa ma, ri ga ma pa dha ni, sa sa ni pa, papa, ni pa ni ni.* Other prayogas are : *sa sa ri ri, ri ga ma pa dha ni, sa sa ni pa, sa sa sa sa sa, ri ga ma pa ni pa sa sa. sa sa sa ni pa sa sa sa sa ni* is found as *Thaya prayoga*. The *prayoga* in *Prabandha* is : *ga ma pa sa sa, ri sa sa ri sa sa, ni sa sa ni pa ma ma ri sa.* The *suladi prayoga* is : *sa sa ni pa ma ma ri sa sa sa.*

Venkatamahin after mentioning the aforesaid *Lakshanas* further says *shadja* in *Nata* is *vadi, panchama is samvadi, rishabha and dhaivata* are *anuvadis* and *gandhara* and *nishada* are *vivadis*. The last two notes are called *vivadis* because they come, in between *shatsruti rishabha* and *madhyama* and the other between *shatsruti dhaivata* and *shadja* with only a resultant semi tonal interval on each side. In other words these notes bring about a succession of three semitones consecutively.

Sangita sudha gives the same lakshana and like *Chaturdandi Prakasika* mentions *Nata* as first among *Ghana Ragas*. But *Tulajendra* mentions *Nata* as second, only for the reason that he considered it auspicious to mention *"Sri"* first. In the fifty *melas* and *ragas* of *Vidyaranya* described in *Sangita Sudha* it is the first. It is also one of the fifteen *melas* given therein. It is called *Nata.* It is derived from *Pinjari* considered to be *Bhasha raga* of *Hindola* which itself is traced to the *Grama ragas*. It is in this sense that *Venkatamahi* and others call it a *Bhashanga.* This is one of the few ragas whose origin and identity is traced back to the period before *Bharata*, viz., to the era of *Grama ragas.* As in the case of this *raga,* it should be possible for patient research to establish the identity of most of the modern ragas, except for such changes as time in its progress must introduce in all things, with their prototypes of remote antiquity.

Somanatha positions it as his 22nd of the 23 *melas* and calls it *Suddha nata.* The notes are the same as that of *Nata*. *Ramamatya* gives it as the 9th of his 20 *melas* and also calls it *Suddha nata. Pundarika Vitthala*'s description of the raga is identical. *Lochanakavi* does not mention *Suddha nata*, but other varieties, which are placed under his *Kedara* which, corresponds to *Sankarabharana mela*. This raga is remarkable in the history of ragas. It is a very difficult raga to render. Only eminent *Vidwans* with high *lakshana gnana* can do adequate justice to it. It has, therefore, remained exclusively with the most learned section of *Gayakas* and *Vainikas*. Unlike *Anandabhairavi* and other popular ragas it has suffered to no distortion. The result is *Nata* has continued absolutely unchanged for more than two thousand years and this is one of the reasons why *lakshanakaras* have traced it to the *Grama* period. *Chalanata* is the name of the *mela* under the *Melakarta* system now current as well as under the system attributed to *Venkatamakhi*. The modern *lakshana* even as given in recent publication has not changed. Though strictly speaking the *arohana* is full, yet in practice, the full complement of *svaras* is used only occasionally. *Chitta tanas* in this raga are numerous. In truth it is very much a *vainika's* raga and eminently suited for *Madhyama kala* or *tana* rendering. It must be handled with vigour and spirit. If played in the beginning of a concert, it has the effect of shaking off lethargy and dejection. The high pitch of its notes produces this result. It is the best illustration of what is known as a *Ghana raga* as contrasted with a *naya* or *rakti* raga like *Punnagavarali* or *Nadanamakritya*. Tyagaraja's "*Jagadanandakaraka*", one of the *Ghana raga pancharatnas* in this raga is unmatched for its grandeur, dignity, and beauty. His '*Ninne Bhajana*" is widely rendered. Dikshitar's "*Swaminatha"* is short and comparatively simpler. There are many *Gitas, Prabandhas,* and *Suladis* in this raga.

2. Gaula

Gaula as a *mela raga*:

(a) '*Gaulastu gandhara varjyah sthardora mela samudravah*
Tritiya praharotara geyah' *(Ahobala)**

Melakarta:

(b) *Brahmadi Dhenusamamikshara nedhasudha*
Madhyi piko haranishadamayiti gaula
Santhyajya mesha mavarohati vanikaisthu

---

*From the Personal collection of Manuscripts of Padmashree, Prof: Leela Omcherry

Tatshadavou drura gane pariganya gitam

Sarimapah sudha sadharanou gah tatalinistadah

Mesho gih *(Parameswara)**

(C) *Gaulo malava gauliya*

Melajo dhaivatonjitah

Shadavo migraho ragago

Ayam sasvat pragiyate//

Asmin - rage - gandharo -

Madhya mandraroha krama - Evagaschati,

Shadja Paryantaroha krame - Nagaschatiti

Tana shadja nishada dva- rishabha shadjava

Dhyarohakrama - avi - gandhara nagaschaliti

Gandhara hinon durva murchana tana – eva

Eva – shadava murchana tanascha - //

Asyodaharanam - r m p n s r g m r r s

S n p – m p r s – n s n p m r – Iti

Sacharini chaturtha mukutila tana

Prayogah / R R s n S S - Iti shadja sthai

Dhaye/

R s r p m m - r g m - r s n s s - Iti

Dhaya prayogah/

R s r s n s r g m - Iti shadjadi taya –

Apurva prayogah/

N n n d, m m m g, S m m m n d -

M g m n n n d n n S n d u - Iti Prabandha

Prayogah

R r m p n s r s s m P   S s n P m r g M

Ma ri mulatimaa... ....   ma ti maka danti la lou   -

*Iti suladi prayogah//**

(d) *Nishadansa grahanyaso gowtah panchama varjitah*
Syadangam dakka ragasya prayah sringara virayoh

*(Somaraja)**

Gowdasyat shadja ragangam sanyasamsa grahastihtah

Varjasya Pnahcame nysa rasavire niyurte

Jyateshchangam nishadivyo vadanti ratinme matam

*(Jagadeka)**

Gowdah ragah shadavah syit

Nishadamsa grahanyaso gowdah syit Panchamojita

Virasringaragorgiyam divante virala rishabha

*(Narayana)**

Laskhmitat gowda ragasya pratishta rishabhayotrana

Swasthane thatita schayam

Giyate gitayedibhih

*(Etaditi Sriraga Paramritayate)**

Nyasomsya syat shadjah Panchamakinasta

Rishabha grahanah

Sphritakya gamaka mibido gowdasyat

Dakka ragaswasadrushyah

*(Nanya)**

Dakka ragena sadrushyah Panchamena virarjitah

Shadjanmsa nyasa sampanno gowdasyat drusha kampanam

*(Matanga)**

Tato gowdabhidho raga dakka raga samudbhava

Nyasamsa graha vanisha nishedi panchamorjitah   *(Haripala)**

Raganga rageh
Dakkasyangam bharit gowdah
Panchama swara varjitah
Nishadamsa grahanyaso varshasu karunematah
*(Bhatta madhava)**

Goula satu gadha varjyastad
Gauri mela samud bhih *(Ahobhala)**

Brahmadi dhenu samamiswara mesha sudha madhyam
Piko hara nishada maye ta goure
Santajya meshavarohita vainikastu
Tat shadavandua gane parigapyagritam
Sa ri ma pa h sudha / sadharana gah/
*Kakali nishadah/ Meshog*ah/ *(Parameswara)**

Gaula is considered to be the derivative of Malavagaula mela by many authors (if the older could be deemed the offspring of the younger). It is a shadava, dhaivata being varja. Nishada is its graha. In this raga gandhara comes only in *madhyamanta arohanakrama* that is when the phrase in the aroha goes only as far as madhyama. It does occur in the *arohanakrama* sanchara which goes to *shadja*. Even in the strict *avarohanakrama* from *nishada* and *shadja, gandhara* does not occur. The inference is *gandhara* comes only in *vakra prayogas*. The *shadava tanas* include *gandhara hina audava tanas*. It will be seen that these remarks will be found to be in agreement with the practice prevailing at present. *The tana prayogas are: ri ma pa ni sa ri ga ma ri ri sa sa ni pa, ma pa ri sa, ni sa ni pa ma ri; sa sa ri ri ga ga ma ma ri ri sa; ri ri sa ni sa sa; ri sa ri pa ma ma, ri ga ma ri sa ni sa sa' ri sa ri sa ni sa ri ga ma.* These are the various prayogas in alapa. The *suladi prayoga* is: *ri ma pa ni sa ri sa sa ni pa, sa sa ni pa ma ri ga ma*. The *prabandha prayoga* is: *ni ni ni dha ma ma ga sa*

From the Personal collection of Manuscripts of Padmashree, Prof: Leela Omcherry

ma ma ma ni dha, ma ga ma ni ni dha ma ni ni sa ni dha ni. It will be seen that in the *prabandha prayoga, dhaivata* is present and *panchama* is absent.

Probably *Tulajendra* was citing here a *prabandha* in a different raga for it is difficult to believe that *Gaula* which has been carefully cherished in the *vainika sampradaya* would have changed in material aspect. *Venkatamakhi* calls this a *raganga* quite consistently for he gives to it the status of a *mela raga.* He states that *ri* and *ga* are *vadi-samvadi.* By no stretch of imagination can the two notes be in *vadi-samvadi* relations. *Sangita Sudha* mentions *nishada* as *vadi* and *gandhara* as *samvadi*. This is appropriate. The *graha* and *amsa* according to it, as indeed according to all, is nishada. Furhter *Sangita Sudha* refers to *rishabha* of *Gaula* as amsa owing to its frequent use. This description is quite modern considering the time when the book was written which was more than three centuries ago. The author gives *Gurjari* for the mela name only for the reason of *Gaula* being *shadava*, while the objection to Malavagaula was that it was not so well-known as *Gurjari*. If a conclusion could be drawn from this, the *Gaula raga* was at least more famous as, if not more than *Gurjari*. Most writers describe this raga under slightly different names such as *Gaura, Gauda,Gauli* etc. That *Gaula* was a well known ancient raga prevelent in all parts of India is certain. Further it has in the main retained its individuality notwithstanding slight local variations in the practical renderings. It is a *ghana raga* well suited for *madhyamakala* renderings, the delight of *vainikas*. There are many *kirtanas* and *suladis* of *Purandaradas* in this raga. Tyagaraja's "*Dudukugala*" one of the pancharathna pieces gives a masterly presentation of the beauties of the raga. Dikshitar's songs *"Sri Maha Ganapati"* and "*Tyagaraja*" have become popular. This raga is the second of the series of five ragas known as ***Ghanapanchaka*** which with or without further additions formed a permenent feature in the *vainika sampradaya*. Those who are steeped in classic traditions still maintain this feature in their concerts.

3. *Varali*

(a) *"Varali melaragam*
Brahmadi dhenuvidhi mesha viruda madhya
Panchadi dhaivrasiradanthi tatho bhayata

Purnabhidhe brahula kalpa naya varali

Rago chamatkritim maneka vidham vadanti

Sarigapadha sudhah prati madhyamamh kakalinishadah"

*(Parameswara)**

(b) ***Varali Raga Dhyanam**:*

"Vividha kusumabhusham samrutalim sadalim

Madhura mridula vakyo sthosha yantim valantim

Valabhidu palanitam bhargave dhyanalolam

Mamamasi sadalam chuitaye Sri Varalim"

*(Raga Sagara)***

(C) *"Sudhah syuh sarigah sudhapanchamah*

Sudha dhaivatah//

Kakalya khya nishado vikrita panchama madhyamah

Etaih pusta tayukta samgrahamsa /

Bhinna panchama bhasheyam sarvayameshu giyati//"

(d) *"Bhinnadi bhudasya cha panchamasya*

Prokta vibha straiva varadikeyam

Mamandra ka dha amsa yuta dha tara

Shadja grahantacha sama swara syat" *(Moksha)**

"Vibhasha raga rajasya

Panchamasya varadika

Amsa shadja grahanyason

Nitara mandra madhyama

Soma resha swara purna

Sringare yashti kodita" *(Jagadeka)**

"Atah param vasaditi

Gathito raga uchyate

Ragajjata sthiato raga
Rajapanchama samjuakam
Dhaivatamsa maho nyasa shadjo
Sou tara dhaivatah
Madhyamastu sampurna
Swara sesha samobhavet" *(Hari)**

"Samasvara cha purnacha
Ri tara mandra varjita
Varadi panchama nyasa
Gahamisa khita kathyate// *(Matanga)**

"Rishabhaka tara purna mandra tya kta
Sama swarabhoga
Nyasamsa graha panchama yukta
Prokta varadika bahubhih *(Nanya)**

"Asyah trai vidhitham
Ratna malayam sudha varadi, Dravivaradi,
Vesa varadi tiuktam//
Kai mutyam tu shadava madhye gamita" *(Narayana)**

"Grahairavartato geya
Bh*inna panchama vatsada/*
Shadja nyasa grahamsousha
Varadi bharato dita// *(Narayana)**

"Sadyanta samsa samyukta
Varadi Ragaja mat" *(Madana)**

"Bhinna panchamaka syangam
Varadi syat sama swara
Dha amsa shadja graha nyasa
Mandrama tara dhaivata
Grishme prak prahare geya
Sampurna kamage rase// *(Bhatanayaka)**

"Vibhasha raga ragasya
Panchamasya varadika
Samasesha swarapurna
Sringare yashti ko di ta// *(Hammirah)**

"Shadja grahamsaka nyasa
Varadi kathita budhaih
Prattma murchanayasyam
Sampurna kirti vahini
Sa ri ga ma pa dhani sa". *(Damodara)***

Varāli

Varali is a Mela as it has been to almost everyone of his predecessors. It takes Suddha Shadja, Rishabha, Gandhara, Panchama and Dhaivata with kakali Nishada and Vikrita panchama Madhyama. It is Sampurna. It is Bhasha of Bhinna panchama. (This is practically unintelligible in current lakshya. According toTulaja it can be sung at all times. The Udgraha, Sanchari, Thaya and Prabandha prayogas as illustrated by Tulaja are all regular in ascent and descent. No vakra prayoga is to be seen. The nomenclature is significantly different as seen from different works on Music; Varali, Suddha Varali, Suddha Varatika etc.. Certain North Indian scholars while writing on the Sanskrit works have given the name as Barati. In Bandyopadhyaya's 'Origin of Raga', the raga- name, given as Varatika in the sanskrit sloka in the Sangita Makaranda, is given as Bharatika in the English translation. Sangita Makaranda, roughly to be placed between 7th and 9th

centuries A.D. mentions Varali as one of the sampurna ragas. It is a feminine raga to him. Narada assigns Varatika to evening.

Parsva Deva's Sangita Samaya Sara to be placed roughly prior to Sangita Ratnakara mentions Varali (as he calls it), as one of the Raganga ragas. He says "Vibhasha raga ragasya Panchamasya Varatika". He gives Dhaivata as Amsa and Shadja as graha and Nyasa. Dhaivata is Tara and Madhyama is Mandra. He associates varali with sringara. The mention of Dhaivata as Amsa Tara and Madhyama as Mandra seems to fall in line with current thought. Sarngadeva of the 13th century A.D. mentions Varali as one of the Purva or Prasiddha ragas.

The trio Ramamatya, Somanatha and Venkatamakhi mention varali in their respective treatises. Ramamatya speaks of Varali as a Mela and calls it Suddha Varali. Shadja is graha, amsa and nyasa. This raga can be sung at all times. Furhter he says that it is an uttama raga (Sampurna)-free from any kind of mixing and also suitable for singing composition, elaboration and for Thaya. The svara nomenclature given by him are Suddha Shadja, Rishabha, Gandhara, Panchama and Dhaivata. Chyuta panchama madhyama and chyuta shadja Nishada. No doubt the Madhyama and Nishadja of Varali are rather too sharp, beaning perfect consonance with each other. Rarely do these notes stand in any exact position. Somanatha in his Raga Vibodha speaks of one Suddha Varali corresponding to our 45th Mela Subhapantuvarali. He mentions Gandhara as Sadharana for his Suddhavarali. The Madhyama is also Tivratara and no Chyuta or Mridu Panchama Madhyama. Somanatha gives the svara as Sudha in respect of Shadja, Rishabha and Dhaivata. To him, it is a raga to be sung in the day. Somanatha does not seem to have taken note of our present Varali.

Chaturdandi Prakasika of Venkatamahi (1635 A.D.) speaks of Varali as a raga but deems Suddha Varali as a Mela. In his Mela prasthara it is the 39th Mela. (He assigns sruti values, for the svaras taken by suddha varali mela) Shadja, Rishabha, Gandhara, Panchama and Dhaivata are Suddha. He designates the Prati madhyama itself as Varali madhyama and Nishada as kakali. Even for the raga like Suddha Ramakriya and Kalyani, Venkatamakhi gives the Madhyama as Varali Madhyama which looks rather incongruous in current lakshya. The Madhyama of kalyani and Ramakriya are definetely not so sharp as in Varali. In the Mela prakarana (Slokas 155-157) of his Chaturdandi Prakasika Venkatamakhi assigns sruti values for Varali as: one sruti for Shadja, three surtis for Rishabha, Two srutis for Gandhara, Seven srutis for Madhyama, one sruti for Panchama, three srutis for Dhaivata and five srutis for Nishada, thus twenty two surits.

In the raga chapter Venkatamakhi describes Varali as taking Shadja for graha, amsa and Nyasa. In slokas 51-53 he says that Varali is a Sampurna raga in the sense that it possesses the full compliment of the sapthasvaras. He mentions Shadja as Vadi, Madhyama and Panchama as Samvadis, Gandhara and nishada as Vivadis and Rishabha as Anuvadi. Venkatamakhi could rightly have designated Madhyama also as Vadi in Varali in view of its importance as Bharata says 'Yo Yatramsah: Ya tasya Vadi'. According to modern understanding Shadja – Panchama, Madhyama – Nishada, Rishabha – Dhaivata and Rishabha – Madhyama too are Samvadins to one another.

Rishabha-Gandhara are Vivadins to one another and the rest are Anuvadins. Besides Shadja and Panchama, Gandhara and Madhyama are, to say, Vadins in as much as thye constitue the amsas. To Venkatamakhi Varali is a raga sung at all times of the day. Suddha Varali is one of the 19 Kalpita Melas or Purva Prasiddha Melas of Venkatamakhi. Venkatamakhi is the lakshanakara who decided the status of Varali as the 39th Mela in his scheme of permutations and combinations that could be derived on the basis of the 'Prasiddhairdvadasa svaraihi'. In the earlier kanakambari nomenclature, when seventy two Melas were named for the first time, the 39th Mela was Varali. Govindacharya in his Sangraha Chudamani called the 39th Mela as Jhalavarali. The author (not known) of the later Kanakambari nomenclature chose to have it named as Dhali Varali (Subbarama Dikshitar's Sangita Sampradaya Pradarsini is the evidence). Govindacharya does not mention the raga name Varali as such but only Jhala Varali as the 39th Mela. He gives two ragas, kokila panchama and Bhupala panchama as the two janyas of JhalaVarali. While giving in notation the lakshana gita for JhalaVarali, Govindacharya Says: Prati madhyama Kakalisvara itara sudha – Aroha avaroha sampurnam– Sagrahannyasamsa". For the first time the mela mnemonics are given for the melas. Rishi – Go is Jhalavarali, e., 3rd mela in the 7th chakra. Sangita Sara Sangrahamu in Telugu, a work of the so called Akalanka also follows suit with regard to varali.

The Sangita Sampradaya Pradarsini of Subbarama Dikshitar gives an apt description of the present status of Varali. He gives the arohana-avarohana as: sa ga ri ga ma pa da ni sa – sa ni da pa ma ga ga ri sa. It is Raganga, Sampurna, Shadja graha, Ghana raga and can be sung at all times. Subbarama Dikshitar stresses the importance of the prayoga sa ga ri ga ma and janta gandhara in the avarohana. He says that while the prayoga is found in Gita and Tana, sa ri ga ma is also found in Kirtanas. As usual, he quotes Gita and Tana of Venkatamakhi and his own sanchari in Misra jati eka tala besides, two kritis of Dikshitar 'Mamava Meenakshi' in Misra Eka and 'Seshachala' in Rupaka Tala. It is most significantly worthy of note that the Gita cited in the Pradarshini in the name of Venkatamakhi contains the raga mudra as Dhali Varali. This amply testifies to the fact that the name of the author given as Venkatamakhi is incorrect; Venkatamakhi whom we know as the author of Chaturdandi Prakasika could not have been the author of any nomenclature for the 72 Melas in as much as he could only visualise the remote possibility of a good number of melas. He knew only the 19 kalpita melas and nothing more and he did not know or coin any nomenclature for the 72 melas.

In current practice Varali is one of the most concert worthy ragas. It claims its rightful place anywhere in the sequence of the concert. Its beauty becomes greater when rendered in tana either vocal or instrumental. It is failry well represented. One of the earliest editions of Tyagaraja's Kritis published in 1908 records 7 kritis of Tyagaraja in this raga. The darus in Varali in Nowka Charitam are of course not found in the said edition. Tyagaraja as a composer has established the full melodic worth of this raga Varali. We have a Tana varnam in Varali in Chaturasra Ata Tala composed by Ramnad Srinivasa Iyengar.

4. Arabhi

(a) "Arabhi Sadageya aroheganivarjita
Kvachidaroha Samyukta nishado nigraho bhavet"

(Chaturdandi Prakashika)**

Sankarabharana mela ragah

Adharabhyam Samarohe

Meshakunjara Vayanam

Ganyolopah (Parameswarah)*

Mela ragah

Dhira sankarabharana mela janyah

Aro: s r m p d s

Ava: S n d p m g r s *

Arabhi

Arabhi is an ancient raga of our music, in as much as, it could be traced out atleast to the 7th century A.D. One of the Thevara pans corresponds to Arabhi. Arabhi is one of the ragas described in the Sangitha Sudha of Govinda Dikshitar in which the fifty ragas listed in the Sangeetha Sara of Holy Vidyaranya, are embodied. Vidyaranya's treatise on music is the very first attempt made for bringing back to life the art of music which had suffered along with other Arts, in the South, from 1300 to 1400 A.D., on account of Muslim invasion and occupation. This raga, therefore, appears for the first time in the treatise written after the bifurcation of the system of music of the land into Southern and Northern. The Suladis of Purandara Dasa include Arabhi among the ragas used. Arabhi is found here and there in the copper plates of the songs of Thallapakam composers, as edited by the T.T.D. Tirupathi. Arabhi is also a raga eminently suitable for singing semi-poetic forms like Churnikas and Dandakas (A little tinge of Devagandhari may incidentally be noticed in some cases).

It looks strange that the raga name Arabhi is not found in Brhaddesi, or, even in the Sangita Ratnakara which is a comprehensive compilation of many of the earlier works. There are three ragas by the name Abhiri in these texts. One is derived from the Grama raga Panchama, The second from Malava Kaisika and the third from Kakubha. The description of these three ragas lends support to the conjecture that either the first or the second Abhiri may be same as Arabhi. In the first Abhiri, Panchama is the Amsa Graha and Nyasa. Its Nishada is Kakali and it is used in war-like scenes. In our Arabhi too, panchama occupies the most important place. Nishada is Kakali and all the svaras are energetic. Thus a similarity is noticeable. In the second Abhiri, Gandhara and Nishada have alpatva. This feature is found in our Arabhi as well in current lakshya. It has Madhyama for its amsa and nyasa and has for its rasa 'Nirveda' or despondency. It has, therefore, features similar to our current Abheri where the notice of despondency is clearly felt in pieces like 'Nagumomukana leni' of Sri Tyagaraja. So, we may sum up to say that our present Arabhi combines in itself some of the features of the first two Abhiris referred to above. However, this is only a partial analogy. As a matter of fact the very nomenclature of the raga brings in not even a partial semblance (ABHIRI-ARABHI). The cream of phraseology in Arabhi extends from Dhaivata (Manara) below to panchama above (Tara). The other features may be developed as follows:- Rishabha and panchama exhibit their Vadi Samvadita (consonance) in the ascent, while Madhyama and Shadja exhibit their consonance in the descent. Rishabha is more prominent than Shadja. Similarly Rishabha has got two samvadins, Panchama and Dhaivata. But, panchama is more prominent than Dhaivata. Dhaivata has a prominent samvadin in Rishabha, and pratically ignores its consonance with Gandhara. Gandhara and Nishada are alpa in Arabhi. Both Gandhara and Nishada are given negligible emphasis in the descent. They are treated as extent, to longhana. In Arabhi, there is no descent without passing at panchama. The sthayisvara alankara of the svaras of this raga is Prasannanta. But, in the Alapas and Thayas given by Shahji, one cannot help wondering as to how Gandhara and Nishada are found, not only in the descent, but also in the ascent.

A survey of the textual tradition revelas that this raga name Arabhi, as such, could be traced only after the partition of the system of Indian music into Southern and Northern, Northern text book writers of music have left the raga unnoticed, while the Southern authors have mentioned this raga. However, we do not come across this raga in Svara Melakalanidhi of Ramamatya and in Somanatha's Raga Vibodha which is partly Northern and partly Southern in the treatment of the subject. This raga has however been very popular during the 15th, 16th Century A.D. in as much as, Arabhi is found as one of the ragas employed by Thallapakkam Composers for their innumerable sankirtanas. From the 17th century onwards, we have a cogent lakshana and lakshya tradition mentioned for this raga. They are not atmuch variance with each other.

Tulaja mentions Arabhi as a janya of Sankarabharana Mela. It is a sampurna raga in the sense that it takes the full complement of the sapthasvaras in both the arohana and avarohana put together. It is an evening raga, with the added attribute 'Subhaprada'. Among the illustrative prayogas we find 'dha ni sa', 'pa dha ni dha ni sa', 'ri sa ni dha ni sa'. Once of his phrases goes like 'ga ma pa dha ni sa'. These phrases are unacceptable in current lakshya. Sangitha Sara Sangrahamu in Telugu however, gives the Arohana of Arabhi as sa ri ma pa dha ni sa. This is a much later work comtemporay to Sangraha Chudamani, which could roughly be located either in the last quarter of the 18th Century or the first quarter of the 19th Century A.D., Sangraha Choodamani says that Arabhi as a janya of Dheera Sankarabharana Mela taking Chatusruti Rishabha, Chatusruti Dhaivata, Antara Gandhara, Kakali, Nishada and Suddha Madhyama. It omits Gandhara, Nishada in the Arohana and Avaroha is Sampurna; Shadja is the graha, amsa and nyasa as in the case of many other ragas the work discusses. At the end of the edition of Sangraha Chudamani, in the ragas listed out, we find the arohana-avarohana of Arabhi as 'sa ri ma pa dha sa – sa ni dha pa ma ga ri sa'.

In the Sangitha Sudha we find the treatment of Arabhi elaborate. The description is taken through the stages of Akshiptika, Raga Vardhani followed by Vidari, tara ,shadja sthayi prayogas, madhya shadja sthayi, Vartani and finally Nyasa.

In slokas 57-59 of the 'Raga Prakarana' of the Chaturdandi Prakasika, Venkatamakhin gives the lakshana very briefly. Arabhi is a janya of Sankarabharana and is a Sampurna raga. In the raga lakshana given in Chaturdandi in Sanskrit and also in the Tamil translation thereof, the treatment runs as follows:

> "Arabhi sadageya aroheganivarjita
> Kvachidaroha samyukta nishado nigraho bhavet".

According to the above verdict the raga deletes Gandhara and Nishada in the aroha but rarely nishada occurs in the arohana too; Nishada is graha; The raga can be sung at all times. One can not accept the above verdict as the nishada does not occur in the ascending phrases in current practice. Not only that, no where do we find nishada employed as graha. It is a widely acknowledged fact that nishada is an alpatvasvara subject to anabhyasa if not langhana. The above treatment is quoted verbatim in the Sangitha Sampradaya Pradarsini (P-846 Tamil Trans) under the authorship of

Venkatamakhi. Subbarama Dikshitar adds of course his own raga lakshana for Arabhi. Upanga raga, Sampurna raga; Shadja graha; Gandhara and Nishada are varjya in the arohana too. Ghana araga can be sung at all times. By Ghana raga Subbarama Dikshitar evidently means that Arabhi is more eminently suitable for Madhyama Kala or Tana singing.

It is needless to say that Tana varnas and kritis in Madhyama Kala are the most suitable musical forms to project this raga. Subbarama Dikshitar specifies that in negotiating the phrase 'sa ni dha pa ma ga ri', there is a sort of of 'Nokku' which goes technically as 'Tirupa' in the panchadasa gamakas. Subbarama Dikshitar is of the opinion that the very phrase 'dha ni sa' can occur in this raga. He has incorporated one 'dha ni sa' prayoga in the Mandra sthayi in the 6th avarta in his Sanchari – Tam – Tran). Whatever might have been the past, the phrases, 'dha ni sa', 'ni dha ni sa', 'sa ni dha ni sa' and 'ga ma pa' have all gone into obivion. On the strength of lakshya pradhanam Arabhi exists at present as a simple audava sampurna raga to be reconed as a janya, of Dheera Sankarabhara. As far as the raga features are concerned in between Sankara-bharanam and Arabhi the semblance is an emphatic nil. The Dirgha Kampita Rishabha and Dhaivata of Sankarabharana are seldom heard in Arabhi. We have no occasion for a stable unshaken gandhara in Arabhi, as we have in Sankarabharana. The pronounced nishada of Sankarabharana has no place in Arabhi. Gandhara and nishada are not of any pronounced nature in Arabhi. This is quite evident from some versions of Sadinchane without nishada altogether. Arabhi can be classified under the scale of Dheera Sankarabharanam rather than technically being reckoned as a janya of Sankarabharanam.

Lastly, it could be summed up by quoting a few of the most important and appropriate phrases of Subbarama Dikshitar which contribute, in all its essence, to the real form of the raga. 'Ri Ri – Dha Dha Sa SA Ri Ri – Ma Ga Ri Ri – Dha Dha pa pa ma ga ri Ri – sa ri Ma ga Ri Ri – sa ni da pa ,ma ga Ri Ri – Sa Ni Dha Ri Sa'. The Arabhi Raga Tana Varna beginning with the words 'Sarasija Mukhiro' (in Adi Tala) of Pallavi Duraiswamy Iyer is the concise 'Oxford Dictionary' for Arabhi for ready reference. 'Sadinchene' –(ghana raga pancharatna of Thyagaraja and his 'Chalakallala-dukonna' 'Jutamurare' are compositions of high lakshya value, Dikshitar's 'Marakoti' and Thyagaraja's 'Sundari ninnum varnimpa' are in a somewhat slow tempo.

5. Sri Raga

Ashtadasabdah smara carumurtih
Whirollasat pallava karuapurah
Shadjadi sevyoruna vastra dhari
Sri raga rajah kshiti pala murtih (Sangita darpanam)*

Sri ragah sac vikhyatah satrayena vibhushitah
Puruasaruaguno petah murchana prathama matah
Kechintu kathayantiena rishabha traya sammatam (Damodara)*

Veerasanam Sinha mukhagrahastham
Manickya totiravi bhasitam sada
Pasvadaya sthabja mukhi kadambham
Sriraga devam bhajatam manome (Raga Sagara)**

Kechidenam gaura Varna mashta bahum
Pancha pasankusachari bija pmaka pusthakan
Vibhranam Paneeshatakena Vina Sakta Karadvayam
Brahmananiva hamsena gachantam jaga due budha (Kumbha)*

Athanyashtaka raganga Sri raga madhya taraka
Gandhara mandra rishabha pancha mambhyam Vivarjita
Nyasa grahamsa vanshadje Samasvara vibhushita (Hari)*

Melakarta:

Chatur Sruti ridhou yatra bhavetam nijata
Sadharano pi gandharo nishada kaisiki punah
Vinika vishaye sudha shadjamadhyam panchama
Sri raga sthapi meloyam kathito gayakotamai
Dinante giyate ghadjagrahamsa nyasa sobhita
Aadha murchanaya purna sriraga vatha gojhita// (Sri Kanta)*

Shadjash chatursruti vrushontaramesha Sudha –
Madhyopikashta danukaisya nishada era
Sri raga evamatha vakragatis thu meshe
Dhaivena varjita tatha sa tu shadavakhya//
Sa ma pah sudhah/ rish chatursrutih/
Gaantarah /Ni kaisikah/Dha varjitah/Vakragatih/ (Parameshwara)*

Shadjamsa nyasa samyuktah Sampurna saptabhisharaih/
Antotitastu svasthane pravishtatrasha bhavintah//
Avarohapi gandharah kkapi kkapi prayujyate/
Gandharo durbalashchayam sri ragah parikutitah// (Someswara)*

Nyasamsaka grahapada sthita shadjatana –
Shadjibhavatsvaladhu panchama kashcha purnah
Gandhara tara dhruta madhyammandra bhaiah
Sri raga ityabhihitah samasosha nadah// (Nanya)*

Sri raga as raganga raga:

Sriragashtaka sambhutah panchama prabhavarjitah
Grahamsanyasa gandharah karune pravrushi – smrutah
(Bhattamadhava)*

Shadjam dvigunamasthaya sthayinam Todathastanam/
Sthayinam ca Vidhayath dvitiyam chaturyakam//
Tritiyam Sthayinam sprushta dvitiyamutu Vilambyacha/
Sthayi svara yadanyasah Sri ragah Sa tada bhavet/
Sva sthana mathami varusosya dirtiyo dasayate grahat// (Vemah)

Eka eva guruyatra pratipadam vyavasthitah
Dhru vakya sa tu mantavya hastanyuli vikalpanat//
Matra chatushtayenasan gamaniya prayoktubhi//

Layo Vitambita kshasminnavapadi Chatur vidhah
Chachatputhena talena ragashchatra rasasritah//* (Nanya)

Melotbhaveshu rageshu sri rago datra chiram ta naih
Ghama ragaiti prokto raganga raganga miti kaschana
Sri rago raga raji tayam sarva sampat pradayakah
Ityam chato tetra lakshyna tulajendrana dhimata
Sir Ragah paripurah sa grahamsa nyasa samyuktah
Goyah sayahra samaye hyatha tana vivanjitah
Sudhah syuh samapah panchsmiti rishbha dhaivata
Sadharanakhya gandharah kaisikyakhya nishada kah
Etaih sapta svaraiyukto yo mela statra ehadimah
Sri raga stan mela jatnu dhisamiha kaschanah
Sri rago raga rago ta tha ragah kannada goulakah
Deva gandhara ka khyascha tatha salaga bharavi
Tatha syach sudha desicha syan madhava manohari
Madhyama grama ragasha saindhavi kafi kadada hvayah
Huseri inti sampurna yatra raga undahrutah
Sri ranjani malavasir statha deva manchari
Jayanta sena samjnascha manirangushca shadavah
Madhyamati statha sudha dhanyasi sonduvon maton
Shadavondava sampurno raga otra nidasitah
Tulajendrena sanita saramruta its sphutam //
Asya raga syalpo dhaivatah
Arohavaraha - Murchana tanayaorayam
Samdarbho atra sanga schatetayam sandarbho
Na sangachana ityetanischayartham
Prachina gita prabandha thayalaparupah

Chaturdandi suladi prabhutyodaharana legha

Nena sphudam yatha bhavati tatha likhyato

Asyashadja eva grahamso nyayascha

Asyodaharanam:-

S - s n s - r g r g r s - s s g r s – s r s s s n p

PpMr – m m p p n n p - m p m p u n s – n s r g r g r s –

S n r g r S n s g r s - g r s - s r s s s p n -

M p m p u n g s - N N s - r g r S s n s – r g s - s n p

"Etat shadja sthayi nithaye"

r g r s - s n p - p n p p m r m m p - m p n n s -

n s r m m m - p p u m p p s s – s n p - p n P p m –

m p m r r g r s - Iti thaya prayoga.

R r m P n s P n p m p

Aa a a a u mirdha na dha na

M p r r g r s

Vam tu ka – risale - Iti svara khantah

R m p n p p m r m r s s n p

.... Thodhi domdam dham dhi

g r S s n P

mi ki ta - Iti prabandha prayoga.

S S n d p d n p m m P - Ityatgrahe prayogo asthi /

Asmin raga Sari ga meti nagaschati,

Ma ga ri sati nagaschati,

Itya dhyana gaschanto aneka prayogah santi//*

Sri Raga

Tulajendra makes it clear that in Sri raga, Dhaivata is alpa. He gives sancharas and points out permissible and non-permissible prayogas in accordance with Gita,

Prabandha, Thaya and Alapa or the Chaturdandi as well as Suladi. Shadja is mentioned as Graha, amsa and nyasa.

The following is given as Shadja Sthayi in Thaya: Sa Sa ni sa, ri ga ri ga ri sa, sa sa ga ri sa, sa ri sa sa sa ri pa pa pa ma ri ma ma pa pa ni ni pa, ma pa ma pa ni ni sa, ni sa ri ga ri ga ri sa, sa ni ri ga ri sa ni sa ga ri sa, ga ri sam sa ri sa sa sa pa ni ma pa ma pa ni ni ga sa, ni ni sa, ri ga ri sa sa ni sa, ri ga sa, sa ni sa. Thaya prayoga is as follows:- ri ga ri sa, sa ni pa, pa ni pa, pa ma ri ma ma pa, ma pa ni ni sa, ni sa ri ma ma pa pa ni, ma ppa pa sa sa sa ni pa, pa ni pa pa ma, ma pa ma ri ri ga ri sa. You will find the second set of svaras given above is nearer modern usage. The Sthayi sancharas which are given in the first set conform to the ancient orthodox mode of rendering which is not now followed as such. Next Svara Khanda is given as: ri ma pa ni sa, pa ni pa ma pa, ma pa ri ri ga ri sa. The prabandha prayoga is given as: ri ma pa ni pa pa ma ri, ma ri sa sa ni pa, ga ri sa sa ri pa. Then he mentions sa sa ni dha pa dha ni pa ma ga ppa as occuring in Udgraha. The modern practice, however, is to use the dhaivata not in the intial phrases but only in one or two of the final sancharas. He takes care to caution that in this raga the svaras do not proceed as sa ri ga ma or as ma ga ri sa. It will be seen how the Sri raga has continued unchanged for centuries. Tulajendra was in fact deriving the lakshana of it as contained in old compositions and the raga as illustrated there in no way differes from the modern version of it. The author praises its antiquity and classifies it as an evening raga. Now, rightly or wrongly the noon seems to claim it more often than other parts of the day.

Venkatamakhi enumerates the same svaras for Sri Raga mela. His statement of the dhaivata being chatussruti though correct according to modern conception was from his point of view a mistake, for in giving the srutis of Dhaivata, he says they are five. In all other ragas for the same note he uses only the term Panchasruti Dhaivata. It might interest you to note that the mela by means of which you first become acquainted with twenty-twp srutis, is also the mela bearing number twenty-two in Venkatamakhi's scheme of seventy-twp melas. Venkatamakhi is also of the opinion that the raga is sampurna with ga and dha varja. The exact significance of this statement is, as we have already seen, explained by Tulajendra. In Sangita Sudha too the raga is described as taking the same notes as mentioned above, and all various stages of alapa are detailed as in the case of all ragas it discusses. Ramamatya has nothing new to say. He had named the srutis of the notes of Sri raga mela in the same manner. Somanatha who is generally very clear in his sruti discussion mentions this raga as taking tivratama madhyama. This is obviously a mistake. Pundarika Vithala who wrote works both on the Southern and Northern systems of music describes Sri raga as Tulajendra has done, but appropriately calls rishabha and dhaivata as chatussrutis. Lochanakavi who wrote his book Raga Tarangini in the fifteenth century mentions only twelve scales of which he gives Bhairavi as the first. He is moe a lakshanakara of the Northern system thatn the Southern. It may be assumed that during his time that divergence whose increase began after the era of Purandaradas a century later, was not very marked. The Bhairavi described by Lochana Kavi is not the Bhairavi of the present Hindustani system which corresponds to our Kharaharapriya scale or from the precise sruti point of view, our Bhairavi in its aroha. In fact Lochana Kavi was well aware of the Bhairavi as rendered by us for he expressly refers to the use of Komala dhaivata in Bhairavi and has no hesitation in condemning it as improper and not pleasing. The Bhairavi of Lochana Kavi is thus the Sri raga which we have been considering and corresponds to the Kafi Thata of the Northern system and he is clear that it was the suddha scale. It looks, therefore, very probable that long ago Bhairavi had its avaroha exactly like its aroha without komala dhaivata. When in course of time komala dhaivata crept in and came to stay in the avaroha and upon analogous principles in certain sancharas of aroha also. Tyagaraja thought fit to resurrect the old Bhairavi as kharaharapriya with a slight sharpening of ri, ga, dha, and ni to give it a distinct form. Those who can recall "Viriboni" varna as rendered at the beginning of this century can perceive how komala dhaivata has been making inroads into Bhairavi.

The Dvidiya Ghana Raga Panchaka

1. Kedara

Tulaja describes Kedara as a janya of Sankarabharana mela. The vital expressions like 'Dhaivata varja', Shadava soyam and 'mavakra svaragati' are particularly and significantly noteworthy. But, in the main part of the lakshana sloka Tulaja says it is sampurna. In the illustrative phrases we find no dhaivata at all. But, we must note here that, even in the current mode of phrasing as 'ga ma ni Pa ma ga, the nishada is noticeably soft. It has no assertive pronouncement. It sounds almost like 'ga ma dha pa ma ga'. It is only dhaivatha stroke for the instrumentalist.

Subbarama Dikshitar's treatment of Kedara gives a picture of the raga as it prevails at present. As usual a lakshana sloka in the name of Venkatamakhin is given:

> Kedara shadavo rago dhaivatasvara varjitah
>
> Arohe vakragandharah shadjagrahasamanivatah**

Murchanarohanavarohana is 'sa ma ga ma pa ni sa – sa ni pa ma Ma ga ri sa'. The dirgha madhyama as indicated in the avarohana as given above is to be noted. In addition to dirgha madhyama, the dirgha gandhara and deergha Rishabham as in 'ma Ga, ri Ri, sa Sa:' Is now the trend in present lakshya. Subbarama Dikshitar says that Kedara is bhashanga; shadava: Dhaivata varja; sa graha; Gandhara is vakra in the arohaha. Excepting the aspect of bhashangatva the rest of the details could be found in line with the treatment of Kedara as found in the Raga Lakshana appendix of Chaturdandi prakasika (Academy Edn). Subarama Dikshitar says that Nishada and madhyama are the important ranjaka svaras and it is quite so. The phrases cited by Subbarama Dikshitar give no doubt a picture of the raga Kedara as it prevails now. The illustrative prayogas are "Ni pa sa – Ma ga Ma pa – Ma Pa Ni Ma – Pa Ma ga ri Sa – ma ga ma pa sa sa – pa ni Ma ga ri Sa – Sa ni pa Ma ga ri sa – no pa sa ma Ga ri sa ni Sa". Subbarama Dikshitar specifically adds that 'sa ga ma pa ma ga – ri ga ri Ma ga ri sa' is to be found in raga lakshya geeta meaning perhaps in musical compositions in general. It may be obseraved that one phrase 'sa ri ri Ga sa' has found in roads into Kedaram in current lakshya. It is not known how. Even in standard compositions like Ananda Natana Prakasam of dikshitar and for that matter in the sanchari of Subbarma Dikshitar himself, a do not come across 'sa ri ri ga sa' at all.

Curiously enough Sangraha Chadamani, Sangita Sara Sangrahamu and Gana Bhaskaram give the arohana-avarohana as 'sa ma ga ma pa ni sa – sa ni pa ma ga ma dha ma ga ri sa', 'ga ma dha ma' is absolutely unwarrented. 'ga ma pa ni pa ma ga ri sa' may perhaps be construed to sound like 'ga ma dha pa ma'. The Sangita Svara Prasthara Sagaram of Nadamuni Pandithar puts it correctly as 'sa ma ga ma pa ni sa – sa ni pa ma ga ri sa'.

Further details regarding the raga kedara may be given as follows: A madhyamakala Pradhana raga, that is why some anonymous author has chosen to list this as a ghanaraga belonging to the dvitiya gana panchaka group. This raga creates a brisk atmoshphere. It is most suitable for tana varna and kriti forms. It creates the requisite musical atmosphre when sung at the commencement of concerts. A morning raga – to be sung between 7 and 9 A.M. But this Ganakala is not mandatory.

2. Narayana Gaula

'Syan Narayana gaula stu Sampurno nigrahan vitah
Arohe gandhara varjascha Vinyasa dvidyate kvachit'**

(Chaturdandi Prakashika)

Narayana gaula is a janya of Kambhoji mela. Nishada is the graha, amsa and raga and is the jiva svara. According to Tulaja it is an evening raga and this raga does not take 'pa da ni sa' in the arohana. He puts the arohana and avarohana as follows: 'Sa ri ma pa ni dha ni sa – sa ni dha pa ma ga ri ga ri sa' The phrases ni da pa ma and pa dha ma ga ri sa can be seen in Veena kuppaihav's Varna in this raga. In this varna ma pa ni ni sa and ma pa ni dha ni sa both are prominent. This varna can be taken as an aunthetic source of Narayana gaula as Veena kupparha was know as an expert in this raga and was even known as Narayana gaula as Veena kuppihar. The phrase ni ga ni ga sa ri occurs twice in this varna.

The first janya raga that is taken up by Tulaja under Kambhoji mela is Narayanagaula. It is sampurna of course, in the sense that it takes all the svaras in both arohana and avarohana taken together. Nishada is an important jiva svara or raga chaya svara. Regarding the ganakala of the raga, Tulaja says – 'Yame turiyake' – it is evening. There is a specific mention by Tulaja that 'pa da ni sa' does not occur in the arohana.

'Nidhanisadhanisa ityevgacchati padhaniseti nagacchati'

All the illustrative praoygas given by Tulaja go to confirm that the rohana and avarohana could safely be determined as follows: 'sa ri ma pa ni dha ni sa – sa ni dha pa ma ga ri ga ri sa', Tulaja could also have speicified that 'ni dha pa ma ga ri sa' is not allowable. The phrases 'ni dha pa ma' and 'pa dha ma ga ri sa' seem to be very common as evidenced by the tana varna of Veena Kuppayyar in Narayanagaula. This varna is an encyclopeida in this raga. Veena kuppayyar himself was known as 'Narayanagaula Kuppayyar' 'ma pa ni ni sa' and 'ma pa ni dha ni sa' are both equally prominent. In the varna quoted abovem there are occurances of the phrases such as 'Sa ni dha pa – Pa ma ga ri – sa Ni sa ri ma ma pa (last charana svara). Similarly in the mukthayisvara we find 'n d n p' – 'ma ga ri Sa'. In both these phrases, we find the elongated 'Pa', prior to 'ma ga ri sa'. In the mukthayiswara after dirgha madhyama we get 'ga ri sa' as:- 'ni sa ri ma Ma; ga ri sa Pa pa... ni sa ri Ma ga ri sa ga ri sa ni'. The varna starts at the very outset as Ma Ga ri ga ri ga Sa'. The phrase 'ni sa ni ga ri ga sa ri' occurs in both the sthayis (with 'ni' in the mandra and also in the madhya sthayi). Similarly 'ga ri ga sa ri' occurs in both the madhya and tara sthayis. In these phrases the combination of kaisiki nishada and antara ghandhara is not a very wholesome one and here the practical tendency makes the ghandhara slightly falttened though not upto the level of sadharana gandhara. It is amazing to not as to how and why Subbarama Dikshitar, the doyen of musicology did not take congnisance of this fact, though in a similar situation (both in a lesser degree) in the phrase 'sa ri ga ri sa' in Khamas, he takes care to speicfy that gandhara speaks less in sruit. The phrase 'ni ga ri ga sa ri' occurs twice in the famous Narayanagaula varna of Veena Kuppayyar. In 'Sro Raman' of dikshitar, we see the occurance of 'Ni ga Ri ga' in Naradadi'. The dirha dhaivata, though occasional, is another salient feature in Narayanagaula. The anupallavi of 'Sri Ramam' of Dikshitar starts with 'Dha Pa Ma' (Dee ragra) and then again in the charanam 'ri Ma pa Ni Ni' Da' (kusa lava tatam) This sort of a deergha dhaivata is not to be seen in the Narayana gaula varna of Kuppayyar. The dhaivata in the varna is given as deergha only for two aksharakalas and never more than that. Only dirgha madhyama and nishada are highlighted in the varna; Dirgha rishabha does not seem to have been given a place. In this varna, the raga hovers over a full range of two thayis from mandhra madhyama to tara madhyama. But in the kriti "Kadalevadeu' of Tyagaraja and 'Sri Ramam' of Dikshitar, we find only the mandra panchama and tara rishabha (perhaps gandhara also) touched.

We apparently find a difference between the effect created by Tyagaraja in his 'Kadalevadu' and by Dikshitar in his 'Sri Ramam'. In the former the madhyama is rather plain, while in the latter it is solftened, as per certain version in 'Ro; Ma; Ga Ga Ri ga ri' Sri ramam ravi.

Dirgha gandhara is also to be noted here in this context. This is of course a rare phenomenon. In Tyagaraja's dealing, we find a regular descent as 'ni dha pa ma ga ri sa ri' as in 'Kadalevadu' May it be a difference in version perhaos ut us 'dha pa ma ga ri ga Ri'.

Rishabha, madhyama and nishada are the eminent jiva svaras, raga chaya svaras. Nishada is however not to be found employed as an assertive graha svara, though the intermediary phrases have nishada at the beginning. The raga is not characterised by any dirgha graha and nyasa, except perhaps for dhirgha madhyama being employed as graha in 'Kadalevadu' of Tyagaraja. This raga further does not provide much scope for jhanta, dhatu, ahata and pratyahata combinations of svaras. Only the movement of single noted phrases seem to dominate. Madhyamakala dominates this raga. That is why some anonymous author has created a place for Narayanagaula in the dvitiya ghana lpanchaka group. The very conception dvitiva ghana panchaka is faulty in as much as Saranganata and Bowli are mentioned as belonging to the group. Narayanagaula is eminetly suited for varna and kriti and not for other types of compositions. It is more of the type of 'madhyama' raga in the classification of ragas by Ramamatya into Uttama, madhyama and adhama ragas.

Subbarama Dikshitar's treatment of Narayanagaula is very concise but the essence of it is there. The lakshana sloka quoted by him, under the anthorship of Venkatamakhin, is found in the Raga lakshana appendix printed at the end of the text of the Chaturdandi Prakasika both in Sanskrit and the Tamil translation thereof as brough out by the Music Academy and it reads thus:

'syan narayanagaulastu sampurno nigrahanvitah
arohe gadhavarjasca vinyasadvidyate kvacit'**

The murchanarohanavarohana is given as follows: 'ri ma pa ni dha ni sa – ni dha pa ma ga ri ga ri sa'; upanga raga; nishada is graha. Gandhara and dhaivatha are varjya in the arohana, but occur in vinyasa; can be sung at all times.

The specific note provided, rather added by Subbarama Dikshitar is significant. The commencement of the murchanarohana and avarohana with rishabha and nishada respectively, make these notesa s graha and thereby the most important jiva svaras and amsa svaras. He quotes the poorvacharyas Bharata and Matanga in this context. When in a raga a svara is mentioned as graha, it implies the other two, ie., the same note much be amsa and nyasa also. Srngadeva too mentions such a point. He says that if, of the graha, amsa and nyasa svaras, one is mentioned, it implies the other two as well. But this statement does not carry weight uniformly in all cases, say for instance, gandhara of Sahana. It is the dominating jiva savara but seldom occurs as a graha and nyasa. Similarly dhaivatha too.

Here in Narayanagaula it is reported wrongly under the authorship of Venkata-makhin that gandhara and dhaivata are varjya in the arohana. Gandhara is no doubt varja in the arohana but how about dhaivatha? The phrasing ‘pa ni dha ni sa’ is as frequent and appropirate in usage as ‘ri ma pa ni sa’, perhaps the former being rather more so, as evidenced by standard lakshyas available. Subbarama Dikshitar adds further that though nishada is the important graha, amsa and nyasa, rishabha too is an important nyasa svara. He furhter says that though ‘ma ga ri ga ri sa’ is incorporated in the murchana, the phrase ‘ma pa dha ma pa ma ga ri’ sounds more beautiful in raga. He concludes by saying that the phrase ‘pa ni sa’ is in usage. This is a very important point to be noted.

Subbarama Dikshitar quotes a Kaivara Prabandha of Venkatamahi. ***In the ‘Mudra Khanda’ of the prabandha, we come across:***

Sankaramunimata pratisthavana
Kovidu govindhadhvarina
Ragambikasuta venkatamahi. **

The above kaivara prabandha contains all sorts of phrases quite line with the current phrases occuring in the Raga Narayanagaula. Subbarama Deekshitar’s sanchari is well expressive of the form of the raga as illustrated through the kritis of Tyagaraja and Dikshitar.

To trace the history of the raga at least with reference to the nomenclature, we do no come across the raga either in Sangita Makarandha or in Sangita Samaya Sara or even in Sangita Ratnakara. Pandit Srinivasa mentions Narayanagaula in his work written exclusively on the music of the South. Panditaradya Charita of Palkurukki Somanatha Kavi does not mention Narayanagaula.

Holy Vidyaranya mentions Narayanagaula in his 50 janya ragas as authoritatively reproduced in the Sangita Sudha of Govinda Dikshitar. It is the only janya of Kedaragaula mela as reported in the Sangita Sudha.

'Narauanagaueamsaya kedaragaulayasya ca melaekah

Nyasograhom saya nisada eva'**.

The lakshana slokas as given in the Sangita Sudha in general with regard to the akshiptika, raga vardhani, vidari, shadja – madhyama – panchama sthayi etc. are not very much intellgible with reference to current practice; illustrative phrases could have served better. But certain key statements are significantly noteworthy.

We do not come across Narayanagaula in the ragas adopted by Tallappaka Annamacharya. We find only Narani, Narani Desakhi. Similarly we do not come across Narayanagaula in Lochana Kavi's Ragatarangini, Ramamatya's Svaramelakalanidhi or in Somanatha's Raga Vibodha.

The next treatise worthy of note is the Chaturdandi Prakasika of Venkatamakhin. In the Mela Prakarana of Chgaturdandi Prakasika, Venkatamkhin mentions and describes only the 19 purva prasiddha or kapita melas and kambhoji is one among them. In the Raga prakarana while enumerating ragas with nishada as graha, amsa and nyasa., Venkatamakhin mentions Narayanagaula as one such. In the very brief description of the Janya ragas one by one in order, Narayanagaula is mentioned as a janya of Kedaragaula. The sloka in Chaturdandi Prakasika goes thus:-

'Narayanagaulastu sampurnah

Prakirtitah kedaragaula melotthasah'*

The above is the edition of the text of Chaturdandti as done by Pandit Subramanya Sastri and T.L. Venkataramayyar, printed and published by the Music Academy, Madras.

This gross mistakem whether it is a typographical error or a printing error is repeated in the Tamil translation of the text also as done by Pandit Subramanya Sastri and published by the Music Academy, Madras. We have to take refuge only in the defence counsel projected by late M.S. Ramaswamy Iyer, when he protects Ramamatya against the scorching citicism by Venkatamakhin, of certain viewpoints of the former: "What sort of a copy of the manuscript of the work fell in the hands of Venkatamakhin copied and recopied by different indifferent copyists!" Besides it can also be inferred here that though Venkatamakhin lauched his own creative mela system, he still had in the innermost recesses of his heart, what his father had to say about Narayanagaula. We know pretty well that Govinda Dikshitar described Narayanagaula as the only janya of Kedaragaula mela on the authority of the treatment of 15 melas and 50 janyas by Holy Vidyaranya; It is very definite that to Venkatamakhi Kambhoji alone was the mela. Elsewhere in the description of Kedaragaula itself Venkatamakhin says that Kedaragaula is of janya of Kambhoji mela. ***Sloka 98 of Raga prakarana of the Chaturdandti Prakasika of Venkatamakhi of the same edition thereof reads thus*:-**

'Kedaragaulah sampurnah
Kambhojimela sambhavah'**

How can one and the same raga be both a mela and janya

In the very first nomenclature for the 72 melas evidently appearing in the Sangraha Cgudamani of Govindacharya, the 28th mela is found only as Kambhoji. It is only in the later Kanakambari mela nomenclautre the 28th mela became, Harikedaragaula, evidently with a view to replace the bhashanga raga Kambhoji by Kedaragaula and still further as Harikedaragaula to fulfil the Katapayadi requirments to get at the correct serial number of the mela in the scheme. But still there is the question as to where is the documentary evidence abd oriif that Kambhoji is a bhasanga raga. But no doubt there has been a tinge of bhashangatva in kambhoji as could be traced to the rendering the tevara hymns in Takkesi pan. Definitely from the 18th century A.D. pnwards, Kambhoji has been only a bhashanga raga in practice if not in books.

In the Sangita Chadumani of Govindacharya, Narayanagaula is recorded as a janya of Harikambhoji, the 28th mela with the folowing arohana – avarohana 'sa ri ma pa ni dha ni sa – sa ni dha pa ma ga ri sa' ***In the lakshana gita it is recorded as*** :

> '*Arohagavarjya vakra avaroha*
>
> Sampurnam nigrahanvasamsa
>
> *Harikambhojimelajanita narayanagaularagah'.**

The illustrative phraseology is however not in variance with the current trends. Raga Pravaham quotes one version of the arohana – avarohana Narayanagaula as 'sa ri ma pa dha ni sa – sa ni dha pa ma ga ri ga ri sa' The arohana is not in line with current practice Gana Bhaskaram of K.V. Srinivasa Iyengar follows Sangraha Chudamani and Sangita 'Sara Sangrahamu in giving the arohana – avarohana as 'sa ri ma pa dha ni sa – sa ni dha pa ma ga ri sa' Everything said and donem though; 'pa ni dha ni sa' is favourable. 'ma ga ri ga ri sa' is more favourable than a 'ma ga ri sa' in the descent Sangita Svara Prastara Sagaramu of Nadamuni Panditar, a work of commendable value (Telugu) gives Narayana-gaula as a janya of Harikambhoji with 'sa ri ma pa ni da ni sa – sa ni da pa ma ga ri sa' it will do well to retains this, though a regular descent as 'ni dha pa ma ga ri sa ri' occasionally is not prohibitory. We find this phrase in 'Kadale vadu' of Tyagaraja, as, noted earlier. This phrase 'ni dha pa ma ga ri sa' and also 'pa dha ma ga ri sa' are incorporated in the authoritative lahshya prabandha – the varna of Veena Kuppayyar.

3. Bauli

Bauli is an upanga raga and janya of Mayamalavagaula. One of the Upa Ghana ragas, this is a shadava raga as Ma is vanga. Nishada takes place in the avarohana as ni dha ni sa is an occasional phrase. In the current practice nishada is altogether omitted in the arohana.

Tulajendra then describes the Bauli raga. It is born of Malavagaula mela. It is an upanga. Ma is varja and therefore it is shadava. But what is extraordinary is the statement that ma is its graha and that it is an evening raga. Nishada in aroha as in dha ni sa is

(*Sloka 102 in the Chapter, "Raga Prakarana" of Chaturdandi Prakasika of Venkatamakhin)

occasional. In modern practice nishada is altogether omitted in aroha. In the avaroha nishada is regularly present. The tana prayoga is; sa ri ga pa dha ni ni sa, ni dha pa dha ri ri sa dha ni sa ri, sa sa dha ni ni sa, ni dha pa dha, ri ri sa dha ni sa ri, sa sa dha pa ga ga ri; in thaya the prayoga is : ri ri sa ni dha pa dha; ga ri sa ni dha dha pa ga, dha dha ni dha dha pa ga, dha pa ga ga ri; sa ni sa sa. Gita prayoga is : (ma) pa ga pa (ma perhaps in a misprint for dha) dha sa dha sa ri ri ga sa pa ga ri sa ni dha pa ga. The tanikarana prayoga is given as: ni dha pa ga pa ga ri ga, sa ri, ga pas dha sa ri ga pa ga ri sa. The prabandha prayoga is noted as : ri ga ri sa ni dha pa ga ri sa ri ga. Venkatamakhi's description is exactly what Tulajendra gives. Sangita Sudha discussed the appropriateness of making madhyama the absent note as grahasvara and says that in practice only the shajda is grahasvara. The mention of madhyama as the grahasvara is perhaps a survival of the priod when the scale of the raga started from madhyama as funamental. This raga is described by most writers with the name Bahuli under the Malavagauda scale. It has now become the mot popular of the Udaya ragas. It is curious how it was once regarded as an evening raga. The presence of the Komala rishabha and gandhara with the absence of the madhyama imports the character of the morning raga. Revagupti, Bhupala, Malayamaruta are alike in this respect. Bilahari and that Desakshi having affinity to it, assume a similar complexion not withstanding their rishabha is not of the Komala variety and perhaps for this reason come a little later in the morning. On the principle of inductive reasoning Bauli should be a morning raga and practice as it now prevails is in conformity with sound reason. The gandhara and nishadha of this raga are slightly flattened, without however their being made to lose the Antara and Kakali character respectively. Tyagaraja's "Melukovayya" and Dorai-swamy Iyer's Aruno-dayamaye" are fine examples in this raga.

4. Saranga Nati

The next Janya of Malavagaulamela is Saranga nati with shadja for graha, amsa and nyasa. It is an evening raga. Venkata-makhi states its vadi is shadja, samvadis are madhyama and panchamam anuvadis are dhaivata and rishabha and vivadis are gandhara and nishada. Tulajendra avers that the arohani is from madhya shadja to tara shadja, but the gandhara and nishada do not occur in the regular course. These notes should be used according to sandharbhawhich can only mean tradition and usages. The tara shajda tana praoyaga is : dha sa sa ri, sa ri ma ga ri ma ma pa ma pa dha dha pa, ma pa dha sa sa. The avarohi dhaviata tana prayoga is : ni sa ri ma ga ri ga ma pa, pa pa ma. It is difficult to understand how this can be regarded as dhaivata tana in the total absence of dhaivata itself. The panchama sthayi is given as : ma pa dha ni sa, dha pa ma ma pa ma ri. Theya prayogas are : dha pa dha ma pa ni sa ri,m ri sa dha pa, sa ni dha pa, ma ma pa ma ri ma ga ri sa, ni sa. Prabandha prayoga is given as : ma pa dha ni sa ri, ma ga ri sa ni dha pa, ma ga ri sa. Sangita Sudha severely criticises the view of those writers, who place the raga Saranga nata under the Salanga nata mela which takes the sharp rishabha and sharp dhaivata and that other janyas stated under it are, to be classed under different melas. Evidently the author of Sangita Sudha is of opinion that no raga ort mela of the name Saranga nata existed apart from Saranganata described by him as janya of Gurajari mela. It is not Ramamatya alone who speaks of Saranga nata with sharp rishabha and sharp dhaivata under a mela of the same name. Somanatha mentions Saranga nata as a janya of Mallari which in the notes taken corresponds to Saranganata of Ramamatya which is practically Sankarabharana. The janyaragas which Govinda Dikshitar complians of as wrongly placed under Salanganata and disposed by him under different melas, are also placed by Somanatha under Mallari. Paundarika Vithala also places Saranganata under Kedara which takes sharp rishabha and dhaivata. The common inference from these facts is that ragas having the same name came to be rendered differently in different parts of the country or in different ages, the variable notes being changed. For instance while Bhupali of the Sourth takes flat varieties of rishabha, gandhara and dhaivata, the raga of the same name in the north is sung with the sharp varieites of these notes. The notes themlsevles are not chanted but their variety. As we proceed with other ragas, many instances of this change will be found. Pratical music in a wide country like ours cannot always continue unchanged. A lakshanakara should take note of these chantes and explain. Nothing, therefore, seems more appropriate than the inclusion of brief history of the raga in the books that give its lakshana. In Sampradaya Pradarsini only one compositions of Diskhitar is given. No song of Tyagaraja in this raga appears in the printed editions of his songs. It seems as if this raga went out of vogue ecen in

***(Slokas 419 – 420). (Note: Sangita Parijaga of Ahobala as quoted in this anthology is the edition of the text by Kalivara Vedantavagisa and Sarada Prasada Gosh and published by Basanta Lata Mitra – The New Sanskrit Press Calcutta - 1879.**

Tyagaraja's time. The use of rishabha and dhaivata was evidenlty unsettled both in the svarakrama as well as their sruti values. One the other hand, Saveri was straight and unambiguous in its notes and did not in bhava, differs substantially from Saranganata as a janya of Malavagaula mela and came to be favoured more to the gradual exclusion of the dubious raga. When there is a violent difference as to the lakshana of a raga it is not unusual for practical artists to abandon it particularly when there is another raga almost like it. This is one of the reasons why Vasanta came to be favoured more than Lalita, it looks as if Saranganata ceased to be current for more than wo centuries. It is true Dikshitar has composed a song it it. It was one of his aims to revive disused ragas. Tyagaraja also revived extinct ragas but he did so only when they had a chance of independent existence, and clear identity. It will not be a surprise if Tyagaraja has not composed in this raga. It may be pointed out that the distinction between Saranganata and Salaganata now made is illusory.

5. Riti Gaula

This is a janya raga derived from the 22nd mela, Kharaha-rapriya as it is used today. But different treatises on ragas give us various suggestions about the lakshana of this raga. ***The lakshana sloka given in the raga lakshana anubandha of the Chaturdandi prakashika is as follows:***

"Nigraho ritigaula kyo arohe tu dha varjutah
Sampurnascaisa gatayakovidaih"**

The sloka gives a view that the dhaivata would not iccyr ub tge ascending phrase as dha ni sa. This view is totally contradictory to the news and versions of shaligi and Tulaja. According to Subharana Dikshitar it is a raganga and Sampurna raga. Nishada is graha svara – ascending to him. He further gives details such as Dhaivata is varjya in arohana (as mentioned in Chaturdandi prakashika), a ghana raga, can be sung in the

---

***From the Personal collection of Manuscripts of Padmashree, Prof: Leela Omcherry**

**** Slokas from Treatises- Sangita Darpana, Shiva Tatva Ratnakara, Sangita Parijata, Raga Sagara, Sangita Damodara, Chaturdanti prakasika, Sangita choodamani and also from the book, A Historical Study of Indian Music by Swamy Prajnananda (Chapter- The Iconography of Indian Music)**

evening, Ni sa Ri ga and Ma are jiva, and nyasa svaras. Subbarama dikshitar gives same illustrative sancharas and prayogas of this raga in order to establish its character. The phrases included even sancharas like 'Sa ri ga ma' 'ni pa ni ni', 'pa ni ni sa' 'ni pa ni ni sa'. The pancha should occur only in the phrases in mandra sthayi, not in the madhya sthayi phrases. He mentions the usage of only one dhaivata ie., Sudha dhaivata in this raga.

Subbarama Dikshitar also mentions about the raga lakshana appendix given in Chaturdandi parakashika of Venkatamahi where the 20th melakarta raga is formed as Nari ritigaula but the raga is described only as Ritigaula.

The discription about this raga by shaliji is as follows: It is an evening raga; it is a janya of mela, Bhairavi; a sampurna raga, nishabha vajya in the arohana. Rishadha appears only in the phrases like 'sa ga ri ga ma' and in phrases in like sa ga ga ma, ma ga ga ma rishabha is varja. He puts Panchama as an alpa svara with no significance. According to him the dhaivatantya phrases are also very rare in the raga. The probobility of the occurance of sudha-daivata is restricted to minimum. Probebly the only phrase where sudha daivata occurs is 'padhadha ma'. And this phrase is not detrimental to raga bhava. The chatusruti dhaivata in its trisruti form only features in Ritigaula.

In 'Sangita ratnakara' of Sarangadeva of 13century A.D, it is mentioned about Ritigaula as Prak prasidha raganga and Riti as a Prak prasidha Desi raga. Vidyaranya describes Riti gaula as janya of Sri raga which takes Pancha Sruti dhaivata. Similarly, Ramamatya mentions Riti gaula as one of his 30 melas and discribes further about the notes taken by the raga as follows: Sudha shadja, Rishabha, gandhara, Madhyama, Panchama and Panchasruti dhaivata and Kaisiki nishada. He further mentions Ritigaula as one of the madhyama ragas and he describes it also as a sampurna raga with nishada as graha, amsa and nyasa svaras.

In his 'Ragavibodha' Somanatha (1609 A.D) mentions Ritigaula as one of his 23 melas. Somanatha also gives the svarasthanas Shadja, Rishabha, gandhara, Madhyama and Panchama as sudha. His Dhaivata as he calls it is Tina tasa Dhaivata, which is equal to the pancha sruti Dhaivata mentioned by Rama matya. He does ot call Riti gaula as a janya raga According to Venkatamahi Riti gaula is a janya of Bharavi mela which takes the svaras shadja, Pancha sruti rishabha, sudharana gandhara, Sudha madhyama, Panchama Sudha daivata and Kasikinishada. Nishada is graha, amsa and nyasa svara.

The Raga lakshananubandha mentions Nari Riti gaula as 20th mela. It is also mentioned as one of the 'Ashta ghana ragas'. As the character of a ghana raga is well brought out in the 'tana' performance on in the madhyamakala, then Riti gaula is really one such raga as it is suitable for 'Tana' performances. In the Raga lakshananubandha it is further mentioned that this raga is an evening raga and describes nishada as graha, nyasa and amsa. It further says that Dhaivata is varja in the arohana.

Ahobala in his Sangita parijata (1660 A.D.) treates Ritigaula as a sampurna raga with panchama as varja in the arohana. Sangraha choodamani of Govindacharya which can be considered as almost contemporary to the Trinty period, puts Ritigaula as janya of Natabharavi, the 20th mela and gives the following arohana and avarohana: 'Sa ga ri ga ma ni dha ma pa ni sa – sa ni dha ma pa dha ma ga ri sa'. The lakshana gita conforms this version as the text of the *gita* says: "Chatursruti rishabha, Sadharana gandhara, Kaisiki Svaram, itara sudha aroha avaroha sampurna vakra sangraha nyasamsa triputa yukta Natabhairavi mela janita Riti gaula raga": The gita does not mention about two dhaivata occuring in it.

In the sangita swra sangrahamu Riti Gaula has been mentioned as a janya of the 22nd mela, Kharaharapriya. The arohana and avarohana are given as follows: Sa ga ri ga ma pa dha ni sa – Sa ni dha pa ma ga ri sa. K.V.Srinivasa Iyer gave in his work 'gana bhaskaramu has mentioned Riti gaula as janya of 20th mela, Nata bhairavi and gives aorhana and avarohana as follows': "Sa ga ri ga ma da ni sa – sa ni dha ma ga ma pa ma ga ri sa".

The Sangita Svara prasthara samgrahamu of Nadamuni Panditar treats Riti gaula as the janya of 20th mela Nata bharavi. He gives the arohana and avarohana as follows: "sa ga ri ga ma ni ni sa–sa ni dha ma pa dha ma ga ri sa ni pa ni sa". The 'Raga lakshana- nubandha' of Muddu Venkatamahi puts Riti gaula as one of the 'Ashta ghana ragas'. It is interesting to note that different authors have came out with various versions of the lakshana of ragas and through ages some new version has got established in practicality.

In practice today Riti gaula is considered as the janya of 22nd mela, Kharaharapriya and sudha dhaivata phrase is totally negligible and the dhaivata takes trisruti. However, as one goes though the history of this raga, it is more established that this raga is a derivatioin of the 20th mela. This raga is suitable for madhyamakala which again establishes that this is one of the eight Ghana ragas mentioned in various treatises.

Apart from these two sets of ghana ragas, these is another set of right ghana ragas mentioned in some treatise in which the five of the first set in, Nata, gaula Varali Arabhi and Sri and present and two of the second set such as Riti gaula and Bauli are also appear. Another raga which does not came in these two sets of ghana raga ie., Melava sri is one of the 8 ghana ragas. What is interesting is the two ragas in the second set of Ghana ragas such as Narayana gaula and Saranga Nata do not appear in the list of these 8 Ghana ragas. It is should be assured that the ghana ragas are basically the ragas suitable for thana prayogas and it can be seen from the Veena tradition that these ghana ragas are usually played at the commencement of a concert.

Celebrated composers like the *Trinity* have employed these ragas in their compositions in order to suit to the requirment of the particular composition. It is really amazing to see the list of compositions in which these ragas are employed by various composers of different periods such as the Pre-trinity period, Trinity period and Post-trinity or contemporary period.

These ragas manifest in different musical forms like Prabandha, Gita, Svarajatis, Varna, Keertana, Kriti etc., which is dealtwith in the chapter on *Musical Forms.*

5

Ghanaraga Panchaka in Musical Forms

In the post trinity period, musical compositions (kritis) have emerged as manifestation of ragas in their fullest form as they could bringout the bhava or character of ragas while giving realistic appearance to the otherwise formless ragas. After the musical trinity the composers have started composing kritis and gradually it has become the most essential item of Carnatic music. In concerts kritis are chosen as the main piece when the artiste shows his ability to render Ragalapana, Niraval and Kalpana svaras in the particular raga in which the kriti is composed. If one analyses the kritis composed by the trinity and other great composers in various ragas, it is easy to know how the ragas have been interpreted according to their lakshanas (the Characteristics) given in the treatises. They give us a clear picture about how a particular raga is to be sung. The sangatis introduced in kritis have also given an out line of the important phrases of a raga.

Brief Dèscription of Major Musical Forms:

The Ela Prabandha

"Nibadha: shadbhi ragaischa-

Chaturbhir datu bhischaya:

Svarougha: Sa prabhandha: sjat"*

(Sangit ratnakara)

(The group of svaras that consists of 6 angas and 4 datus is called prabandha)

The Angas of Prabada:

The 6 angas and their definitions are as follows:

1. Swaram:

'Sarigadya sapta varna: Shadjadi dvani vachaka:

svarabhivyakti samyukta: svara sabdena keertita:'

The seven musical notes like s r g etc. are called 'Svaram'*

2. Birudam"

"Sambudhyanta padainava neturyadupabadhyate

Varnanam dhairya somjader bindam nama tammatam"*

The words and syllables that show the valient nature of the hero like - dhairyam, Samyam etc are called Birudam

3. Padam

"Kariyakaraka sambandha rupena yadi badhya te

Tadeva dhairya sourya der varnanam tatpadam smrutam"

The incidents used to describe the hero are called Padam.*

4. Tenakam

"Tenati sabda stena: syanmangalartha prakashaka":

"Tena" denotes to the 'Parabrahma'*

5. Paatam

'Paato vadyaksharotkara:'*

Paatam literally means cholkettu. The syllables that emerge from the percussion instruments are called "Paadam'.

Eg. Dim, Tadim, Gina etc.

6. Talam

"Kalo laghu adi mitaya kriyaya sammitomitim

Gita dervidadha talam".*

Tempo set by the tala angas of laughu, drutam, Plutam in the gitas is known as Talam.

Dhatus of Prabandha:

There are four types of dhatus as follows:

1. Utgraham

"Prabandha syadi mo bhaya utgraha:

Pariteirlita:

Atavut gruihyata gita mava narabhyate yata"

The first part of prabandha is called as Utgraha.*

2. Melapakam

Mitho melana hetu tva dudgraha dhruvayor dvayo:

Melapaka: Prabandhasya dvitiyo bhaga uchyate:

As Melaapaka forms the Utgraha and Dhurva it is called 'Melapaka'*.

3. Dhurvam

"Dhruvatrad dhruva samjnasma tritiyo vayava smruta:

As dhruva is a constant part, the third part of the prabandha is called dhruva:*

4. Abhogam

"Prabandhasya yada bhogam paripurtirm karoti tat
Abhoga: sa: prabandhasya tooriyavayava: smruta:"

It denotes completeness; this part is called 'abhoga'*.

There is another part of Prabandha called Antara which is seen in some gitas with those Khantas (Parts).

The five jatis of Prabandha:

There are five jatis of Prabandhas namely:

Medini

Anandini

Deepini

Bhavarni

Taravali

"Tatra svaradibhi: Shadbhiram

Gair yukthatu medini

Anga panchaka samyukta jatiranandini smruta

Chatmangayuta jati dipiniti prakirtita

Jati ranga dvayopeta taravatya bhitiyati"*

*** Sangita Kalpadrumam- Section-II, Chapter-9- 'Prabandha Prakaranam'**

Medini consists of 6 angas and Anandini, Deepini, Bhavani and Taravali consist five, four, three and two angas respectively. The Prabandhas are usually named after the jatis.

There are three more varieties of Prabandhas such as Sudam, Ali and Viprakeernam. Sudam is further divided into eight kinds such as Ela, Karanam, Dhenki, Vartani, Jhombadam, Lambham, Rasam and Ekatali.

Ali Prabandha is further categorized into 24 types such as Varnam, Varnasvaram, Gadyam, Kaivadham, Angacharini, Kandam, Turagaleela, gajaleela, Dvipadi, Chakravalam, Kranchapadam, swarartham, Dvanikatini, Arya, Gatha, Dvipathakam, Kalahamsam, Todakam, Ghadam, Vrittam, Matruka, Ragakadambakam, Panchataleswaram and Talarnavam,

Similarly Viprakirnam is categorized under 36 heads such as Srirangam, Srivilasam, Panchabhagi, Panchananam, Umatilakam, Tripati, Chatushpati, Shadpati, Vastu, Vjayam, Tripatham, Chaturmukham, Simhaleela, Hamsaleela, Dantakam, Jhampadam, Kandukam, Tribhangi, Haravilasam, Sudarsanam, Swarangam, Srivardhanam, Harshavardhanam, Vadanam, Chachari, Charya, Padhadi, Rahadi, Virashri, Mangalacharam, Dhavalam, Mangalam, Ovi, Loli, Dhollari and Danti.

The Five Matras of Prabandhas:

There are five kinds of matras used in prabandhas as follows:

Chhaganam: This consist of six matras eg.'girisa tanaya'

Paganam: This consist of five matras e.g., 'gajavadana'

Chaganam: This consists of four matras. E.g., 'Purahara'

Taganam: This consist of three quatras e.g., 'girisa'

Daganam: This variety consists of two matras. E.g. 'Hara'

Five types of Desa ela Prabandhas:

These are five kinds of Ela prabandhas written in regional languages such as: Karnata, Lada, Gauda, Andhra, and Dravida. They are named according to the language in which they are written.

These Prabandhas are composed in the Ghana ragas. A list of few prabandhas composed in Ghana ragas are given below:

Jaya Jaya Sangita (Sri Vardhana) - Nata raga - Rupaka tala

Dugu dugrijhan jham (Kaivara prabandha) - Nata raga -Rupaka tala

Tom tom ga dadhimi - Sri ragam - Dhruva tala

Note: The prabandhas with notation are furnished in the Appendix.

Thayas

References of Thayas can be found in treatises like Brihaddesi, Sangita parijata, Sangita samayasara. Thayas are also known as Thana as in the treatises.

Definition of Thayas

Group of foum svaras when sung or played in arohana or avarohana under they are called Thayas eg., s r g m, m g r s, r g m p , p m g r etc.

According to Sangita samayasara, Thayas are sung in groups of four swaras and gradually sung in five, six and seven respectively so as to give the raga bhava. They are also to be sung in different speeds.

According to Saranga deva's 'Sangita ratnakara' Thayas are 'Thanams' sung systematically as groups of svaras in akara.

According to Chaturdanti prakasika, Thana or Thayas are sung as per the requirement of a particular raga. Thana can be sung based on one particular note. Then thanas should be sung with the 'combination of four svaras in ascending and descending order. After certain phrases are sung, it takes rest on the particular note which is placed at the centre of the phrases used. This kind of Sanchara is called 'Eduppu' or 'Makarini'.

There are Thanas composed in the Ghana ragas. Some gita Prabandhas are also called as Thayas by some scholars. Eg. Rare Thanas in Saranga Nata raga and Jaya jaya Sangita in Nata raga. Though these gitas do not match the lakshana of thaya as mentioned in treatises, most of the Thanas are in the Ghana ragas as the Ghana ragas are suitable for thanas. (Examples for thanas are given in the appendix.)

Gitam

'Giyate iti gitam' is the short and general definition of gitam. According to this definition any verse that is sung is a gitam but here, to be more specific on the word Gita in the musical sense, a gita is a song other wise known as 'Salaga sudam'. The word salaga sudam has its origin from the words chayalaga and sudam.

According to Venkatamahi there are seven kinds of gitas such as 1. Dhruvam, 2. Matham, 3. Prati matham, 4. Nissarukam, 5. Ata talam, 6. Rasakam, 7. Eka tali.

1. Dhruvam

There are two main angas (parts) in this kind of gitas. They are Udgraham and Abhogam respectively. According to Bharata there are sixteen kinds of dhruvas. There are guide lines in respect of name, tala and rasa to be employed in these 16 dhruvas.

E.g., The first dhruva is called Jhayantarm and it has to be set only to adi tala and the proposed rasa is Sringara the second one called as Sekharam is set to the tala 'Nissarukam' and rasa is Vira.

2. Matham

Matham takes one or two jatis in the anga Udgraha. This has to be set to Matha tala. There are six types of Mathas. They are all set to the varieties of Matha tala such as Jaganam, Bhaganam, Saganam, Raganam, Naganam and Matha visesham.

3. Prati Matham

This is almost like Matham except for the tala used and has four varieties. The talas employed are: one guru, two drutam with one vishamam and two laghu; three laghu and a viramam; and one laghu with a viramam and a laghu respectively.

4. Nissarukam

These kinds of gitas are only set to Nissaruka tala and Nissarukam has six verities.

5. Ata talam

These kinds of gitas are set to Ata tala and Ata talam has six verities.

6. Rasakam

They are set to Rasa tala and Rasakara has four verities.

7. Eka tali

These gitas are essentially set to Eka tala or Eka tali have three varieties.

Gitas help establish the phrases that are to be used in a raga and establish the identity of the raga. Usually there are three different khantas in a gita such as Udgraha, Abhoga and Mudra khanta. After each Khanta is sung the first khanta is repeated. The dhatu of a gita is always simple and the matu in desiya bhasha (regional languages). The syllables like aiya, aya, thiya, am o, re, tuma, kuma are often seen in the sahitya of a gita. They are known as 'Matruka padas'.

Gitas are mainly of two kinds such as Lakshya gita and Lakshana gita. Lakshya gita is further categorized under Sadharana gita, Samanya gita, Sanchari gita and Sthuti gita. In lakshana gita, the lakshana of a raga is described such as its graha, amsa, nyasa, arohana-avarohana, sanchara etc.

There are gitas composed in the Ghana ragas such as Nata, Gaula, Varali, Arabhi and Sri. These gitas are called 'Ghana raga gitas'

E.g.					
	1. Sri Sambho	-	Nata	-	Ata tala
	2. Rere Balagopala	-	Nata	-	Triputa tala (Saravalaghugitam)
	3. Govinda gokula	-	Nata	-	Dhruva tala
	4. Gana vidya	-	Nata	-	Dhruva tala (Saptatala gita)
	5. Kamalaja	-	Arabhi	-	Dhruva rupaka tala
	6. Jaya jaya	-	Sri	-	Dhruva tala
	7. Aare svara	-	Gaula	-	Triputa tala
	8. Dhirutu	-	Bauli	-	Dhruva tala
	9. Areare	-	Saranga Nata	-	Rupaka tala

Note: The Ghana raga gitas with notation are given in the Appendix.

Swarajati & Jatiswara

It is difficult to trace the origin of svara jatis from old treatise as they do not mention away lakshana for these forms. They are comparatively modern compositions and have the history of hundred or hundred and fifty years. Swarajati has three parts such as Pallavi, Anu Pallavi and Charana. The sahitya usually deals with devotional themes, sringara etc. The celebrated composers of svarajati are Syamasastri, Adiyappayah, Swatitirumal, Chinna Krishna dasa and others.

There is no sahitya employed in Jatiswara unlike Swarajatis. Swara jatis are also called as 'Swara pallavi'. There are svarajatis & Jatiswaras composed in the Ghana ragas. Some composers have used the Ghana ragas to compose the swarajatis & Jatiswaras. There is a pancha raga svarajati composed by svatiturumal. (Selected swarajatis & jatiswaras are given with notation in the Appendix)

Varnas

Varnas are scholarly compositions and have great importance in the field of Karnatic music. A Varna introduces all possible sancharas of a raga in it and it gives the raga bhava to a great extend.

There are four main categories of Varna such as: Chouka varna, Pada varna, Tana varna and Dharuvarna.

1. Chouka Varna

It is consists of a Pallavi and Anupallavis and a charana. Charana is also called as Edugada Pallavi. Matu of a choukavarna includes sahitya, svara and jatis. The Chitta svara appears after the pallavi and the Chitta svara consists of sahitya as well as Cholkettu. The anupallavi consists minimum of four avartas with sahitya and cholkettu. The Charana is followed by again chitta svaras of one, two, four, eight avartas.

2. Pada Varna

Pada varnas are almost of the same format as chouka varnas. In pada varnas, unlike in Chouka varnas, chitta svaras are sung followed by the svara sahitya.

3. Tana Varna

Tana varnas are usually set in madhya makala (medium tempo). It is practiced in three degrees of speed. It consists of Pallavi, Anupallavi, and Charana etc. like chouka varnas. Sahitya can be only in Pallavi , Anupallavi and Charanam.

4. Daru Varna

It consists of Pallavi, Anupallavi and charana and has 6 angas like svara, sahitya, Jati, ragam, talam and rasam. The theme of the sahitya is usuallys. Varnas are very popular musical forms and composed ragas and even as raga malikas. Varnas are also seen composed in the Ghana ragas. (Few example are given with notation in the Appendix)

5. Dhruva

This kind of composition can be traced from the very early stage of the development of Indian music. Dhruva ganas were used to sing for dramas according to the scene. Many old ragas were employed to compose these Dhruva ganas. One such frequently used raga probably is Varali, one of Ghana raga panchaka. This establishes the prominence of this raga from the very early age.

(Few examples for dhruva gana in Varali are given in the Appendix.)

Kriti:

The most important and prominent music form in the sabhagana today is kirit. Kritis occupy the major part of a concert where as the forms like Pada, Tavali, Thillana etc are not sung for more than once during a concert. Largest number of compositions is also found to be kritis. Though the kriti is identical to keertana, an imperative is given to its music while composing. Though kirtana is an older form to the kriti, kritis have got more prominent place in classical Carnatic music. It is only at the time of the Trinity; kirti has become popular as the trinity composed numerous kritis in order to express their musical ideas.

(1) There are countless kritis composed in the Ghana ragas and it is interesting to know how the Ghana ragas are handled and employed by different composers. E.g., The Ghana raga pacharatna of Tyagaraja in the raga nata does not take sampurna svaras in the arohana. Similarly Sri raga as it appears in 'Endaromahanubhavulu' does not have the prayoga pdnpm r g r s. All this helps one to understand how the interpretations of ragas vary according to the view of the composer.

There are also forms like Pada, Thillana Javali, bhajans etc, composed in the Ghana ragas, composers like Maharaja Swati tirunal has composed many padas in Ghana raga eg. 'Valayannika' Malayalam padam set to rupaka tala. There are many musical forms that are used for dance like alarippu, kirtanas, Kavutuvams etc, where Ghana ragas are employed like the vanampadi kavutuvam in the raga Nata set to aditala.

Alarippu in Nata raga set to Khanta chapu, kirtanas like Orukal Siva chidambaram in Arabhi raga set to Adi tala and composed by Muthutandavar, 'Vijaya vinayaka' in the raga Nata, set to Adi tala and composed by Saravana bhavanandan, Vinayaka stuti in Nata raga set to Adi tala etc.

In Tamil music also the manifestation of the Ghana ragas are very obvious. There are many Tevaras sung in Ghana ragas some of them are:

1. Todu daiya cheviyan - Pan Natapadai (Nata), set to Tisra laghu by Tirunana sambandar
2. Piraiyani - Natapadai - (Nata) Adi - Choma Sama sundaram
3. Chiraiyandam - Pazhamtaka (Arabhi) - Triputa - Charna soma sundaram.
4. Churaiyaraum - Pazhamtaka (Arabhi) - Adi - Jnana sambandar.
5. Angamum - Nata padai (Nata) - Rupakam - Sambandar.

There are tirupugal composed in Ghana raga but as they are not strictly sung in the traditional way as in the case of Tevara, it is difficult to mention the original ragas in which they were composed. There is a divya prabandha "Tiru pallandu" in Natapadai set to chapu and composed by Periyalavar.

6

The Great Composers and Ghana Raga Panchaka

The great composers who have dedicated their lives for the development of music contributed so much with their invaluable compositions to the realm of Karnatic music. Composers who belong to the three different times viz., Pre-trinity period, Trinity period and post – trinity have enriched the repot ire of Karnatic music with the compositions in various ragas. Few composers have dealt with the Ghana raga panchaka with special significance as they composed group kritis, compositions grouped and composed in the five Ghana ragas e.g., the Ghana raga Pancharatna of Tyagaraja, Ghana raga Malika varna of Veena Kuppaiyar, the nava raga malika svara jati of Swati tirunal etc. Here are the biographical sketches of some of the composers who dealt with the Ghana ragas as a group.

1. Tyagaraja

The qualities of Tyagaraja's compositions are not easily assessable, but if any one probes into them, a few aspects can be presented. His compositions are highly philosophical with simplified language dipped in literary and aesthetic beauties.

The songs of Tyagaraja are like the scriptures in thought and word. It is apt to call them 'Tyagopanishad'. They are highly philosophical and impetus to one's creative thoughts. They are also moulded in a spiritual charm and beauty. For they have tremendous power to capture the minds of the music lovers.

Every musical composition has its two main divisions such as Sahitya and Sangita. The Sahitya or lyrics of the song are essentially made of words but they also contain thought, a musical and philosophical thought that carries and caters the musical ideas and philosophy of the composer. Similarly the sangita or music (Dhatu) of the song has two aspects, raga (melody) and tala (rhythm). The raga is the vehicle to transport the feelings that are hidden in the sahitya to the listeners and the tala keeps the tempo, which gives the right rythm apt to the mood of the song. These four essential aspects make a song beautiful. In Tyagaraja's compositions every one of these qualities is present and thus his compositions become perfect in nature. This might be the reason why Tyagaraja as a composer is accepted and appreciated by all the music lovers irrespective of the countries and systems they belong to. His approach in composing songs with literature that up holds humanity or mankind has given him wide acceptance from all walks of life.

Tyagaraja had dealt with different subjects for his compositions. He stands distinguished among the composers in dealing with topics relating to Sangita Shastra (science of music) as the main theme for his compositions. 'Nada tanu", Sobhillu", 'Sogasuga' are few of this class. He was trying to reach Rama through his music as he considered the both identical. This quality of his compositions also caters happiness to the musically educated and laymen alike.

Though Tyagaraja was the staunchest adherent of ancient tradition, one can see that he had lots of revolutionary ideas as composer. The infusion of Sangatis by him to the kritis totally changed the pattern in which the already existing keertanas were sung. It paved way and made new waves of art music different from the existing recitative style of singing.

The art music was taken to the platforms, which put the musicians to creative phase of music, and the artistes' fancy embellished the set beauty of the Prabandhas. The introduction of Sangatis by the composer not only enriched the raga bhava and raga sancharas and the beauty of the compositions but it also helped bring out the exact feeling of the melody of the song. The notes he employed while composing a song is note worthy as he employed low notes or octaves when he wanted to express his feelings and talk to his own self. E.g., in the song 'Teratiyaga rada', speaking of himself behind the curtain of darkness, he seems to be using the lower octave.

Unlike other composers, he mainly used Adi tala in abundance and Triputa rupaka, jhampa and chappu to a lesser extent. But his compositions have varieties of 'Eduppu" (the rhythmic point where a composition is started), Kala and Jati in familiar talas. He composed Kritis in the Pallavi pattern as one can witness that some of his kritis have 'Arutis' like Pallavi and they also gave wide scope for the raga in which a particular kriti is composed. Tyagaraja employed a large number of ragas to create his pieces. The ragas he handled may come to around two hundred and sixty according to the available sources. In the major and familiar ragas there are numerous compositions and it is amazing that in none of them the music is the same to the other.

The language of Tyagaraja is highly poetic, adorned with picturesque similes, grace and charm of diction, with easy flow of measured syllables. They are like the sutras of scriptures, suggestive of infinite meaning and yet most familiar like the simple dialect of the common man. Consider for instance the expression "Kaddanu variki kaddu kaddu". Even the unlettered can understand it easily, yet it contains all the profundity of meaning that students of Vedanta are familiar with and is like its Biblical parallel, "to him that hath shall be given". It enunciates the cardinal principle that faith is the foundation of religion as distinguished from philosophy. He is a lyrical poet of the highest order. He conceives Rama in all possible relationships and pours out his songs which are the outflow of the most feeling heart, as lord and master in "Banturiti", as parent in "Sitamma", as companion in "Vinarada" as spouse in "Chanitodi", as child in "Merusamana". What language simpler and thoroughly modern than "Undedi Ramudokadu" can convey so vast an idea as in Shelley's like "the one remains, the many change and pass". There are many songs, which are exquisite word pictures like "Vachamagocharame" and "Ramabana".

It cannot be forgotten that most people regard Tyagaraja as composer first and foremost, and his modernity as such should interest us as supremely important. While he composed in all the ancient and time honoured ragas, he avoided such sancharas in them as had even during his time become archaic. In this respect he presents a contrast with his distinguished contemporary, Muthuswamy Dikshitar, who had a particular partiality for obsolete phrases. Further, Tyagaraja anticipated the musical expressions, which were likely to go out of use, and avoided them. For instance, in the raga Salagabhairavi while the old lakshana mentions s r g m as admissible, only s r m was in extensive use in his age. In the sancharas of the raga as given by Tulajaji in his Sangita Saramrita, s r g m occurs only once whereas s r m occurs frequently. In his composition "Padavi nisadbhakti" he employs only s r m and not s r g m. He was quite aware of the old sanchara but did not adopt it as it had ceased to be current.

In the creation of new modes he shows the most amazing insight into future and has produced most fanciful melodies, which have furnished at the inspiration for later creative effort. He knew that the ages to come would expect a variety of new scales and ragas with compositions in them. He has accordingly left us a treasure of priceless gems in the forms of kirtanas in apurva ragas. To separate the raga from them and elaborate it as a mode is apt to end in failure. The genius of Tyagaraja was able to impart a melodic individuality to it. In the hands of anyone less talented the mode would suffer in the alapana, either by the frequent repetition of the most characteristic phrase as ma ga ri ga ri in Kapinarayani or by rendering the svaras of the scale in raga syllables without rasabhava as in the raga of "Entavedukondu". Even niraval and svarakalpana in these apurva ragas should be reduced to a minimum. It may be noted that Muthuswamy Dikshitar and Syama Sastri, unlike Tyagaraja, confined themselves to old and current ragas and if they departed at all, it was only by way of exception. Of these two Dikshitar revived certain antique ragas, while Shyama Sastry did not handle any but the most popular ragas of his age. Tyagaraja anticipated the trends of the future, created new modes extensively and composed in them. It may sound surprising to-day that even familiar ragas like Karaharapriya, Harikamboji and Devagandhari are his gifts. His magic touch could transform any scale into a living raga.

The trait of modernity is perhaps best illustrated in his principle of variation by sangatis of the original and musically effective parts of composition such as the pallavi, the anupallavi and the latter part of the charana in so far as it follows the music of the anupallavi. The first half of the charana is generally left free of set sangatis of the composer so that the musician may have full scope for the play of manodharma. It may be pointed out that sangatis as such were not new even in the days of Tyagaraja. But they were features only of the manodharma pallavi where the musical expression of prescribed words is varied without limit within the scope of the avarthana in the chosen raga. The sangatis in the kirtanas of Tyagaraja are definite except in so far as the singer makes his own additions to them. They are not matters for improvisation as in the pallavi of manodharma but form an integral part of the composition. In leaving the earlier half of the charana free of sangatis Tyagaraja allows extensive scope for manodharma sangatis by way of neraval. Oftentimes the musician chooses the pallavi or anupallavi for neraval. The choice, however, is a matter entirely of taste, though, generally, the initial part of the charana is best suited. Tyagaraja's compositions in this way effect a most harmonious integration of the ancient kirtana paddhati and the later manodharma pallavi. In Hindusthani Music Tyagaraja's achievement would be representative of both the Drupad and Khyal styles. Modern taste cannot be gratified by mere recitative type of music. Only Tyagaraja's genius could see so far into the future as to shape his songs to meet the progressive development of taste. He is the one composer whose music can never become stale even in the most distant ages to come.

His modernity is equally manifest in the variety of musical forms where as he outwardly portrayed the beauty of kirtanas. The kirtanas is a bhakti pradhana prabandha. All his compositions are kirtanas as they are in praise of God irrespective of the other themes included in them. He did not compose any other type of music like Varna or javali. He was one of the greatest bhaktas of Sri Rama and could not conceive the dedication of his songs to any other being. While he pours out his love and devotion to his ishta devata in every song of his, yet he had so composed as to make certain pieces resemble types other than the kirtana in sangita rather than in bhava. In music alone "Dandamu bettanura" is a Gita, "Najivadhara" a Varna; "Kshirasagara" is a Pada and

"Chanitodi" a javali. Here again Tyagaraja's powers of invention in keeping the and spirit of the kirtana and yet imposing the beauty on it other forms of composition areas marvellous as they are heroic.

It is considered high poetic merit to make the sound echo the sense, as in the expression "the murmur of innumerable bees". Tyagaraja with equal felicity has made music reflect or suggest the bhava. There are many examples of this excellence in his compositions but I shell content myself with citing but one instance. In the pallavi of "Teratiyyagarada" it will be found that the initial phrase referring to his own

Ignorance within the low notes of the mandhara sthayi are used, but the music moves to the tara sthayi when he addresses the exalted Deity standing high on the hills of Tirupati. Here is a fine illustration musically of a modern poetic virtue.

In the field of rhythm too his achievements are unequalled. He employed only simple talas like adi, rupaka, triputa and Jhampa. Adi tala however predominates. Within the limits of these plain talas every variety of eduppu, gati and svara vibhaga is employed to enhance the delights of rhythm. Tyagaraja subdues rhythm and enriches the melody. In a very simple kirtana, "Nadatanum", he describes Siva the embodiment of Nada as svaravidyalola and as vidalita kala; that is, ostensible as one who destroys Yama, but really as one who subdues time. It is clear that in his opinion raga must predominate and tala be subordinate. His marked preference of melody to tala as the principal element of sangita shows how modern he is.

Tyagaraja's Pancharatnas are the greatest creations of musical art. They stand un approached for beauty of word and music, of sound and rhythm, and every kind of artistic excellence. The ghana panchakas of the classic vainikas are the five mighty ragas, which furnished the melodic foundations of the compositions. The principle of svara sahitya finds fullest application in them. In one of them, "Sadhimchane", the ethugada svaras as in the regular varna, are appended to the charana. They are in the regular varna, are appended to the charana. They are the most celebrated examples and models for those who do svara kalpana. In concert as in pedagogy their merit and value are supreme. Even if Tyagaraja had composed nothing more than these Pancharatnas, he would as now be immortal. No vidvan should consider himself competent unless he has mastered all the five masterpieces. These gems will outshine all other songs for ever. The wheel of time cannot depress them. They are the embodiment of the eternal elements of truth and beauty in art, music and literature, in spirit, love and sentiment.

The Ghanaraga Pancha Ratna

(Tyagaraja's Five gems)

The great saint-singer and composer of music, Sri Tyagaraja, needs no introduction to any music-loving public. Classical Karnatic Music (at its best, of course) owes its popularity largely to this mighty genius that attained immortality through his musical contributions.

The main form of homage that musicians and music students pay to their Parama Acharya is the singing of his Pancharatna Kriti-s or the five gems of composition which are set in the foremost five Ghana Raga-s of the classical tradition, viz., Nata, Goula, Arabhi, Varali and Sri. These ragas lend themselves most admirably to Tana or Madhyamakala treatment, i.e., medium tempo. Tyagaraja's songs amply bring out the beauty of Madhyamakala inherent in these ragas.

Masterpieces these assuredly are, but they are not typical compositions of his. They are of an unusual type-unusual and almost unparalleled, in fact, in the whole field of 19th century Karnatak Music. His typical compositions are noted for brevity in the use of words and a musical structure, which admits of imaginative improvisation. Here, in these Kriti-s, insofar as the charanas are concerned, every svara and letter is fixed and there is generally one letter for every svara. To a superficial observer, therefore, it would appear that these songs are overburdened with words and that the literary aspect reigns supreme. But, on close scrutiny, it will be found that the words sub serve a greater cause which is purely musical. Though the richness in spiritual content of these, as indeed of all Tyagaraja's compositions, is undeniable it is not on that their fame rests. It rests on the architectonic beauty of this ensemble, which is a fantasy of melody and rhythm, words being there not merely for the sake of verbal sense (at any rate, during the singing of them) but to lend euphony and majesty.

A characteristic of these Pancharatna Kriti-s is that each of them has a number of charana-s, about ten of them, all set to different dhatu-s (melodic-rhythmic lines). Also, they are generally sung as svara and sahitya (text) alternately. Traditions, however, vary. While there is near unanimity in regard to the Kriti-s in Nata, Gaula, Arabhi and Sri raga-s, the same cannot be said of the kriti in Varali. This raga has suffered a serious handicap all alone in that, owing to sentimental and irrational objection, it has not been directly passed on from Guru to Sishya. Musicians who cared to learn the Pancharatna song in Varali from masters other than their own have been few and, even amongst them, there are different versions in regard to the music of it. Some schools do not sing svara for the charana-s of this song.

Musical Set Up

From the music point of view, the Pancharatna kritis are highly sophisticated compositions in which the ragas are developed step by step in their logical progression culminating in a grand finale. The ettugada swaras come in waves with an originality and daring that are breathtaking. The nuances of each raga have been woven into the rhythm of the pieces in a meticulous manner. It is noteworthy that all the five pieces are in the Adi Tala, the tempo of which has, however, been varied by Tyagaraja in different ways to suit the mood of each song in the group. The sarva laghu dances equally merrily in the brisk Arabhi piece and in the sedate Sriraga kriti. One may say without any doubt of contradiction that Tyagaraja has, in these compositions, exhausted all the possible combinations of the ragas handled and has left no room for further innovation.

The Sahitya

The words of the Pancharatna Kritis are primarily ancillary to the music but they are also supremely worth conning from the literary and aesthetic points of view. Tyagaraja was a poet and his songs are often described as 'poems set to music'. They are the most splendid specimens of the literary strucutre of a kriti, the grammer of which has been spelt out by Tyagaraja himself in the kriti 'Sogasuga' in the raga Sriranjini.

The beauty of the language to which music is set has a great deal to do with the performance and popularity of the music itself. The diction most suited for music has to be euphonious and composed of words, which are not, flowing, and melodious, with no harsh or discordant combination of syllables to great upon the ear. The Pancharatna kritis are unrivalled for their sweet phrasing. According to Kalluri Virabhadra Sastri, the Telugu commentator on Tyagaraja kritis, they have the lakshanas of a Mahakavya built in as defined in the Alankara Sastra as they deal with a Nayaka who, in this case, is none else than the Lord Himself. The first Kriti 'Jagadanadakaraka' is in Sanskrit and the remaining four in mellifluous Telugu. A brief assessment of the special features and import of the kritis is attempted below.

Jagadanandakaraka

As a close follower of tradition, Tyagaraja commences his first piece in Nata with the use of the word 'Jaya' in the pallavi. In olden times, Nata was invariably sung at the beginning and Surati at the end of concerts and hence the adage 'Adi Nata, Antya Surata'. The first song of the Todaya Mangalam, which is also in Nata, runs as follows:

"Jaya Janakiramana
Jaya Vibhishana sarana
Jaya saroruha nayana
Jaya dina karuna"

Following this tradition, Tyagaraja has employed the phrase "Jaya Janaki prananayaka". Each phrase in this magnificent kriti has a special significance in relation to its hero viz. the Upanishad truth that the Lord is the stressed is portraied in the opening phrase itself. The anupallavi starts with the phrase" Gaganadhipa Satkulaja" (born in the noble solar dynasty) after the fashion of Valmiki who starts his epic with the sloka:

"Ikshvaku vamsa prabhavo
Ramo nama janaih srutah"

The various divine qualities of Rama are then brought out in a series of delightful combinations like "Nigama nirajamruta poshaka" and 'Satkavi hridalaya'. Valmiki is given a new title, as 'the Sun among poets'.

Dudukugala

After the majestic Nata comes the plaintive Gaula, in which the composer passes into a mood of introspection and self-reproach. After the manner of the earlier saints, he asks in wonder "which Lord will save an incorrigible sinner like me?" Courched in simple Telugu the kriti proceeds to catalogue sins of omission and commission, which include the teaching of music to people, like dancers, gallants and women with the sole aim of winning them over. To Tyagaraja music was not an art, profession or a form of entertainment but yoga sadhana as he considered the bartering away of this treasure the most heinous crime one could commit.

He deplores how he (which, in fact, applies to all human kind) wasted his youth in useless arguments without a thought of God and devotion to Him. This noble human birth was put to all kinds of abuse as a result of pride, jealousy, greed etc, and the entire life wasted in the service of one's family and for acquiring wealth. The kriti stresses the transient nature of worldly pleasures and invokes the grace of the Lord for getting liberation from them.

Sadhinchane

Despite the plaintive appeal in 'Dudukugala' the Lord did not appear before him and Tyagaraja now embarks on a bold 'ninda stuti' of feint praise. He accuses Him as being a cunning God who always betrayed His own teaching and achieved His own ends. When Devaki and Vasudeva wanted Him as their son, He was born unto them but denied them the pleasure of His company. When Yasoda caroused. Him as her own son, He sarcastically laughed up His sleeve. When the Gopis wanted union with Him, He teased them without acceding to their request.

A unique feature of this kriti is that Tyagaraja alternates between Rama and Krishna; he praises Rama as a soft-spoken hero who treated other women as His sisters. He reserves all his sarcasm for Krishna. In the end he reconciles himself with the advice given by the Lord "This is the lot of all true devotees. Do not grieve; keep no company with people who turn their faces away from God and take the rough with the smooth".

Kana Kana Ruchira

Tyagaraja finally proceeds to describe the divine beauty of the Lord that 'grows more and more charming as one looks at it'. This kriti is based on the sloka:

"Kshane kshane yan navatampaiti
Tadeva rupam ramaniyatayah"

(Beauty is that which assumes a freshness and charm every moment). He sings of His effulgence like the rising Sun, His Lotus-like eyes, His shining cheeks, His dazzling crown of gems and His forehead with its Kasturi mark. It was a beauty that thrilled Sita. Tyagaraja cites a long list of witnesses who feasted their eyes upon that divine splendour. These include Dhruva, Anjaneya, Siva, Narada, Parasara, Suka, Saunaka, Indra, Parvati and Sita. This moving piece in Varali bears Tyagaraja's characteristic imprint.

Endaro Mahanubhavulu

In the end Tyagaraja offers his salutations to the perceptions and purvacharyas of yore, as mentioned in the sloka 'Punyan iman parama bhagavatan smarami'. And what a galaxy of acharyas, bhagavatas, munis and devotees he presents! In the anupallavi he stresses that only adepts in yoga can see in their hearts the form of the Lord "whose radiance is like that of the Moon". These include nada yogis who sing His praises in svara, laya and raga, those who look upon the world with nectar flowing their eyes and those who know the mysteries of scriptures. This grand piece rounds off the Pancha Ratna group on a soothing note.

The five kritis are thus an unrivalled group of compositions both from the music and the sahitya points of view. Tyagaraja must have composed them when he was at the peak of his career as a composer. The pieces are scholarly without being pedantic. A continuous rendering of them in chorus ushers in an atmosphere of peace, tranquility and devotion. Those who wish to pay their homage to Tyagaraja and all that he stood for, cannot do better than to arrange for these kritis to be sung in all festivals connected with the saint.

The Sahitya and Its Meaning

'Jagadanandakaraka'

Pallavi

You give joy to the entire universe! Beloved consort of Sita, Victory to you,

Anupallavi

Your are a scion of the noble solar race, King of Kings, a repository of auspicious virtues, an object of worship by the Gods and a source of all goodness.

Charanas

You shine like a Moon amongst the galaxy of Gods who are like the stars. You are the perfect God, free from all sins, the (Kalpaka) tree that fulfils all the desires of Gods, the stealer of pots containing milk and curds, a God with a beautiful countenance and speech like nectar, the kind shepherd, the yoyo us Lord, the consort of Lakshmi, the ever youthful God who protects His devotees.

You flourish by the nectar emanating from the Vedas. Your are the destroyer of the enemies of the Gods. Garuda is your mount and the hearts of good poets, your abode. Countless monkey chiefs serve at your feet.

Your body has the hue of a sapphire. The Sun and Moon are your eyes. Your splendour is beyond one's imagination. You are the father of Brahma, the Lord of Creation; You are the Universe; You sleep on Adi Sesha, the king of serpents and worshipped by Lord Siva.

The touch of your feet dispels the curse of the saga (Gautama). You are the protector of sacrifices, a master of the mantras (Bala and Atibala), a God with a serene mind, the consort of Siva and a giver of boons to Brahma.

Your are the Creator, Protector and Destroyer of the Universe, fulfiller of countless wishes of devotees, a Lord with a matchless figure, an object of worship by Indra, a dispeller of the Sea Lord's vanity and the Hero of the epic (Ramayana) which contains the essence of devotion and music.

You are the Moon that rises from the ocean called the pure minds of virtuous men; the rider of the celestial chariot called Pushpaka Vimana. Hanuman, the killer of Surasa, the demon, serves at your feet. You are the destroyer of evil nature. You are Eternal. Lord Brahma pays homage to You.

You are like parrot in the cage called Omkara (Pranava), The Trinity, Sova, Brahma and Voshnu find their culimination in You. You are the killer of Ravana, the father of Indrajit. You are the friend of Siva, who wears the crescent on His head; the merciful Lord who protects His devotees and dwells in their hearts; the Supreme without a change; the essence of the scriptures.

Arrows are your weapons; You vanquish the demons and give protection to Gods and Brahmins; You are the hero of the epic (Ramayana) written by the Sun among poets (Valmiki) who was born in an ant-hill; Tyagaraja pays his homage to you.

You are the Ancient Lord; the son of an Emperor; the Savior of your devotees; the killer of Khara, Viradha and Ravana; the immaculate Lord whose charms attracted the sage Parasara; the changeless God Whom Tyagaraja adores.

You are a repository of all auspicious qualities; the golden cloth (Pitambara) is your attire: You felled the seven Sala trees. Your feet are lotus-like in colour; Your glory is immeasurable; Your abode is in the hearts of sweet poets; You are the protector of gods and sages; the consort of Lakshmi who emerged from the ocean; the lion that destroys the elephants called sin; the Supreme worshipped by devotees like Tyagaraja.

'Dudukugala'

Pallavi and Anupallavi

Which Lord except you can protect an intractable sinner like me who, attracted by sensual pleasures, indulges in sin every hour?

Charanas

You are the Moon that blossom the lily that is the heart of Lakshmi; You are beyond the reach of one's minds and speech.

2, 3, 4 & 5, Little did I realize that it is you who pervades all animate beings; I discarded the path of worship and indulged in worthless arguments; I coveted the wealth of others with greed and demeaned myself to pleasure them so that I could fill my belly; I spent my days under the illusion that to lead a comfortable life was the SUMMUM BONUM of existence.

I taught (music to) dancer, gallants, mend of low caste and women to gain their favour; being completely ignorant of the mysteries of music I arrogated myself to the status of a devotee although my heart was as hard as stone.

Lord of Lords! I placed my trust in members of the fair sex, mansions, children servants and wealth, which are attractive to the eye and forgot to worship at your Lotus feet.

Forgetting your beautiful countenance, I approached men blinded by pride and getting involved in evil

Thoughts I became weak-minded, unable to disentangle myself from my evil desires

I forgot that the human birth is the most coveted among all creation and I fell a victim to pride, jealousy, greed and miserliness. Although born in the highest of castes, I demeaned myself by indulging in the professions of men of low castes. I kept company with men of evil character and misbehaved in my attempt to adopt worthless beliefs.

I spent a part of my life in the company of women part for acquiring possessions and the rest in protecting my children and amassing wealth.

'Sadhinchene'

Pallavi and Anupallavi

O Mind! Belying the teaching, which He Himself uttered, the Lord worshipped by Tyagaraja carried out His desires and evaded appearing before me.

Charanas

1 & 2. He uttered Words suitable for the occasion. He put Devaki and Vasudeva to many trials. He is the Lord of the stage called the world, the source of the river Ganga and a traditionalist in music.

He taunted the Gopis without fulfilling their hearts' desire.

He would always make women pine for Him and surrender to Him. He is the Lord of the Universe. He smiled cunningly when Yasoda kissed Him under the impression that He was her son.

He is the most compassionate of all Gods, a veritable ocean of good qualities, eternally stainless and a dispeller of the sins of the Kali age. I eagerly expected that He would free me from the trials of his world and meditated on Him in my lotus heart.

Here Ramachandra! You are a scion of the Raghu dynasty! Your speech is sweet and you like a brother to all women. You are birth less. Your mount is Garuda and you are worshipped by emperors. You are eternally youthful and sinless. Your eyes are like lotuses. I prayed to you to save me but you evaded protecting me.

Lord Venkatesa of Divine splendour! Highest of all Gods! Dweller in the minds of righteous men! You are the wearer of the golden attire and shined with your crown and dazzling ear rings. I sang your praises as the emperor among men but you belied my hopes.

He advised me that this was the lot of all devotees and lovingly accepted my worship. He advised me not to lose my composure and not to keep the company of godless men. He counseled that I should accept even sorrow when it comes. The Lord who blesses men with peace and serenity did not however come near me but fulfilled His own desires.

'Kana Kana Ruchira'

Pallavi and Anupallavi

The more I lovingly perceive you, day after day in my mind' he more beautiful you appear.

Charanas

Your charming countenance radiates majesty and unbounded glory.

Sita, with her effulgent face, derives great pleasure by glancing at you in her modesty.

You wearer of a golden attire with the hue of the rising Sun; Your neck is adorned with necklaces studded with gems. Your eyes are like lotuses. Your cheeks shine and your crown Is radiant.

Did not the boy-devotee Dhruva, who felt mortified by the sharp and insulting words of Suruchi his step-mother, attain bliss by meditating on your glorious form?

Your forehead is adorned with musk, You are the saviour of Jatayu, the king of eagles. Did not the description of your floury, given by Hanuman, transport Sita with you?

You are the source of all joy. You are the wind that dispels the clouds called atheists; You dwell in the hearts of Liberated souls; You are the Kalpaka tree for your devotees; Your qualities are exemplary; Your form is bliss itself: Your mount is Garuda: Your weapon is the disc (Chakra), Yet you are the most merciful Lord, a veritable ocean of compassion and the dispeller of fear.

The witnesses to this experience of mine are Hanuman, who lovingly bears your lotus feet in his hands, Lord Siva, who revels in the chanting of your name, and also Narada, Parasara, Sukam, Saunaka, Indra, Parvati and Sita, You reside in the ocean called joy. The more your devotees gaze at you the more beautiful you appear.

You are eternally worshiped by this Tyagaraja with his heart filled with love. Your face surpasses the Moon in its luster.

'Endaro Mahanubhavulu'

Pallavi

My salutations to all great souls of the world (past and present).

Anupallavi

To those who derive supreme joy (Brahmananda) by always seeing in their lotus hearts the Divine form and effulgence of the God whose hue is as white as the Moon.

Charanas

Oh Lord who delights in Saman music and possesses the beauty of Cupid! My salutation to those who are foremost among the ones blessed by you;

To Those who stop the evil wanderings of the monkey called the mind and concentrate it on your Divine form;

To those who unhesitatingly offer their lotus hearts at the holy feet of the Lord;

To those who understand the mysteries of Svara, Laya and Raga, sing the praises of the Supreme Lord, who is the saviour of the downtrodden, (and follow the true and virtuous path);

To those devotees on whose necks the gem-like qualities of Lord Hari shine like necklaces and who look upon the world with nectar-like looks and protect it with wisdom solicitude and compassion.

To those who see before their mental vision the Lord with a majestic gait and getting immersed in that ocean of joy; feel enthralled by the transcendental bliss;

To those great souls, supreme devotees and sages like the Moon, the Sun Sanaka, Sanandana, the protector of the eight directions (Dikpalakas), the Gods (Devas), Kimpurushas Prahlada, Narada, Tumburu, Hanuman, Lord Siva, who wears the Crescent, Suka, Brahma and the noble Brahmins who enjoy the bliss of the realization of the Lord.

Oh Lord of the Raghu dynasty! To those who delight in adoring the beauty of your form the efficacy of your name and your qualities like prowess, courage, composure of mind, compassion and truthfulness and who, knowing your aversion to, false faiths, discard them and always sing only your praises;

To those who have understood the hidden truths of scriptures like the Bhagavata, Ramayana, Gita, Veda, Sastras and Puranas and the mysteries of the six faiths like Saivism, the minds of the thirty-three crores of Gods of the Hindu pantheon and who, acquiring longevity through the joy of music, attain everlasting bliss through bhava, raga, and laya and thus become Tyagaraja's friends and well-wishers.

To those who, with overflowing devotion, mediate upon His holy name and become the true servants of the Lord who is the tutelary deity of Tyagaraja, the Rama Bhakta.

The Kshetra Pancharatnas of Tyagaraja

As the term suggests in music, a 'Pancharatna' is a group of five compositions. Apart from Ghana raga Pancharatna he composed 7 sets of Pancharatna kritis composed on the presiding deities of the five temples at 1. Tiruvaiyaru 2. Tiruvottiyur 3. Kovur 4. Lalgudi and 5. Srirangam. His contemporary composer and one of the trinity, Muthusawamy Dikshitar is also a prolific composer of Kshetra kritis.

Tiruvaiyar Pancharatna

Tiruvaiyar literally means 5 rivers in Tamil. Tiruvaiyaur is situated in the midst of five rivers, Kaveri, Arasalar, Vennaru, Vadayar and Kudammurthi. The deity of this place is also called Panchanadeesa. The following are the five Kritis composed by

Tyagaraja on the deity which are known as Tiruvaiyar Pancharatna:

1. Sari vedalina	-	Asaveri	-	Adi
2. Ilalo pranatharthi	-	Atana	-	Adi
3. Ehi tri Jagadeesa	-	Saranga	-	Misrachapu
4. Muchata brahmadulaku	-	Madyamavati	-	Adi
5. Evarunnaru	-	Malavasri	-	Adi

In the group, Apporva raga like Malavasri is employed which has not been handled by probably by any post – Tyagaraja composer.

Tyagaraja's two set of Pancharatna kritis on goddess Dharmasamvardhani are given below:

The first set is

1. Bale Balendu	-	Ritigaula	-	Adi
2. Amma dharma samvardhani	-	Atana	-	Adi
3. Viddi chakradulaku	-	yamunakalyani	-	Rupaka
4. Sive Pahimam	-	Kalyani	-	Adi
5. Karuni judavamma	-	Todi	-	Adi

The second set is

1.	Innalla vale	-	Desya Todi	-	Chappu
2.	Mara vairi	-	Nasikabhooshani	-	Rupaka
3.	Nannukannatalli	-	Kesari	-	Desadi
4.	Parashakti	-	Saveri	-	Adi
5.	Nivu brovale	-	Saveri	-	Adi

Kovur Pancharatna

This is a set of Pancharatna composed on the Lord Sundaresha:

1. Shambo maha deva	-	Pantuvarali	-	Rupaka

2. Korisevimparare	Kharaharapriya	Adi
3. Sundareswaruni	Sankarabharanam	Adi
4. Ivasuddha nivanti	Sahana	Adi
5. Nammi Vachina	Kalyani	Rupaka

The word 'go' literally means 'cow' but it also refers to the goddess Mahalakshmi. The goddess of Govur is called Soundarya nayaki. The temple is said to have built by Raja Raja chola. During the festival in the temple for nine days, this set of Pancha ratna is sung.

Tiruvottiyur Pancharatna

The temple of this place is known for its deity the Lord Shiva in the form of Svayambhu linga. The goodness of the place is Tripurasundari. This set of Pancharatna is composed on Devi Tripura Sundari. The following are the kritis:

1. Darini telusukonti	Suddhasaveri	Adi
2. Sundarini	Kalyani	Adi
3. Kanna talli	Saveri	Adi
4. Sundari nannindarilo	Begada	Rupaka
5. Sundari ninnu	Arabhi	Misrachappu

Another speciality of these kritis is that they all contain Sthalamudras.

Lalgudi Pancharatna

This set of Pancharatna is believed to have composed during Tyagaraja's visit to Lalgudi. The name of the Lord is Saptarishisvara and goddess Pravidya Srimati. In this Pancharatna he has composed the first two kritis on the Lord and the next three on the Goddess. They are

1. Isa pahimam	Kalyani	Rupaka
2. Deva sri	Madyamavati	Triputa

3. Mahita pravudhe	-	Kambhoji	-	Adi
4. Gatinivani	-	Todi	-	Adi
5. Lalite Sri Pravadhe	-	Bhairavi	-	Adi

The devata mudras are found in these kritis. The composition in Madyamavati and Kambhoji are in Sanskrit language and the rest in Telugu. The kritis are apt examples for prosodic rules and their application in Kritis.

Sriranga Pancharatna

This Pancharatna is a set of compositions on Vaishnavite deity, Lord Ranganatha unlike other Pancharatnas. The Tamil Periyakoil refers to Srirangam and Lord is known as Periya perumal. The pancharatnas are:

1. Jutta murare	-	Arabhi	-	Rupaka
2. Vinaradana	-	Devagandhari	-	Desadi
3. Rajuvedala	-	Todi	-	Rupaka
4. Karunajudavayya	-	Saranta	-	Adi
5. O'ranga sayee	-	Kambhoji	-	Adi

Here, Tyagaraja uses Paryaya Nama of the Lord such as Kasturi ranga, Vaibhoga ranga, Kaveri ranga, Rangasai and Ranga pati. All the Pancharatnas are the rare varieties of gems and they have tremendous capacity to travell along with the time and thus they became eternal and the composer immortal.

2. Muthu Swamy Dikshitar

The contribution of Muthuswamy Dikshitar to the sphere of Karnatic music is invaluable and unforgettable. He had deep knowledge of the classical tradition of music that existed in the past. His genius, originality and creativity was all the cause for the resumation of old praygas the fashions in ragas and antique modes that were varnishing from practice. He succeeded in revising many obsolete and divised phrases and modes by breathing fresh type and cha to them. He handled the ragas in a unique way as it is evident in his compositions. He has to his credit the largest number of group kritis as many as 12 sets each consisting 5, 8, 9, 11 or 12 songs in it.

Muthuswami Dishitar's services to the cause of music, culture and religion, are unforgettable. He had a deep reverence for classical tradition. His genius, originality and creative spirit were largely directed in the resurrection of old prayogas and sancharas in familiar ragas as well as antique modes that were vanishing from currency. Purandaradasa and finally systematized every branch of Carnatic Music and Venkatamakhin had widened its foundations. True to the principles laid down by these two great purvacharyas, Dikshitar enriched and enlarged the heritage in a manner all his own. He succeeded in reviving many obsolete and disused phrases and modes by breathing fresh life and charm into them. His pieces form a golden link with the music of the past. To the student of music they are a mine of inexhaustible treasure. Dikshitar is an ardent supporter of the Carnatic traditions of Purandaradasa in the faithful adoption of the suladi sapta talas for his compositions and in the resuscitation of the prayogas in gita, thaya and prabandha.

It is remarkable that the classicist par excellence was equally at home in the invention and improvisation of new modes for which the mela system of Venkatamakhin afforded such ample scope. He could compose with as much facility in Rasamanjari as in Bhairavi raga. Like his great contemporary he could create living raga forms of exquisite beauty from the dry bones of a meager scale. Let it not be supposed that this is an easy task. Only those can successfully achieve this result to which it is given to penetrate the dark veil that surrounds the mysterious universe of sound where dwells the supreme spirit, Nadabrahman. To weave a few notes into a song is simple, but to create a new raga which is a recognizable entity by itself is the work of highest art.

Dishitar is original in the structure of his pieces. He does not follow the method of the typical kirtana composer of making the second half of the charana correspond with the anupallavi in the musical setting. The pallavi, anupallavi and charana have each a different dhatu. His songs are fashioned somewhat on the archaic type like the gita and the prabandha with varied khandas and angas. Rhythmic variety is provided by quicker tempo in parts of the song. The niyama of yati and prasa, however, as in the case of the typical kirtana, is scrupulously observed. His compositions are endowed with such excellences as solkattu svaras and with that musical and literary figure of speech known as srotovaha or gupuccha yati where the svaras and syllables are arranged in series of increasing or diminishing quantities. They are master creations of the noblest art, carefully conceived, elaborately developed and consummately finished. Languor, indifference and are altogether absent from them. The perfect blend of sangita and sahitya is a marvel of synthetic artistry.

It is however for the richness and beauty with which raga forms are portrayed that his compositions are most remarkable. Raga is the supreme achievement of Indian Music and the value of a composition is entirely dependent upon the fidelity with which the raga form is presented. From this point of view the songs of Dikshitar are unsurpassed. They are examples of every principle of musical excellence and embodiment of all that is best in lakshya and lakshana sangita, like the constant use of vadi, samvadi, harmony, graha, amsa and other features of raga, the employment of every variety of gamaka and alankara and the assimilation of the beauties of the Northern and Western systems of music. If it is permissible to call architecture frozen music, it will not be amiss to describe Dikshitar's music as ethereal architecture of raga forms.

Dikshitar's style of music is characterized by power. It is the vainika's style of music is characterized by power. It is a sampradaya in which seldom is a plain note rendered as such. Every svara receives its oscillation, slide or shade of other notes. This embellishment known as gamaka with all its varieties, endows the svara with beauty and vitality. The svara is the soul and the gamakas the limbs and body of the rendering. In vilambitalaya, Dikshitar employs the slide and the continuous transition from note to note simultaneously with anusvaras that the suddha Karnataka bhava is admirably maintained. His pieces are forceful illustrations of the genius of Carnatic Music found in the incessant flow of melody and rhythm where note succeeds note in a continuous bond of linked grace and sweetness. This style is mainly the contribution of the vainika who invariably plays the higher note from the lower fret. It is evidently for this reason that Yagnavalkya said that only the mastery of the secret of vina play will lead a man to salvation, certainly to salvation in music. To give a concrete example, Dikshitar's style is the style of the famous Varna known as "Viriboni" of Adiappayah, except for difference in tempo. I am not aware of any composition ancient or modern, which embodies in a greater measure the genius, power, beauty and rhythm of Carnatic Music that the Bhairavi Varna. "Koluvaiyunnada" "Balagopala" and "Kamashi" are the result of its inspiration. In fact, that piece has influenced the style of the three master-composers. The successful play of that Varna is so difficult that it would seem to strain the vina not to say the player to the breaking point. It is therefore called vina goddali. If you have understood the profundity of that Varna, you have the key to the appreciation of Dikshitar's music as well as that of his illustrious compeers. The musical ideas of these composers are so rich and so suggestive of infinite potentialities, that you never feel queasy with surfeit however often you may sing or play their pieces. Every time you sing them you fancy you get new ideas for interpretation and your rendering of them has always the charm of freshness. The individualistic character of our music is not confined to ragas alone, but extends to song renderings. Recital as such has no place in our music. Every rendering is in some measure a creative expression. The more often you sing the compositions of Dikshitar and others like him the more meaning you read into their music. Your aesthetic experience gets enriched and stimulated for further efforts. You can read a play of Shakespeare or Kalidasa and hear or render a song of Diskhitar or Tyagaraja for a thousandth time and not lose interest. The creations of these master-minds, literary or musical, possess a universe of meaning, which becomes clearer and clearer by the intensive application of our minds to them. You can never tire of Hamlet or Sakuntala, Kaddanuvariki, Sri Subrahmanyaya or Brovvamma. Dikshitar's song therefore is invested with the eternal elements of truth and beauty and will endure for ever. Repeated rendering will only enhance their charm.

The Sahitya of Dikshitar does not posses the human interest, lyrical and emotional exuberance so characteristic of the sahitya employed by Tyagaraja. The attraction of Dikshitar is more for the music, which the language bears. Yet the sahitya has dignity and intellectual appeal. It is replete with profound references to yoga and mantra sastras and many other branches of learning and a close study of it will profit those who have a predilection for esoteric studies. Sangita as you know has three main branches, gita, vadya, and nirtta, the soul of each being respectively bhava, raga and tala. While Tyagaraja, Dikshitar and Syama Sastri did the amplest justice to bhava, raga and tala, yet it is permissible perhaps, to represent each of the elements dominating in the three composers in the order respectively. It will not, therefore, be amiss to treat raga as the forte of Dikshitar tacks is more than made up by the bhava of raga. It is often said that music is a language by itself. Truly it is the language of the entire universe. It is understood by the different races of mankind speaking different tongues. It sways animals and plants and the very elements. Music may not succeed in expressing the subtle shades of complex thought. Nevertheless, it is most admirably suited to give utterance to the eternal longing of the soul, to joy and ecstasy, to pain and sorrow which are fundamental and common to all existence. Thus emotion, sentiment and rasa are the very essence of raga. Thus music is the truest poetry of basic feelings. The compositions of Dikshitar are raga poems presenting rich and gorgeously coloured portraits of deep feelings that stir humanity. Composers are the tone-poets of the world and Dikshitar takes his place among the foremost of them. The appeal of their works knows no limitation of language, time or country. The compositions of Purandaradasa and Tulasidas, of Bach and Beethoven of Tyagaraja and Muthuswami Dikshitar and others like them will continue to endure and flourish so long as the phenomenon of sound shall exist in the universe.

Dikshitar provided pilgrims with kriti-s to sing at all shrines and before all forms of the personal God; he placed at the disposal of those initiated into the esoteric worship of Devi, kriti-s that could be used in Her worship; he gave those who felt the impact of the Stars, songs to pray to the Planets. Dikshitar also produced kirtana-s for popular use on festive occasions, at speical annual Vrata-s and Puja-s Ganesha, Varalakshmi Sarasvati and so on. Among those that are popularly sung, the Chamara (Shanmukhapriya) piece Siddhivinayakam has reference to Ganesh Chaturthis; Sri Vara-lakshmi in Sri is for Varalakshmi Vrata observed by women. Sri Venugopala in Kurunji refers to Jayanti, i.e., Gokhulashtami when Krishna just born is worshipped. Sri Satyanarayanam in Shiva Pantuvarali similarly describes the Satyanarayana Vrata.

Dikshitar adopted the Sanskrit language as the medium of his work as this was the prevailing practice among the great composers; in the immediate past, he had his own father (to some extent) and the complete Sanskrit composers Narayana Tirtha, Sadashiva Brahmendra, Upanishad Brahmendra and last but not least Margadarshi Shesha Ayyanar who served as a model for Shri Svati Tirunal. Among his two contemporaries, Shyama Shastri wrote in Sanskrit before changing over to Telugu and Tyagaraja had several songs in pure Sanskrit. The Sanskrit medium established the continuity with the classical past, and, what is more, provided the most suitable vehicle for the kind of thought and ideas that Dikshitar had to convey. Sanskrit established here the necessary link with sacred literature, Veda, Mantra, Tantra, Kshetramahatyma. It also lent dignity to the diction and proved an aid to the elevating effect of his compositions.

Although the olden age of Gita, Prabandha etc., was nearing its end, these forms still appeared in the Lakshana and Lakshya-gita-s of the different raga-s. Ramaswami Dikshitar still composed a Lakshya-prabandha for his creation Hamsadhvani. Appearing during this transitional phase, Dikshitar's compositions gave a new direction to kirtana-s, along with those of his contemporaries. But a very important point of difference in Diskhitar's Kriti-s which distinguishes them from those of others (like Tyagaraja's) is that the charana-part is one integral whole and no part of it could be skipped; the musician can sing one charana of Tyagaraja's piece and leave out the rest. This is possible because the charana-s are in the same setting and can be dispensed with. This is not possible in Dikshitar's kriti-s Madhyamakala passages of varying length are a regular feature of Dikshitar's kriti-s and give a needed variation, as the prevailing tempo of his compositions is the slow one (vilambita); often they alternate with the vilambita passages in all parts of the compositions. Several songs have svara passages and also a few have jati-s. They have the embellishment of prasa-s, initial, medial and final, but they do not fall into metrical patterns as songs of composers in the Telugu medium do. They employ the Yati-s of Gopuccha and Srotovaha, decrease and increase, syllable by syllable, a feature seen also in old Devaram music. Examples are: Anandabhairavi,-Tyagaraja-yoga-vaibhavam, Raja-yoga-vaibhavam, Yoga-vaibhavam, vaibhavam, Bhavam, Vam; and in the same piece, taking the reverse order, we have the increase, Sham, Prakasham, Svarupa-prakasham, Tattvasvarupaprakasham, Sakala-tattvasvarupa-praksham,

Tattvasvarupaprakasham, Sakala-tattvasuvarupa-prakasham, Shiva-shaktyadi-sakala-tattva-svarupa-prakasham. Concert listeners may recall similar passages in Maya tvam yahi and Sri Varalakshmi.

The importance of the compositions of Dikshitar for the theory and evolution of Karnatic music was dealt with above. The raga-s are the crux of this matter. Dikshitar's systematic work put Venkatamahin's scheme of 72-Mela-janya scheme on a strong foundation. In the last piece of his series of illustrative compositions of this scheme, Dikshitar mentions expressly the 72 Raganga ragas. Aware of the importance of the subject, Dikshitar took special care to work into the text of the songs and most dexterously, the names of the raga-s so that doubts or disputes regarding the raga-s of the pieces do not arise in his case as they do in the case of many kriti-s of Tyagaraja.

Of the three aspects of music and composition, bhava, raga, and tala, the beauty of the last, of rhythm, pace and lilt can be enjoyed in Shyama Shastri. Bhava is most patent in the lyrical outpourings of Tyagaraja. Raga may be said to be Dikshitar's forte. This raga importance in Dikshitar may be viewed in more than one aspect. Firstly as a classicist, Dikshitar had a full awareness of the great heritage of the art. In may be seen from the several lists of songs give above under different heads, he brought to life numerous ancient raga-s by composing kritis in them. His kriti-s are, therefore, our sole guide now in the rendering of those raga-s. In some of the rare raga-s, Dikshitar has more than one kirtana. Cultivation of his kriti-s is, therefore, an enlarging of one's musical equipment and knowledge. The full and correct forms of raga-s were formerly determined by different kinds of definitive compositions gita, prabandha, thaya and alapa, referred to, together as chaturdandi. Then came the tana varna-s and daru-s. In course of time, the pada or kirtana (kriti) on the side and alapa on the other became, according to the law of survival of the fittest, the two chief media by which raga-s were not only expounded and enjoyed, but also technically defined and recognized. Between the kriti and alapa, the former is the ready and tangible one. For all the ten characteristics of a raga, the sanchara-s and prayoga-s of master composers in their pada-s or kirtana-s became the chief guide. The kriti-s of Dikshitar form, in this respect, our most precious possession. If as sahitya-s on different deities, his kriti-s are life dhyana-shloka-s of the murti-s of different forms of Divinity, on the music side they are so many Lakshana-gita-s investing the raga murti-s with all the subtleties and graces of the raga-s.

The raga-s, as named and so sung in the kriti-s give rise to some confusion and controversy. The raga-lakshana discussions of the Expert's Committee of the Music Academy, Madras, continued for many years during its Annual Conferences and form the Academy's solid achievement. The detailed reports in the Academy's Journal show that the usages seen in the kriti-s in the same raga-s by the two main composers, Tyagaraja and Dikshitar, figured continuously, producing the idea of two schools, as it were, the Tyagaraja School and the Dikshitar School. From this point of view again, the kriti-s of Dikshitar are valuable. We may leave aside raga-s like Shankarabharana, Bhairavi, Kambhoji or Todi; even in the case of raga-s sung less often although the same notes are used by two composers, Tyagaraja and Dikshitar, the setting of the Dikshitar kriti is such that a different ethos and effect are created. There is then this distinct aesthetic value which we should not deprive ourselves of.

The distinct quality of Dikshitar's music, from the aesthetic point of view, is its style which is derived from the technique of the vina. In his major Bhairavi Kriti Balagopala, Dikshitar calls himself a vainika-gayaka and this gives the key to an understanding and appreciation of the excellence of Dikshitar's style. In the well-known Gamakakriya song on Minakshi, Dikshitar speaks of the ten agamas in the playing of the vina. The richness of gamaka in Dikshitar's music, the grace of the kampa, the odukkal-sadukkal, as they call it in our musical parlance, all this finer quality of his music derives from the vina. Another distinction is the tempo as the full evocation of raga-form could come only in the vilamba-kala. Due to this vishranti, the gamaka-s and the stately diction of Dikshitar's kriti-s produce the impression of a big python, of a state elephant, of a ship on the waters, and of the big temple car of Tyagaraja at Tiruvarur.

Such is the work, such is the high quality of the art of Dikshitar, a scholar and master, a versatile genius. Like the title vainika-gayaka that he gave himself, another is in his Bauli song, Pandita-tara, meaning more scholarly than others'. This offers us they key to an understanding of another dimension of Dikshitar's work and art. I have observed that when a musician grows in knowledge and maturity, steadiness and reflective ness, he begins to develop a greater interest in Dikshitar's kirtanas.

I may conclude with a reference to Sri Aurobindo's exposition of true or great poetry as mantra. When you sit and listen to Manirangu and Mam ava or Navaroz and Hasti-vadanaya or Bauli and Parvati-Parameshvarau, you are under the spell of something transcending a mere song.

Panchbhuta Kritis & Pancha Linga Kritis of Dikshitar

Muthuswamy Dikshitar has to his credit the largest number of group kritis on various themes. Two among these group kritis are the two sets comprising five kritis each namely, Pancha bhuta kritis on the five elemental forms of Lord Shiva – Prithvi (earth), Appu (Water), Tejas (fire), Vayu (Air) and Akasha (shy). These pancha bhutas are enshrined in temples at Conjeevaram, Jambukesvaram, Tiruvannamalai, Kalahasti and Chidambaram respectively. The panchalinga kritis on the five Siva lingas are enshrined in the temples of Tiruvarur, Achalesvara, Hatakeswara, Valmikeswara, Anandesvara and Sidheswara.

The Saiva tradition hails Siva and his manifestations in to five different lingas (the Pancha lingas). The five lingas are associated with the temples in different places. E.g., In Kalahasti Siva manifests as Vayu-linga. Dikshitar has composed a kriti in praise of this linga (Kalahastisa in Huseni raga). This kriti is are of the panchabhuta kritis. Similarly Pritvi linga appears in the temple at Kancheepuram where he composed the Panchabhuta kritis. 'Chintaya makanda mula' in Bhaivari raga. Another kriti in the Pancha bhuta grasip, was composed on the tejolinga which is the presiding duty at Tiruvannamalai temple. The kriti Annachala natam is composed in the raga Saranga. 'Ananda natana Prakasam' in the raga kedara was composed an Chidambaram temple where Siva manifested as 'Akasa linga'.

'Jampupate' in yamuna kalyani raga was composed on Appulinga the fifth pancha bhuta kriti at Tiruvanikaval.

Another set of five kritis Dikshitar has composed is the Pancha linga kritis on the five Siva lingas enshrined in the Tyagaraja temple at Tiruvavur. These five compositions are: 1. Achalesvara in Bhupala raga, 2. Hatakeswara in Bilahari raga, 3. Valmikesvara in Kamboji raga, 4. Anandeswara in Anandabhairavi raga and 5. Sidheswara in Neelambari raga.

It is interesting to note that Dikshitar has also employed the Ghana ragas as a group in his chaturdasa raga malika 'Sri Viswanatham bhajeham' (The song with notation is given in the appendix.)

3. Syama Sastri

The contribution of the great composer Syama Sastri, to Carnatic Music is of the highest order. His varied pieces are original in all respects and exhibit a marked individuality of style distinct from those of his illustrious comtemporaries. His sahityas are extremely simple and elegant. They may not possess the philosophic profundity of Purandaradasa, the erotic mysticism of Ksetragna, the lyric sweetness of Tyagaraja or the esoteric intellectualism of Dikshitar, but they are replete with the natural pathos and tenderness of the child crying out to reach the mother.

The chief value of the language he employs lies less in its significance, intellectual or emotional, than in the intimacy with which its syllables commune with the svaras. The fortunate circumstance of some of our philosophers and poets being also great composers should not blind us to the essential requirements of classical music whose primary purpose is wholly aesthetic. From the absolute standpoint of art, the only use of sahitya is to sustain melody. In fact, some of the finest melodic pieces of master-composers have very poor sahitya. The ancient gitas deliberately employed expletives and meaningless words to articulate the music. It is pity that at present the dust of political controversy tends to obscure the vision and obliterate the distinction between literature and music on the one hand and between classical music and folk-songs on the other. Those who insist on a particular language in compositions can have but a scant regard for true musical values. They may get the language they want, but not the music they should hope for.

Sangita of the purest kind does not require the aid of sahitya for rasaposhana and if it does, then to that extent, it is attenuated. In the noblest type of music, sahitya does nothing but furnish syllables for the embodiment of the svara, and for the articulation and intonation of the melody. Sahitya in this sense is merely a group of varnas for the incarnation of ragasvara; it is in the perfect wedding of the syllable with the ragasvara that the consummate skill of the great composer is to be seen. This is the only purpose that sahitya has in music of the highest character. Judged from this point of view, Syama Sastri ranks far superior to many composers and stands next only to Ksetragna. Indeed his compositions are marvels of svara-varnasamyoga.

The melodic form of his compositions is strikingly original, unconventional and free. His varna-mettus have a daring grandeur of conception, presenting delightfully fresh phases of raga as rich in emotional spirit as in the haunting beauty of their mode.

Syama Sastri's grandest achievement is perhaps the magical skill with which he applies great rhythmic power to his compositions so that it only regulates, never impedes, the flow of melody. If you would sense the thrill of rhythm, you have to go to chapu tala for it and if you would enjoy its maximum effect, you should find it in the compositions of Syama Sastri.

4. Sri Purandaradasa

In the city of Purandaragada, eighteen miles from Poona, lived a rich banker by name Varadappa Naick. A son was born to him in the year 1484; he was named Srinivasa Naick. At a very early age Srinivasa Naick received his education and attained great mastery in Sanskrit and music. He was also well conversant with all the spoken languages of those parts. He acquired special skill in the assessment of precious stones. He enlarged the business of his father with great care and parsimony. At the age of eighteen, he was married to Sarasvati Bai of a rich and noble family. Her wealth, however, was her least qualification. In beauty and virtue few were her equals. Endowed with a most noble and generous nature, she was a pativrata in the truest sense. Srinivasa Naick with all his learning and wealth was parsimonious. It pained her but she desisted from protesting. Tradition in precious stones and metals he traveled frequently to Bijapur, Gulburga, Golkonda and Vihayanaga; he became so wealthy that he was commonly known in those parts of daughter. His wife was sorry to note that he was impervious to the elevating influence of charity and godliness.

Then, one day, an aged Brahmin with a very young body sought his help for the upanayana of the boy. The Naick turned him out but the Brahmin persisted. Six months passed by and neither would give in. At last, the weary Brahmin approached the Naick's wife in his absence and appealed to her mercy. Her heart melted with pity at the wretchedness of the yachaka, and in a moment of extreme tenderness she gave him the mukhura (her nose ornament) so that the might sell it and get the wherewithal for the upanayana. Her act was desperate. She had not even the presence of mind to pray to be saved from her husband's wrath. The aged Brahmin took the jewel to Srinivasa Naick who was in his business premises and offered it for sale. The Naick immediately grew suspicious, secured the jewel in his safe and asking him to meet him later, returned home and demanded of his wife her jewel. The harassed lady retired to the rear apartment, went to the Tulasi Vrindavan and after offering puja resolved to end her life by taking poison. As she lifted the cup to her lips, down fell into the vessle the mukhura she had gifted away. Her joy and wonder were boundless. She hurried to her husband with the jewel. The Naick was struck by its resemblance to the one brought by the old man; he hastened to his shop to compare them. But, when he opened his safe, it was not there. He returned in fear and wanted to know from his wife all that had happened. She told him everything. The Naick was stupefied. He sat down in sorrow ruminating over his baseness. He realized that human contrivances like bars and bolts and locks and keys were of no avail against the Power which could be invoked by a pure and kindly heart. He even thought that the old Brahmin was no other than the Lord who had come to teach him the great Truth of life, of love and sacrifice. He lost delight in worldly pursuits and longing to see the old man again vowed not to touch food or water till his desire was fulfilled. He fasted for full three days. During the third night, Saraswati Bai dreamt, if her husband gave up all his wealth and became a haridasa, he would have the vision. Srinivasa Naick thereupon walked out of the house with his wife and sons; standing in the street, put a tulasi leaf on the house dedicating it to Lord Krishna. He wandered through the streets with his wife and sons. Tired, he was resting in the corner of a road; then he saw the old man, at whose feet he fell begging for mercy and forgiveness. His mind was now easy. He went round for alms, and the moment he gathered enough for the day, he came back; his devoted wife cooked food which was first offered to the Lord and then shared by all of them. That night he had the vision of Panduranga who directed him to go to Vijayanagar to seek initiation from Vyasaraya: The next day he set out on foot in the company of his loyal wife and affectionate sons. Their way lay through a dark and dreadful forest infested by wild beasts and robbers. Saraswati Bai overcome by fear was unable to proceed; and Srinivasa Naick suspecting she must have in her custody something of value which occasioned her anxiety, examined her small bundle and found she carried the cup of gold he had been using, to provide him with water in case of need. He flung it away and then continued their journey with a free and unburdened mind.

He reached Vijayanagar in humility and sought the asrama where the renowned Rajaguru lived. What a strange contrast! He had visited that famous city unnumbered times in pride of wealth and had sought none but the prince and the richest of the citizens to sell his precious wares. He had not cared then to know Vyasaraya. But now he sat to the feet of the great master to acquire treasures of a different kind. Srinivasa was received into the mutt with the utmost cordiality and after the partaking of the prasada, he and the guru had a hearty and intimate conversation; the latter disclosed knowledge of all the experiences the disciple had undergone. The next day he obtained the holy initiation and was thereafter known as Purandaradasa. The moment he became a dasa he had god-vision; thereafter, he turned out kirtanas of imperishable beauty.

It was his daily custom to go along the principal streets of the city of Vijayanagar sounding his tambura, composing and singing kirtanas with his four sons playing drums and keeping time. His voice was so superb that people thought that none but the gandharvas could sing like him. Those who heard him were stirred to their very depths. Offerings would pour in but he would never take more than what was just necessary for the day taking nothing for the morrow. Sufficient unto the day was the constant admonition he gave his children.

On a certain day when Purandaradasa had gone out as usual singing kirtanas, the wealthy father-in-law of Varadappa (a son of the dasa) called on the dasa. Sarasvati Bai was at her wit's end how best to entertain the distinguished visitor. She hastened to her neighbor from whom she obtained the magic stone which could turn base metals into gold; she soon got a banquet ready for her guest. Meanwhile, Purandaradasa who was feeling perturbed in mind returned home only to find it defiled by the luxurious fare provided by impious gains. He seized the mineral and threw it into the Chakrathirtha thus provoking his neighbour to an unseemly fight. There were occasions when the saint felt bound to administer mild rebuke to his wife when she longed to wear ornaments. His kirtana in Dhanyasi raga in adi tala is an instance.

Krishnadevaraya the King of Vijayanagar who learnt that the fabulously wealthy merchant so familiar to him had turned a dasa, came to the mutt of Vyasaraya and Unobtrusively sat in a corner to listen to the rapturous compositions of Purandaradasa. He invited the dasa to his palace and sought enlightenment. Purandaradasa availed himself of the opportunity to speak out his mind in a song in Dhanyasi raga in adi tala. He was, indeed, not hurting the king, for, humble worshipper as the king was, the dasa could not help pointing out how far superior was the life of the true servant of God to that of a King. Krishnadevaraya in a spirit of adoration showered gifts on the saint who gave them away to the poorest of men, observing that thereby those presents were truly dedicated to God.

The high character of Purandaradasa, the immense popularity of his soul-stirring compositions and the supreme regard that Vyasaraya had for him excited the envy of a large section of the sishyas of the mutt who valued rigid and ceremonial forms more than inward spirituality. They protested against what they conceived to be undue partiality shown by the Swami to a composer of Kannada padas. Vyasaraya who was not to be bullied by these threats commanded that on the sacred pitha should be placed the scriptures and on top of them all the books of recorded compositions of Purandaradasa. There was immediately a violent outcry. The Swami declared he would not prevent anybody from pulling out the obnoxious book from its honoured place. The irate sishyas endeavored to fling it away only to find it resettled in its exalted seat. Vyasaraya remarked that Purandaropanishad was certainly not the book they could lay their jealous hands upon. This incident is alluded to in a composition of Varadappa.

Once when Purandaradasa was sitting in the company of Vyasaraya and others, he was noticed suddenly to rub his garments briskly. When he was asked the reason for the strange act, he replied that the great curtain in front of the deity in Vitthala temple had caught fire and that he put it out. The sceptics in the assembly were struck dumb when a few minutes later the officers of the temple rushed into the presence of the Swami to report how Purandaradasa had extinguished the fire caused by the negligence of the torchbearers. Compositions exist that bear testimony to the occurrence.

Purandaradasa like all other notable saints visited many sacred places and composed songs in honour of the deities of the kshetra. Belur was one of the early centres he visited. There he met Vaikunthadasa who was also a composer of kirtanas. As the latter was childless, it seems, Lord Krishna would assume the form of a lovely child, sit on his lap and humour him. The child appeared to be sacred by his entry; so he sang a kirtana in Bhairavi raga in adi tala to appease the child. Then Melkote, Nanjangood, Srirangapatnam, Abbur, Mulubagal and other holy places in Karnataka were visited and extolled in his kirtanas. While he was still in Karnataka, Narayanappa on whom Krishnadevaraya conferred the title of Kumaravyasa, brought to him for approval Kannada Bharata in appreciation of which he sang a suladi.

Having seen the sacred kshetras of the South, Purandaradasa reached Pandarpur. He remained there for long and composed a very large number of kirtanas. Lord Vitthala would often appear before him and speak to him now as companion and now as sishya and anecdotes relating to them are full of interest to those who believe. One of them, however, is too well documented and circumstantially sustained to be discredited. One morning, Purandaradas called out to his disciple Appanna Bhagavata asking him to fetch a vessel of water. As the sishya who was soundly asleep did not respond, Purandaradasa began to feel the awkward-ness of the situation. Sri Vitthala, just then in the guise of his sishya brought him the vessel. The guru, however, feeling vexed by the delay, hit the head of the supposed disciple with the vessel. Thereupon the sishya disappeared. A few minutes later it was discovered that he who brought water was not Appanna Bhagavata but Sri Vitthala who in infinite kindness served him as his sishya. The same day it was noticed that the head of the image of Vitthala in the temple was swollen and water flowed from its eyes. Purandaradasa, whose influence with Sri Vitthala was well-known, that he was requested to use his good offices in pacifying the deity. The great bhakta went into the temple, prayed for forgiveness and gently passed his hands over the bruised head when all at once the image became quite as before.

In the city of Pandarpur lived a dancer and singer who was an ardent devotee of Sri Vitthala. One day the Lord assuming the form of Purandaradasa entered her house and desired to see her dance and hear her music. The dasi who esteemed the visit of the renowned dasa next only to that of the Lord Himself received and entertained him with unbounded devotion. The visitor too expressed gratification and presented her with a bracelet of rare beauty. The next morning it was discovered that a bangle on the wrist of Sri Vitthala was missing. A search was made. The dasi was forced to confess that Purandaradasa had given it to her. The bhakta was marched into the temple, bound to a pillar and mercilessly flogged. He protested he was innocent, only to aggravate the fury of justice. He then realized it was all penalties for his cruelty and sang in pathetic accents a kirtana in Pantuvarali raga in chapu tala wherein the incidents described are alluded to.

Then was heard from the innermost shrine a voice shouting, "It is I that in the guise of Purandaraadasa gave the jewel to the dasi; worship hereafter the pillar whereunto my bhakta was fastened, as Dasarasthambha". The temple authorities had the image of Purandaradasa carved on the pillar; and ever since it has been the custom for pilgrims to worship the Dasarasthambha before entering the sanctuary.

Worship at Tirupati was dear to Purandaradasa especially when his guru Vyasaraya with Krishnadevaraya visited it during Brahmotsava. His fame had spread so far that many pilgrims during the season desired thirtha prasada from his hands, though his life was one of abstemious asceticism. It somehow happened that offerings proved insufficient to entertain the guests sumptuously. One of these occasions the supply of ghee falling short, he shouted to his sishya Appanna Bhagavata to bring more of it for serving the guests. As the disciple was far away singing and dancing for the delight of those who sat in another quarter, the call went unheeded. When the host was much perplexed he found a person exactly resembling his sishya dashing past with a pot of ghee and lavishly serving it to the guests. It was clear that this was yet another instance of the Lord's mercy and service to His servants; and it occasioned an emotional outburst in a kirtana in Sankarabharana in chapu tala, the first charana recalling the incident.

Purandaradasa's stay in Tirupati was prolonged. Every day he would bathe in Swamipushkarini and say his prayers in a corner of the tank. Krishnadevaraya who noticed it got a special mantapa constructed for the use of the saintly bard, which in time came to be known as dasara mantapa. He would wait until the concourse of pilgrims dispersed from the sanctuary of the temple, and when solitude and silence reigned he would stand in front of the deity and sing his kirtana to his heart's content. His son Madhavapatidasa who was always with him would record the songs. It is said that even the archakas would go out as if unwilling to interpose between him and Sri Venkatesa. The songs that then poured out of his heart are the unalloyed expressionof the ananda that overflowed.

When Purandaradasa returned to Vijayanagar after the pilgrimage Vyasaraya was unable to restrain his emotions of love and joy which find expression in song. This tribute of worshipful adoration paid by the greatest man of the time to one who was his sishya could not but evoke bitter criticism. Vyasaraya gently observed that few could understand Purandaradasa as he did. He would ask Madhavapatidasa daily to recite to him all the padas that were recorded and ponder to recite to him all the padas that were recorded and ponder over the beauty of their music and the depth of their meaning.

Purandaradasa was an ardent lover of peace and harmony. His valued services were always available in composing differences particularly communal. Once in Sholapur when the lingayats and Brahmins were quarrelling bitterly over their religious beliefs,

Purandaradasa interceded and reconciled them to each other, by a song in Madhyamavati in adi tala. The raga was as ever most appropriate for the time of day which was noon and for the occasion which was the elimination of discord. How kindly disposed he was towards the panchamas will be apparent from his songs. The last days of Purandaradasa were spent in perfect bliss. He desired that his son Madhavapatidasa should compose the remaining quarter of a lakh of compositions he had contemplated, to complete his wish. After a life of unexampled service for the cause of music, literature, religion, philosophy and social justice, he left this world to serve the Lord in his imperishable form, on Saturday, Pushyababula Amavasya of Raktakshe year corresponding to A.D. 1564.

Purandaradasa has been justly termed the father of Carnatic Music. He was not merely a composer, but a lakshanakara of the highest caliber. The system of South Indian Music, as we now have it, is entirely his gift. His greatest achievement is that he systematized it, gave it laws and placed it on such secure foundations that it has continued to remain the same in its essentials. All the famous ragas bear the same complexion today as they did in his time. The wonder is not that there is difference in the rendering here and there but that the raga forms in the main have preserved the identity. He was master of both lakshya and lakshana. It was therefore possible for him not only to give correct shape to the ragas but to compose thousands of kirtanas to serve as illustrations of them. It might indeed to be a surprise to some that ragas like Todi and Kalyani had to be reintroduced by him into the southern system. The Tallapakam composers have not used ragas and they do not find a mention in the treatise on music of that period. To him belongs the credit of having rescued Carnatic Music from the chaos and corruption of alien influences from which the music of the North could not altogether escape. He fixed the main outline of all the ragas in vogue in his time with such clarity and precision that there was no chance of their being every mistaken or distorted. Dhanyasi, Mohana, Begada, Madhyamavati, Surati, Sahana, Varali, Arabhi, Nata, Atana, Darbar, Kanada to mention but a few are rendered today exactly as they wre in his day. It is true certain ragas have undergone some change of complexion. It is doubtful if the change is some change of complexion. It is doubtful if the change is for the better. The Trinity scrupulously respected the traditions of Sri Purandaradasa. Dikshitar and Syama Sastri followed him in raga and tala aspects only. Tyagaraja modeled his compositions on those of the great dasa in bhava as well as in raga and tala. Comparative research eve of a superficial kind will show how closely the padas of Ksetragna resemble those of the dasa. There are many Kannada padas which if translated into Telugu will remain undistinguished from those of Ksetragna in world and in music.

The first great change effected by Purandaradasa was to introduce the Malava-gaula scale as the basic scale for music introduction. The ancient suddha scale was Karaharapriya. It was derived by the application of chatussruti interval to sadja panchama and madhyama. Later the sruti values of the notes of the resultant scale were enumerated. In North India as well as in South India the tradition of Bharata's system was forgotten. Ignoring that Bharata's scale started from sadja, the pandits of North India treated the note with reference to which the surits of sadja were given, as the initial and basic note and arrived at the Sankarabharana or Bilaval scale. Purandaradasa, however, adopted the Malavagaula scale as its derivation from sadja, panchama and madhyama was based on a process identical with the derivation of the ancient classic scale with this significant difference that in the derivation a dvisruti instead of a chatussruti interval was used. A dvisruti interval is beyond question easier to negotiate than a chatussruti interval. And that is the reason which underlies the selection of Malavagaula scale.

Not content with prescribing the scale, he framed a graded series of lessons which even today prevails in the teaching of music. The svaravalis, janta varisais, alankaras and gitas form the surest road to the mastery of Carnatic Music with all its intricacies of svara and tala prastaras.

In the number of compositional types he created he has no equal. It is stated on his own authority that he composed four and three-quarter lakhs of songs of which every one was in accordance with sruti and smriti. In every one of them the same-perfect commingling of sense, word and music is noticeable. He was a renowned composer of both lakshya and lakshana gitas. It is unfortunate, however, that only a few lakshya gitas have been handled down to us. All his lakshana gitas have to be unearthed. He was also a prolific composer of tana varnas and tillanas. It is stated that Adiappa Iyah modelled his tana varnas on those of Purandaradasa. It is however the kirtana that forms the largest class of the compositions of Purandaradasa. The lakshanas of the kirtana, its origin and development have already been referred to. The terms pada and devarnama used in the description of his compositions mean only kirtana. A great number of the kirtanas is in madhyamakala. All the varieties of tala are used though chapu and jhampa tala are more favoured. It is significant, however, that as compared with his predecessors he employed the adi tala in a greater proportion. He was equally facile in composing chauka tala kirtanas. Some of his compositions contain the nayaka-nayikibhava and but for the language they are quite apt to be fancied as Ksetrangna's.

The kirtanas form the bulk of his compositions. Many of them have only the pallavi and the charanas. Yet there are thousands of them that have the pallavi, the anupallavi and the charana. It is a mistake to suppose that the music of his kirtanas is of a plain recitative character with little scope for manodharma. There are indeed many songs of his meant merely for sankirtana purposes. But a much larger number of them are surcharged with musical excellence of the highest number of them are surcharged with musical excellence of the highest quality. Except in so far as the composer himself did not impose set sangatis of a sophisticated nature on them, the compositions themselves are the embodiments of raga sancharas of exquisite beauty. As lakshya for lakshana they posses such high value that they are cited in renowned lakshana granthas as unquestioned authority for raga sancharas. Sangita Saramrita of Tulajaji gives the reference to many of his compositions in sangita. In the suladi the theme is the same as in the kirtana, but it has usually seven or eight distinct divisions with elaborate sahitya each of which is set to one of the classical talas. Some suladis have different ragas for the different divisons, and in some others the raga is the same for all the divisions. The suladi is a learned, elaborate and difficult piece giving a most comprehensive view of all the important raga sancharas. Sangita Saramrita of Tulajendra cites numerous prayogas from suladis of Purandaradasa as classic authority for lakshana of ragas described in the work. It is regrettable that the tradition of rendering the suladis is fact disappearing.

A revival of interest in them would be of no small value for the future of the science and art of Carnatic Music.

There is yet another type of composition of his known as ugobhoga. The meaning of this term is again obscure. If an alternative to the classical interpretation may be offered, the following may be considered, viz., that the word is symbolical implying "conducive to the attainment of heavenly bliss". Ugobhoga is an extremely simple type of song undefined into part and almost nebulous in structure. The tala is merely the sarva laghu and the simplest phases of the raga go to make up its music. It is as a musical form even more elementary than the gita. From the point of view of bhava it is supposed to be a direct translation of the thoughts of the composer in the ecstasy of inspiration.

Purandaradasa like his guru also composed what is known as vritta nama. It is a composition in which padya and kritana occur alternately. In other respects the kirtana part conforms to the common type.

5. Maharaja Svati Tirunal

The Royal composer Sri Svati tirunal (kula sekhara perumal) who lived during 1813-1846 A.D. is quite well known as one of the greatest figures in the history of carnatic classical music. He was a great poet, a composer and a patran of all the famous musicians and other artists of his period. He was known as the 'Dikshina bhoja". Considering his valuable contributions to the cause and development of Karnatic music, he deserves to be rankled with the musical trinity.

Svati, as a child was known as balaprabudha, with extreme passion for music and his scholarship in several languages like Sanskirt, English, Telugu, Marathi, Kannada, Hindi , Persian, besides Malayalam his native tangue. Many great musicians of the time have donned svati trinal's cant. Tanjore quartette brothers (the mitya vidwans who had refined and modified the Nritya art into the form of Bharata matya of the present day were prominent among the musicians of svati tirunal's court. The association with the brothers gave the Maharaja an opportunity to learn more about the Bharata natya and detail about Venkatamahi's tradition of the genuine system of the modern phase of classical carnatic music.

He was a prolific composer who has composed more than 300 compositions in various forms during his brief span of life of Thirty three years. Most his compositions are in Sanskrit, same in Malayalam, Telugu, Hindi, Marathi, Kannada and very few in Tamil. Being a devotee of Sri Padmanabha, his family deity, he adopted the mudra in compositions as "Padmanabha" or its synonyms. He composed a variety of compositions in different forms which include Padavarna, Tanavarna, Jatisvara, Svarajati, Pada, Javali, Thillana, Ragamalika etc.

The Group Kritis of Swati

Like the trinity, Swati tirunal has also a good number of group kritis to his credit, such as Navaratri kritis, Nava ratnamalika, Utsava prabandhas, Navaratra malika etc.

The set of Navaratri kritis comprise nine songs in it composed particularly on the Navaratri festivals in order to present each song for each day of the festival.

The group comprises the following songs in it:

1. Devi jagt janani	-	Sankarabharana	-	Adi
2. Pahinmam sin	-	Kalyani	-	Adi
3. Devipavane	-	Saveri	-	Adi
4. Bharati Mamava	-	Todi	-	Adi
5. Janani mamava	-	Bhairavi	-	Triputa
6. Sarouha sanjayaye	-	Pautuvarali	-	Adi
7. Janani Pahi	-	Sudha saveri	-	Triputa
8. Pahiparvata	-	Nata krinji	-	Triputa
9. Pahi parvata	-	Arabhi	-	Adi

The first six songs are whether on goddess saraswati and the rest there on Parvati.

The Utsava sampradaya kritis written in 'Manipravala' language (the early sanskritized Malayalam) are 12 songs and 42 verses. It is further divided into 12 sections each comprises a songs and a four verses in it. The first and the last songs are like introductory and concluding parts respectively. The remaining ten songs are meant for the ten day festival, are each for ten days.

The Navaratna mala that comprises of a 9 songs on Nava vidha bhakti are as follows:

1.	Bhavatiya Katha	-	Bhairavi	-	Adi
2.	Tavakamani	-	Kedaragumala	-	Zhampa
3.	Satatam	-	Nilambari	-	Misrachappu
4.	Pankajasharnam	-	Todi	-	Rupaka
5.	Aradhayami	-	Bilahani	-	Misrachappu
6.	Vande deva deva	-	Begada	-	Zhampa
7.	Parama purusha	-	Ahiri	-	Misra chapu
8.	Bhavati visuaso	-	Mukhari	-	Misra chapu
9.	Deva deva kalpayami	-	Nadhanamakriya	-	Rupakam

He was also a great composer of varnas. He has composed about 23 varnas which include Tana varnas, Chouka varnas and Pada varnas.

His ragamalika swarajati in five ragas Kalyani, Begada, Athana, Suruthi and Todi is very popular. He has composed Thillanas in a ragas like Dhanasri, Bhupala, Todi, Ananda bhairavi, Purvi, Kalyani etc. He has also composed about sixty seven padas in Sanskrit, Telugu, Kannada and Malayalam.

Another pada varna which has become very popular in 'Samasayaka' in five ragas such as Kapi, Kalyani, Khamas, Vasanta and Mohana and it is set to rupaka tala.

He has composed raga malikas on different themes and accordingly selected the ragas and number of ragas. E.g. The ragamalika 'Kamalajasyahruta' explains the ten incarnatics of Vishnu and thus he selected ten ragas in order to depict the dasavatara.

The ten ragas are: Mohana, Bilahari, Dhanyasi, Saranga, Madhyamavati, Athana, Natakurinji, Darbara, Ananda bharavi and Sourashtra. Similarly in the raga malika starts with "Panna gendra sayana" he employed eight ragas viz. Sankarabharana, Kambhoji, Nilambari, Bhairavi, Todi, Suruthi, Nadanaakrinji and Bhupala. Each sections of this ragamalika has eight avartas of sahitya as well as svaras. His 'Bhavayani' is also a popular raga malika even though it was originally composed only in the raga saveri.

The Ghana raga kritana of swati tirunal is noteworthy and is composed a set of 8 kirtanas in 9 Ghana ragas, five in Ghana raga panchaka and three in dvitiya, ghana ragas. The following is the list of this group kritis.

1. Pahi samere - Nata - Rupaka
2. Kamayanaka - Goula - Jhampa
3. Mamava padmanabha - Varali - Chapu
4. Sri ramana vibho - Arabhi - Adi
5. Rinamadadrita - Sri - Chempada
6. Sarasiruhanabha - Kedara - chapu
7. Paripalayamam - Saranganata - Rupaka

Swati tirunal has composed many of his kritis in Ghana ragas. The list of his compositions in Ghana raga is given in the chapter V. They include the Vishnu para Ghana raga kirtanas, Padas

6. Veena Kuppayyar

Veena Kuppayyar who lived between 1798-1860 was one of the celebrated disciples of Tyagaraja. He was popularly known as 'Pata Kuppayyar', Tiruvothiyoor Kuppayyar'. And 'Narayanagaula Kuppayyar'. He was born in Tinvothiyoon, about eight kilometres North of Madras. His father Veena Sambayyar was also a great musician. Naturally kuppayyar learnt music from his father at the early stages of his musical career, though he is probably the most celebrated disciple of Sri Tyagaraja.

Thematically his songs are descriptive of stories from purnas, e.g., In the kriti, "Kaniya dina napai" he is seen describing about Maheswara Swallowing the deadly poison (Kalkootavisha) and the back ground of that episode.

Kuppayar's Pancha Ratnas

He composed two group kritis called 'Kala hastisa Pancha ratna' and 'Venkatesa Pancharatna'. These two classics consist of five kritis each. They are

I Kalahastheesa Pancharatna

1. Konyadinanapai	-	Kamboji	-	Adi
2. Nanu brova rada	-	Sama	-	Adi
3. Birana nannu brova	-	Hamsadwain	-	Adi
4. Samagana lola	-	Salaya bhairavi	-	Adi
5. Sevinta muraramma	-	Sahana	-	Adi

II Venkatesa Pancharatna

1. Mamonu brochu	–	Srihendramadhyamam	-	Adi
2. Nannu brovanika	-	Mukhari	-	Adi
3. Sarojakshuni	-	Saveri	-	Adi
4. Nive dikkani	-	Darbar	-	Adi
5. Bagumeeraganu	-	Sankarabharanam	-	Adi

The above kritis invariably bear the 'Murthy mudra' the name of the deity on whom the respective kritis are composed. i.e., Kalahasteesa on Nagaraja girimivasa or Seshagin mivasa etc.

His contribution to the realm of Karnatic music is invaluable and he has become immortal in the minds of the music lovers though his musical contribution. A distinguished composer of Tanavarnas, he has about 14 Tanavarnas to his credit. His varna 'Intakopa" in the ghana ragas (five from the first group of ghana raga panchaka and four from the second group of ghana raga panchaka) shows the genius composer in him as net many composer have employed both the groups of Ghana raga panchakas together in a single composition. The above mentioned Ghana raga varna with notation is given in the appendix.

So many composers of various periods have composed employing Ghana ragas either individually or as a group. A detailed list of the compositions in Ghana ragas by various composers is given in the **Appendix.**

7

Conclusion

This piece of Research appeared through the preceding chapters consists of the collection and editing of selected manu-scripts on Sangita Sastra and compositions in Sanskrit and other Indian languages. Valuable works as the science of music (Sangita Sastra) existed in India even before Bharata's Natyasastra. Writers who expanded the science of music subsequent to Bharata are numerous. For any research in Indian music, it is necessary and mandatory for a researcher to consult the great works of the celeberated scholars of the yester years. Sarangadeva, Narada, Matanga, Ahobala, Ramamatya, Govinda dikshitar and Venkatamahi have written valuable works which are frequently consulted by scholars.

However, the origin and development of ragas are to be unearthed with the help of manuscripts and old treatises. Though one may not get the practical version of a composition in a particular raga as it is mentioned or given in a script, it is very important to have a script on a particular piece of music, for it is better to have some record of how the ragas were employed in olden days than have none at all.

In This book, I tried to establish a general fact that the 'Panchaka' or number five is a phenomenon that exists in almost all artistic and scientific fields. In order to study the manifestation of Panchaka in the realm of music especially in ragas and musical compositions, it is necessary to understand the importance and significance of Panchaka in other fields as well. It is really amazing to note that the number five or Panchaka had a very important place and significance from the very beginning. As spirituality is the life blood of Indian life, one has to start any research on Indian culture from religion. To look at the facts from a religious point of view, for Indian music also had a religious or mythological origin. A study or a research of Indian music should necessarily enlarge the conceptual area of scales and compositions.

When we analyze the importance of Panchaka in general, it is better to have a study of the theory of elements, and natural divisions of sound.

It is known to all that the universe is composed of the five elements (The Panchabhutas) and we perceive them separately by five distinct senses (The Panchendriyas). A knowledge of what Panchabhutas are and how they are represented in different facets of life is very desirable for a proper appreciation of various factors in them, as they manifest in the field of music.

In iconography, 'Prithvi' or solidity is represented by a square or a cube; 'Aape' or liquidity by a circle, 'Tajas' or radiation by light, bright objects: 'Vayu' or gaseousness by smoke, a globe etc. and the 'Akasa' or Ether by emptiness (sunya), heavenly bodies like sun, moon etc. The five gunas (qualities) thereby are based on the Panchabhutas which is called 'Panchagunas'. These qualities based on the Panchabutas manifest in almost all fields like religion, philosophy, geography, literature etc. which are dealt with separately in the preceding Chapters. In religious Hindu belief, the Pancha-devatas, viz., Siva, Sakti, Vishnu. Surya and Ganesa (Some-times substituted by skanda and kartikya) were the major deities with varying shades of importance. Some of the finest and most popular 'Stotras' and their accessories are accomdated in the treasure house of Indian Culture. e.g.,

The five slokas:

Tvamēva māta ea pita tāvamēva .... (to Vishnu)

Bāneswarāya nara tearnava tāranyaga.. ... (to Siva)

Bhavabhayaharamēkam ..... (To Rama)

Namo brahmanya devaya ...... (to Krishna)

Namah sāvitre jagadega .... (to Surya)

The Mahabharata and the *puranas* especially like the Vishnu, Padma, Skanda, the Markandeya, and Garuda as much as the tantras have similar types of stotras on the Panchadēvatas.

As Indian music had its origin faced on these religious concepts, it is relevant to study and have a look on the developmental process of these concepts through ages coming to the musical development during the Vedic period, we come across the Sama gana or Saman which had five parts in it. The Saman consisted of five parts, Prastara, Udgita, Pratihara, Upadrava and Nidhana. These five parts of Sama gana called by different names in later days such as Alapana, udgraha, Melapaka or Anugraha, Druvaka and Abhoga. These names had their origin connected to the initiator, the narrator, the priests and the people who participated in the ceremonies like Soma sacrifice (The pressing of the Soma plant, the extraction of juice for the gods). Though the number of notes used in this music varied according to different schools, 'gana' was mostly sung with five notes.

Then we find lots of similarities between the Saman and the early church music e.g., the mode of using hand in both the systems (In both the systems, the singers intonate the musical tunes with the help of five fingers)

The Natya Sastra of Bharata is considered to be the Panchama Veda the fifth veda. It is important to learn how the 'Panchaka' has its various forms of manifestation is the cultural domain of vedas. There are two groups of Upa Vedas. The two groups consist of five Vedas each viz., Natya Veda, Gandharva Veda, Dhanur Veda, Arya Veda and Sthapatya Veda etc. This is explained in the Chapter III of the thesis.

Sangita ratnakara gives us detail description about how Panchaka has manifested in *talas*. The Pancha tala was very popular among the Marga talas mentioned in Sangita Ratnakara. The concept of changing the inner pulse divisions governing tala aksharas in a rhythmic cycle is called 'Gatibhedam'. Again there can be only this ultimate number, five as there can only be five gatis (Pancha gatis) such as Tisra, Chaturasura, Khanda. Misra and Sankeerna. So in the case of jatis in tala there are 5 jatis applicable to any tala. As we got through the way the panchaka has been placed from the very early age of music, we come to know that this is a universal phenomenon that appears in almost all branches of knowledge.

For rhythmic area of music from the early period, we come across the five main classes of Tala as the fundamental components. They can be named as: Duration, Pulse, Silence, Tempo and Pattern. The idea of duration appears to be the most neutral of the five as absolute duration remains in doubt in our minds.

Desi tala mentioned in old treatises had two main divisions, Sasabda and Nisabda. The former is an audible sound and the latter was a mental process measuring an interval between beats in terms of rhythmic units stringed together. These days, in solfa corresponding to the five jatis as Takita, Takadhimi, Tadhinginatom, Takadhimitakita and Takadhimi tadhinginatom.

Next is the group instruments where the five, Panchaka has a significant role. Instruments like Panchakamukha Vadya, Pancha Vadya, Pancha maha sabda ,etc.are dealt with in Chapter III.

We can see that the scale of Samaveda is a descending scale of five notes and is connected with the number 'five'. When we review the relevance of numbers in the sphere of music manifested in different facets of music like, Sruti, Swara, Tala and raga, that the fact division of the modal octave is made of 22 intervals became evident. Musical intervals can be accurately defined by psychological correspondences, such as the emotions and feelings or thoughts that evoke in our minds even when our ears fail to appreciate the difference of intervals by emotional correspondence, with the help of other sources.

The Five Families of Srutis

It is interesting to note that the 22 srutis are divided into five groups families or

Jatis. The five Jatis are defined in Sangita ratnakara and Sangita Parijata as follows:

First Jati:

Dīpta (Shining, illustions) contains the srutis : Raudri, Vajrika, Ugra and Tisra to which correspond the *rasas* or emotional expression. E.g., Marvelous, heroic, furious etc.

Second Jati:

Mrudu (soft) to which the corresponding *rasa* is 'love', and contains the srutis: Ratika, Pritih, Kshitih and Manda.

Third Jati:

Āyata (abundant) of which the corresponding *rasa* is coming and contains the srutis: Krodha, Prasarini, Sandipani, Rohini and Kumudvati.

Fourth Jati:

Madhya (moderate) corresponds to the rasa comic and love and contains the srutis. Chandovati, Ranjani, Marjani, Rakta, Ramya and Kshobhini.

Fifth Jati:

Karuna (compassion) corresponds to the rasa pathetic, alions and terible and contains srutis

Eg. Dayavati, Alapini, Madanti.

After this brief review of srutis, it is worth taking a view how the raga chapters are dealt with by the great writers like Saranga deva, Ahobala, Ramamatya and others in their works.

The ragas and their classification and development and talked about in the preceding Chapter IV. Those ragas mentioned in the treatises seem to be changing through ages until the great musical trinity of Carnatic music thrilled the world of music with the soul stringing compositions which have obviously came down through the lineage of their disciples (sishya Parampara) The ragas were classified into many according to their nature of character coming to the Ghana ragas. We find that from ancient time there was a group of ragas that was called as a group of Ghana ragas. There is a mention about the Ghana ragas that grouped eight ragas in it such as, Nata, Gaula, Varali, Bauli, Sri, Arabhi, Malava Sri and Ritigaula. But non of the present day groups of Ghana ragas take Malavasri in it. Both the groups of Ghana ragas are dealt with in detail in the chapter IV.

The ghana ragas have manifested in different forms of musical compositions even before the advent of the Kritis as we see them employed in many Prabandhas and Tayas etc. Many composers have employed these Ghana ragas to compose their Kritis after the trinity. It is probably due to the status given to Ghana ragas by the great composers like Tyagaraja, today these Ghana ragas have become very popular, especially the primary group of Ghana ragas Nata, Gaula, Varali, Arabhi and Sri. Though these ragas existed even before the trinity, credit goes to the great composers for popularizing these ragas. The Ghana raga pancha ratna of Tyagaraja is an apt example and evidence to confirm the role of composers in popularizing these ragas. In short, ragas all existed from time immemorial but to bring out their colourful images to the world of music, we require the immortal compositions in those ragas which can be made a reality only by the great Vageyakaras (composers). Realizing this ultimate truth the great Vageyakara, Tyagaraja would have felt to sing his immortal song which in turn gave Sri raga a boon of immortality when he sang "Entaromahanu bhavulu antariki Vandanamu": (My salutations to all great souls of the world).

LAKSHANAGITAS

Ragam : Nata — **Aro: S r g m p n s**

Talam : Dsuva Rupaka Talam — **Ava: s n p m r s**

2 Dhrva, 2 Laghus, 1 drulam, 1 laghu, 1 dratam & 1 laghu 24 Aksharas

O	O	14	14	O	14	O	14
			I st Part				
r s	s s	S - n p	s n p m	p m	g m p s	s s	s n p s
A -	re -	ya - na ka	dum - du bi	u da	dhi - le va	ta ru	de va - paru
S -	p m	p s s s	r s s n	p s	s n p s	s r	s n s n
Re -	shi ti	ma md da la	bha - - -	- ra	- na ka	ra na	a thi cha thu
P m	p m	p m g m	p s s s	m m	m r p m	m r	s s n p
ra tha	pa ni	ma dhu ra	na ga ra	ma -	- ghu A ne	- ka	vi no - du
			II nd part				
S -	S -	m m m r	S - m m	p p	n s r d	m m	m r s r
A -	ra -	mu ni ku la	sau nu tha	ma ni	mi ra va le	pa ra	- - pa ra
s s	s n	s n s m	m r S -	m m	m r s s	S -	r S - r
Ru -	- pa	ka - mi ni	- ja na	pau -	- cha ba	na -	bha ga tha
s s	s n	p s S -	s r S -	s n	p m p s	n p	n p s n
su ra	- -	dhe - nu	kam sa	sa ra	- - - -	ru gam	- nam- nam
p s	s r	p m m r	s s s n	p s	s m m r	s r	s s n p
ni tha	pa ri	ku va la ya	- pi - da	ma da	- nu keb	la vi	chi th re vi

Ragam : Arabhi
Talam : Misra jampa

1U O = 10 Aksharas
Aro : S r m p d s
Ava : S n d p m g r s

1_7							U	O		1_7							U	O	
d	s	s	R	-	s	r	m	G	r	p	m	g	r	m	g	r	r	s	s
A	-	-	-	-	ra	bhi	R												
							a	-	ga	lak	-	-	-	sha	na	ma	va	-	chi
S	-	s	R	-	s	r	m	G	r	s	s	r	s	r	m	g	r	R	-
A	-	-	ro	-	-	-	hi	-	-	gau	-	-	-	dha	-	-	-	ra	-
d	d	p	m	p	m	g	r	R	s	s	s	r	s	r	p	m	g	r	r
ni	sha	-	-	-	d	a	ra	hi	ta	ma	va	ra	-	-	hi	-	-	-	-
s	r	p	m	p	m	g	r	R	s	R	-	m	g	r	r	p	m	g	r
pur	-	-	-	-	-	-	ha												
							m	-	-	Au	-	-	-	-	-	-	-	da	va
r	p	m	m	p	m	g	r	R	s	s	n	d	s	s	R		m	g	r
saw	-	-	-	-	pur		na												
							m	-	-	saw	-	-	-	ka	ra		-	-	-
d	d	p	m	p	m	g	r	r	s	r	s	r	p	m	g	r	r	s	s
bha	ra	na	jau		yam		-	-	-	ta	-	-	nam	-	-	-	te	-	shu
s	r	s	m	g	r	r	p	m	p	d	p	m	P	m	g		r	r	s
dai	-	-	-	-	va	ta	ni	sha	-	da	sa	hi	tam	nga			sam	-	-
m	m	p	p	m	p	m	g	r	s	s	r	s	s	m	g	r	m	g	r

A	-	ra	bhi	ka	-	-	-	-	ga	Na	-	-	-	-	-	-	ma	-	ka
S	-	r	m	p	d	m	p	p	d	s	r	s	r	r	m	m	p	p	d
ma	-	-	ka	la	ya	n	-	-	tu	sam	-	-	-	-	-	-	to	-	-
r	M	g	r	S	-	-	p	m	p	R	m	m	p	p	d	-	d	p	m
ga	-	-	na	ve	-		-	-	-	ta	-	-	-	-	-		ro	-	m
d	p	m	p	m	g	r	m	p	d	s	r	s	p	m	d	p	m	d	p
sar	-	-	-	va		tan	-	-	-	thre	shu	ku	sa	la			-	-	-
P	m	g	r	p	m		g	r	r	s	r	s	r	r	m	m	p	d	p
va	-	-	di	sam			va	-	-	dya	nu	va	-	-	-	-	-	di	-
r	M	g	r	d	d		p	M	-	s	n	d	d	p	m	g	r	r	s
vi	va	-	di	ka	li		ta	gee	-	-	-	-	-	-	ta				
															m		-	-	-
d	d	s	s	R			m	g	r	S	r	s	r	m	g		r	R	-
pai	-	-	-	da			-	-	-	lan	va	ya	-	la	ne		-	-	-
d	d	p	m	p	d	d	s	S	-	d	s	n	d	p	m	p	m	g	r
ka	-	-	-	-	-	-	-	-	-	-	-	ra	gu	ru	m				
															ur		-	-	ti
d	d	p	P	m	g	r	r	s	s	n	d	d	p	m	g		r	S	-
Sas	-	-	-	-	-	-	tri												
							j	n	a	vi	ra	chi	ta	mi	ma				
															m		-	-	-

APPENDIX

Chaturdasa Ragamalika of Muthuswamy Dikshitar Vilamba Kala

TALA : ADI

PALLAVI

(1) SRI RAGA

R ; ; R g r S r s n r | s n P ; p n | S n r s n S ‖
Sri vi - - sva na - - - | tham - - bha - ‖ je - - ham - - ‖
n S r m p n s R s n p n S |r S n p m p sd |n p m r r g r s ‖
cha tur da sa bhu va na ru pa ra - ga ma ||| ka bha ra na dha ra | nan - tah - ka ra
nam ‖

(2) ARABHIRAGA:

R mg R S S n d d r s | R P; M | m g R S R; ‖
Sri - ta ja na sam - - sa - - ‖ ra bhi lya | - - - Pa ham ‖

Swarasahltyam

P Mg R s D P m g r | r m -Do- | -Do- ‖
A Dhya tmlka di ta pa tra ya ma no - bhltya | Paham |

(3) GOWRI RAGA:

R ; ; G R ; r s R | r s N S r s | r s r m P ; ‖
Sri vi sa ta - - | kshi - - gau - - | n - - - Sam ‖

Swarasahltyam

s r g R s r M p s n r S d | p m g r S r s | -Do- ‖

sa ka la nishkalaru pa sa - cchida nan| da ma ya gau - - | risam ‖

(4) NATARAGA:

N ; M ; P : M m m R | S N; s n | s r G M ; ‖

chl Tra vi tva na ja ka ka sam ‖

Swarasdhltyam

p Mn P s n R s n p R R | S n p m r n | -Do- ‖

ja gat pra ka sa ka bhaska ra sa san ka | ko ti ko - ti pra | Kasam |||

(5) GAULARAGA:

s r G m R s N s r P m p n S | P n P S n | P N S r s ‖

Go - vin- da di vi nu ta gau - lan - gam | kshira kun den du | kar pu ra di vi ‖

r g M r S S n p -Do- |

ja yabha si lod du lt ta gaulangam |

(6) MOHANA RAGA :

d R S r d s d p | s s g d p g r s ‖

gu ru gu ha sam - mo - | ha na ka iin - gam - ‖

Swarasahityam

P G d d P d r S G R | s P D g p d d | s s g d p g s ‖

Pan chi kri ta pancha ma ha bhu ta | pra pan cha di mo - | ha na ka ra lin - gam ‖

MOHANA (1)

GAULA (2)

d P d G p n g n s d S | r g m R s n s | r m p n P: ‖
vi Rin chi vishnu ru dra murti ma yam | vi sha ya pan cha ka ra | hi tam abha yam ‖

NATA (3)

m R S n p m g m p n p s N | r g r S r s n | s r g r S ‖
ni ra Ti sa ya sukha da ni pu na ta ram | ni ga ma sa ram ml . | sva ram a ma ram ‖

ARABHI (5)

SRIRAGA (6)

a N d P m g r m p d i S; | g r s s n p p m | r o r s n p
n s sma Ra ha rampa ra ma si va ma tu lam | sa ra sa sa da ya hri da | ya ni la ya
ma nisam -

CHARANAM

(7) SAMARAGA:

S D : R R; M ; | D P; M | G r g R; ‖
Sa da si vam sa ma ga na vi nu - tam ‖

Swarasahltyam

p M D d S d P p M; | -Do- | -Do- ‖ pra Krutya di sap ta
ro pa sa | magana | vinulam ‖

(8) LALITARAGA

S; R s n s D M D N | R G M D | M g r S: ‖
san Ma - - - tram - la ti | ta hri da ya | vi dhi - tam ‖

Swarasahltyam

M G R s n d m -Do- | -Do- | -Do- ‖
ma Kro dhati ra hi ta lall | Ta hridaya | vidhitam ‖

BHAIRAVAMRAGA

D: P M g M g m p d | n s G M | D P m g R S ‖
da ka - - sa bhi - - - | - ra vam pu | ra ha ram - - - ‖

Swarasahityam

M d P m m G R s r -Do- | -Do- | -Do- ‖
dhi ka pa la tri sU la dha ra bhai | Ravam pu | raharam ‖

SARANGARAGA:

R g m P M m p d n | S; d s D P | p m R g m r s ‖
sa bhe - - savram - - - | sa ran - - - | ga - dha ram - - - ‖

Swarasahityam

P M p m d P s n R sn | -Do- | -Do- ‖
ru ka va na ta po dha na kal plta | Saran | ram ‖

SANKARABHARANA RAGA:

D s S p m g m g r g m p | S r G m p d | n s r N s d p ‖
da sraya mi san ka -ra - bha ra nam | chin ti dar thavi ta | ra na dhu rinatara ‖

Swarasahltyam **(12) KAMBHOJIRAGA:**

M G r d p -Do- | m g p d r s n d | S n p d S ‖
Ma ni kyama ya Sankarabharangam sa d gati da - ya kam | bho ja charanam ‖

Swarasahltyam

D M P g n d p d r S N | p d g R s n d | - s n -Do- ‖
Dhar mar thadi nikhi la pu ru shar tha | pra da sa mar tha ta ra m bhoja charanam |

Swarasahltyam **(14) BHUPALA RAGA:**

p m D p s d M r S -Do- | p d p g r g G | P g d p g r s ‖
va dan Ya do va kriyakho - la nam | vai - dyalih- ga bhu | pa la pa - la nam - ‖

Swarasahltyam

R g P g d p s D g G r S | D p g r s -Do- | -Do- ‖
sri pu Ra nir - ru ti bha ga gar ttatl | ra sti ra ta ra bhu | Pala palanam |

BHUPALA (14) **DEVAKRIYA (13)**

g r G G r g p d P g g p D | p m r S r m p | d s d m P; ‖
gu ru Ga na sa su ra na re sam a ni sam | ku ja bu dha dl gra ha | ga tl vl nutam

KAMBHOJI (12) **SANKARABHARANAM (11)**

m g r s r g s r n d p d S | r g m P n d p | m g g r G; ‖
va ra da ma na la ra vi sa si na ya nam | va na ja chandra san - | Nibha va da nam |

SARANGA (10) **BHAIRAVAM (9)**

p m r g m r S R g m p d N | s s s r g r s m | d d d p m g m ‖
pa ra ma ham sama - na nda nar ta nam - | pa tl ta pa -va na ka | ra nammada ha ranam |

LALITHA (8) **SAMA (7)**

d m g R s n d M D n s r S | r M d D s D | p P m g R ‖
pa ra ta ram pa ra ma ma no la ya ja yam | pa ra di vak pra ka | sa nanda ma yam ‖

Nava ghana raga malika varnam of Veena kuppaiyar

1_4	O	O
Pallavi .Ragam : Nata		
P p m – m m r s – s n r r s – s n p	S n s r s – m r s	P m r – S r g m
In - - tha - - ko - - pa - -	Me - - - la - -	Ra - - - - -
Pm – pnp – snpmgm – pdns	S snp – snp	Mrs – Srgm
Im – ti - - pai - - ni - - -	Sa - - - ni - -	Ni - - ku - - -
Anupallavi – Ragam ; gaula		
S rp pmgm – rrsn – pnsr	S N – srm – rm	Pn – mp NS
Chem – ta - - je - - ri - - -	Na - - - - nu	- - pam - - ta
P n s Rr – p m g m – r r s n p n	S r s Sn – pn	P – pm – gmrm
Me - - - - la - - - ra - - - sri	Ka - - la – has	- tee – swa – ra -
Chitaswaram -Ragam : varali		
P m – d p m G – g r sn – dpdn	S , - r r s – g r	G M – Pd mg
Grs – ggrg – m pdp nndp	Dns – ndp	Grgm p d p
Chitaswaram -Ragam : Arabhi		
M g r – s r m g r – pmg – rmpd	p-mgr-srmp	Dd pm – pds
Pds Rr – srmgr – Rsnd	P dr S – mpd	P – mgr srm (In)

Charanam Ragam : Sri		
P R – s r s n P – p n s n S	N s r g r s – n p	P m r g r s r m
Pan cha sa – ru – ni ba – - ri	Kor – - va – fa	La - - du ra - -
1) P ; ; N ; M ; P	R ; ; G	, R S R M (pancha)
Narayanan Gaula		
2) pndn – Snd – pdmp-gmrg	Rss – N n d p	N d n – S R m (pancha)
Riti Gaula		
3]N n d m – g r g m – d p m g r s n p	N S – n g r gm	Nndn – nnS
N s g r g m g s – g g m g r – ng r	N s n dm – M	Grs – ngrgm(pancha)
Bowli		
4].Pd – gpd gd – pgrg – rsnd	P D – s r g P	D pd – sndP
Dp – dg – pr – gp – gpdsnd – gr	, snd – r Sn	Dp – d P grg (pancha)
Kedaram		
5]S ; ; - sn Pm – Grsn	S ; ; - sn	Sr – sm gm pn
P S – s mgrs – mGr – srsm	P S n p m G	, m g m p n p s
S m g – g r s R , - s r s n p m g	, r s m g r s r	, r s n p s S
Pm – mg gr – smgm – pssngr	S s n – p m P	Mgr – smgm (pancha)

O	1_4	O	1_4	O	1_4	O	1_4
Ps	S s s m	P n	P m g m	P p	S n p s	S s	s r S
Thga	Taga sam	Gi	Ta gama	Thi	Nava thava	Ta -	Mumire
M	M m m g	M p	M m m r	S s	M m m r	S r	S s r s
Vi	- - - ra	Vita	Ranaguna	Chinte	- nani	Ka -	Madhena
S s	S s n p	S n	P p m m	R g	M p s s	S p	M m s s
Tha -	- nu sita	Samma	- - ma	Vai	- - -	-	Bhavaure
M	M p s p	S n	P s s s	M m	M r s	M m	P p
Vi	Svam thara	- -	Bharava	Dada guga	Dada gugithan	Thai	Tom tom
M p	M r m r	S m	M m m r	S s	M r s r	S n	S m p m
I am	Tom gina	Namgi	Namgina	Thata	Dadaguga ahadog	Ddagugu	Da da da gu gu gu gu
R g	N p s s	N p	M m m s	M m	P p	N p	S s s n
Taka	Taka taka tak tom	Dham	Timikita	Dha -	Hamdhimi	Dhimi	Tam tom
S m	M r s r	S s	N p p r	P s	S ;	;	; ;
Tan	Gi n man	Nam	Ginatemane	Che	Re -	- -	- -
;	; np	S s	M m r s	M	M P	S m	M m m r
	Nakha	Mukha	Mukanita	Vi	- na	Nikva	- - - na
M p	M m m	Sm	S r g	M p	M m n s	M r	S r s s
Dala	Ugamma	Budha	Ja – na	Fo -	Tha thir	Tum	Fu nu

Du	S s n p	P n	P p m m	R g	M p s s	N p	M m r s
Na -	- - ra da	Damtu	Ru kin	Na ti	To - -	Sa	Manatuni
M m	P p N	N p	M p m	G m	P s s	S	P s s s
Ala	Sa- re	Re -	- dala	Da -	Lara -	Re	Vara - -
M g	M p	P n	P p m r	S m	M m m r	S m	S r g
- -	Nika	Siro	- - mani	Bala	- karu	Lakan	- - ni
M p	M m r s	S s	M m m r	P	S s s s	S r	S s n p
Na-	Ra – yan a	Pu -	- - ta	Vi	Dya sm	Ha -	Sana - -
P s	S n p m	P n	P p m g	M p	M m r s	P	P m m g
Dhi -	Sarue	Ya -	- sa -	Ra -	- - - ya	-	Ya dara
P	S s s n	P s	S m r s	N s	M m m r	G m	P s s s
Ya	Tu ma cha	Kuma	Mvem	Krde	Man – tri	Racha	Nava gi -
P p	S n p p	M m	R g m p	N p	M m r s	S s	S m p s
- -	- - - -	Var -	Dha – mtu	Praba	- - - nadha	Trya	Ya – da
M p	M m r s						
Ya	A yya						

Jati – Shadjyodichyava *

Kala	Prastara							
1.	s	s	s	s	m	p	g	m
	sai	-	-	-	be	-	-	-
2.	g	m	p	m	g	m	m	d
	sa	-	su	-	-	-	-	mu
3.	s	s	M	g	p	p	N	P
	sai	-	le	-	sa	su	-	nu
4.	D	N	S	s	D	N	P	M
	pra	ma	ya	-	pra	san	-	ga
5.	D	S	s	s	s	s	s	g
	sa	vi	la	-	sa	the	-	ta
6.	D	D	P	D	P	N	D	D
	na	vi	no	-	-	-	dam	-
7.	s	g	g	g	g	g	s	S
	a	-	dhi	-	ka	-	-	-
8.	N	D	P	D	P	D	D	D
	mu	-	dhe	-	-	-	-	udu
9.	s	s	M	g	p	p	N	D
	a	dhi	ka	-	mu	dhe	-	ndu
10.	D	N	S	S	D	N	P	M
	na	ya	nam	-	na	ma	-	mi
11.	y	S	S	s	s	s	s	g
	de	-	va	-	sv	re	-	sa
12.	D	D	P	D	N	M	M	M
	la	va	m	chi	ram	-	-	-

*** Nyasa – Madlyama, Apanyara – Shadja & Dhaivata**

JATI – SHADJI *

Raga – Varadi **Tala- Shatpitaputrakam**

Kala	Prastara							
1.	s Tam	s -	s bha	S Va	P La	nd la	P -	dn da
2.	R Na	gm ya	g nam	G Fn	S Ja	ng -	ds -	D dhi
3.	rg kam	S -	R -	G -	S -	s -	S -	s -
4.	D Na	D ga	N sn	Ns -	Nd Nu	P pra	S na	s Ga
5.	N Ke	D -	P li	Dn -	R Sa	g mu	S -	g dbha
6.	S Vam	D -	dn -	P -	S -	S -	S -	s -
7.	S sa	S na	g sa	S Kni	M Ta	P ti	M la	M ka
8.	S Pam	g -	M -	Dn Ka	Nd Na	P le	G pa	rg -
9.	g nam	g -	g -	G -	S -	s -	S -	s -

* In shadji, shadjam is nyasa and gandhara and panchama are apanyasas.

JATI – SHADJA MADHYAMA *

Raga : Varadi

Kala	Prastara							
1.	M	g	Sg	P	dp	M	nd	nm
	Ra	ja	ni	Va	dhu	-	mu	kha
2.	M	M	s	rg	mg	nd	pd	P
	Vi	la	-	sa	lo	-	-	cha
3.	M	g	R	g	M	M	s	S
	nam	-	-	-	-	-	-	-
4.	M	mg	M	M	nd	pd	pm	gmm
	Pra	vi	ka	si	la	ku	mu	da
5.	D	pd	pr	ng	mg	ng	sds	S
	Da	la	fe	na	sa	-	-	nmi
6.	Nd	S	mgm	M	M	M	M	-
	bham	-	-	-	-	-	-	-
7.	M	M	mgm	md	dp	pd	pm	gmg
	Ka	-	mi	ja	na	na	ya	na
8.	D	pd	pr	ng	mg	ng	sds	S
	hsu	da	ya	bhi	na	-	-	ndi
9.	M	M	dn	ds	dp	mp	f	F
	nam	-	-	-	-	-	-	-
10.	M	mgm	M	nd	pd	pmg	g	M
	Pra	na	ma	-	ma	de	-	vam
11.	D	pd	pr	rg	mg	rg	sds	S
	Ku	mu	da	dhi	va	-	-	si
12.	Nd	S	R	mgm	M	M	M	M
	nam	-	-	-	-	-	-	-

* Shadja and madhyama are nyasa swaras and all the swaras are apanyasas. Used in dhruvaganas.

The ghana raga gitas

(Author unknown)

Raga: Nata

Tala : Eka

Aro: S r g m p d n s

Ava: S n p m r s

1_4				1_4				1_4				1_4			
s	s	s	n	p	s	S	n	p	m	g	m	p	s	s	n
A	ma	ri	-	ka	ba	Ri	-	bha	-	-	ra	bra	ma	ri	-
p	n	s	r	s	s	S		p	n	s	r	m	r	s	r
mu	ka	ri	-	kru	-	tham		du	-	ri	-	Ka	ro	-	Thu
s	s	s	n	p	n	S	r	p	s	n	P	m	m	r	s
du	ri	tham	-	gau	-	Ri	-	cha	ra	na	-	pan	-	ka	jam

Ragam : Gaula

Talam : Rupaka

Author: Paidala gurumurthy shastri

Aro: S r m p n s

Ava: s n p m r g m r s

O		1_4				O		1_4			
R	-	r	s	n	s	r	m	R		r	S
Sri		Ra	-	-	ma	ch	an	-		d	ra
m	r	p	m	g	m	r	g	m	r	r	S
Sa	-	ke	-	-	tha	pu	ra	va	-	-	sa
s	r	r	s	n	P	n	s	R		r	s
mu	ni	ja	na	ma	-	na	sa	ham		-	sa
p	m	p	r	R	s	r	r	m	m	g	m
ni	ki	la	lo	-	ka	pa	-	la	na	dhu	-
r	r	r	s	N	s	r	r	r	s	r	m
ri	-	-	-	-	na	Ka	u	sal	-	ya	-
s	n	s	r	M	r	p	m	r	r	S	-
bh	ag	-	-	-	ya	R	u	-	-	pa	-
R	-	m	m	P	-	p	p	m	g	M	-
wa	-	sa	ra	the	-	pu	-	ra	ya	me	-
r	r	m	g	M	-	r	m	r	r	S	-
Va	ue	ch	am	-	-	ta	va	n	am	they	-

O		1_4				O		1_4			
R	m	r	p	p	m	r	s	m	r	p	m
Pa	-	tha	ka	ma	la	ma	ni	s	am	-	-
R	m	p	n	m	p	s	r	m	p	n	s
K	ra	pa	-	lo	-	ga	-	na	pa	ni	thi
S	r	m	r	m	p	n	s	n	p	m	
Ma	-	Ka	la	ya	-	mu	da	ma	thu	lou	-
R	p	m	r	g	m	r	s	m	r	r	s
De	-	hi	-	me	-	le	ho	-	-	-	-
S	r	r	s	n	p	m	p	r	r	r	s
Swa	-	-	-	min	-	pa	-	la	ya	mo	u
R	r	p	p	m	m	r	m	r	r	S	
Gu	ru	mur	-	-	thi	na	-	ma	ka	m	-

Ragam : Arabhi **Aro : s r m p d s**

Talam : Tisra Triputa **Ava : s n d p m g r s**

(Author –unknown)

1_3			O		O		1_3			O		O	
P		p	m	m	P		m	g	r	s	r	m	g
Re	-	re	Sri	-	Ra	-	-	-	ma	ch	an	-	-
r	R	s	d	d	R	s	R	-	,	R	-	s	r
-	-	-	-	-	-	-	dra	-	-	-	-	ra	ghu
m	G	r	r	s	S	-	p	m	m	P	-	P	-
v	am	sa	ti	la	ka	-	Ra	g	ha	ven		dra	-
p	M	p	m	g	r	r	m	g	r	s	r	s	s
A	-	-	-	-	-	-	-	-	-	-	-	-	-
d	D	r	s	r	s	s	d	S	-	d	d	d	p
A	-	-	-	-	-	-	-	-	-	chri	ta	ja	va
p	M	p	d	s	S		r	s	r	m	g	r	r
po	sh	a	ka	-	re	-	s	ee	-	tha	-	-	ma
m	G	r	m	m	p	m	P		p	P		P	
no	-	-	ra	m	ja	na	Re	-	re	dhi	-	ra	-
p	m	p	d	s	s	r	m	g	r	s	r	s	s
Ra	-	va	na	-	sa	ra	Am	-	tha	Ka	-	re	-
d	D	r	s	r	s	s	d	S		d	d	d	p
A	-	-	-	-	-	-	-	-	-	-	-	-	-
P	m	p	d	s	S	-	S	-	s	d	d	d	p
-	-	-	ge	ya	re	-	dee	-	na	ja	na	ma	n
p	m	p	m	g	r	r							
da	-	ra	Ma	-	ma	va							

Ragam : Sri **Aro : S r m p n s**

Talam : Chaturasra Dhruva **Avo : s n p m r g r s**

1_4				0		1_4				1_4			
m	m	P		P		n	p	n	n	S			S
Me	-	na	-	shi	-	ja	ya	Ka	-	Ma			shi
e										k			
g	r	s	s	n	p	m	p	n	n	S			S
K	am	ka	ti	-	ka	va	-	ma	-	shi			-
R		g	r	S		R		S		s	s	n	p
A	-	pra	ti	ma	-	pro		bha	-	von	-	na	ta
p	s	n	p	s	n	p	m	p	n	p	p	M	
ma	dhu	ra	ma	dhu	ra	sa	-	la	w	ka	-	ra	-
R		M		P		n	s	R		r	g	r	s
om		ka		ra	-	ka	ki	ta		la	-	p	a
R	-	p	m	,	p	r	p	p	m	r	g	r	s
gud	-	da	ma	-	tha	ma	d	hu	kai	-	-	ta	bha
g	r	s	s	n	p	n	p	p	m	r	g	r	s
s	n	p	m	n	s	r	m	m	p	n	p	p	m
R	-	p	p	m	r	r	g	r	s	S	-	S	-
Kar		ti	ke	-	ya	ja	na	ni	-	Re	-	Re	-
R		r	g	r	s	n	s	r	g	r	r	s	n
Ka		tya	-	ya	ni	Ka	-	li	ru	dra	-	-	ni
P		N		S		m	p	n	n	S		S	
vee		na		ni	-	Kva	-	-	-	-		ni	-
n	s	r	g	r	s	s	r	s	s	n	p	m	p
Ka	-	ru	na	Ka	ra	na	Kha	si	Kha	ram	-	ja	ya
p	n	P		M		p	p	m	r	r	g	r	s
ma	dhu	ra	-	la	-	pa	-	-	-	pri	ya	re	-
r	p	m	r	p	m	r	m	m	p	p	s	s	n
A	yi	ya	ti	ge	ya	A	yi	y	am	va	yi	-	ya
P	s	n	p	s	n	p	n	s	r	r	g	r	s
A	yi	ya	ti	yi	ya	A	yi	ya	w	va	yi	-	ya
n	s	r	m	p	n	p	p	m	r	r	g	r	s
-	-	-	-	-	-	-	-	-	-	-	-	-	-
S		s	n	n	p	d	n	p	m	r	g	r	s
Ch		ka	na	-	tha	Sa	-	-	mi	ja	ya	re	-
ok													

Raga : Varali — **Aro : s g r g m p d n s**

Tala : Rupakam — **Ava : s n d p m g r s**

Author – T.S. Raghavan

O		1_4				O		1_4			
P	M	G	G	R	S	G	;	M	;	P	;
Nee	ra	jak	-	shi	-	Ka	-	Ma	k	shi	-
D	N	S	N	D	P	P	M	G	R	S	;
Ni	khi	La	lo	-	Ka	Sak	-	-	-	shi	-
G	;	G	M	P	M	P	M	D	;	P	;
A	-	nau	-	tha	ka	ta	k	-	-	Shi	-
P	D	N	D	P	M	D	P	D	N	S	;
Ak	hi	La	lo	-	ka	sak	-	-	-	shi	-
G	;	;	G	R	S	S	N	S	R	S	;
ka	-	-	ran	-	ya	tak	-	-	-	shi	-
S	N	N	D	P	M	P	M	G	G	R	S
ka	ra	na	-	-	ka	tak	-	-	-	-	Shi
Madyamakala											
G	R	G	M	P	M	D	P	D	N	S	N
kan	-	chi	ka	mak	shi	ka	si	vi	sa	lak	Shi
D	G	R	S	N	D	P	M	G	R	G	M
Ma	thu	rai	mee	nak	shi	sak	ti	ka	tak	-	shi

Lakshana Gitas in Ghana ragas

Raga: Gaula **(U U O O U U = 8 Aksharas)**

Tala: Rupaka Dhruva Talam **Aro : S r m p n s**

Ava : s n p m r g m r s

U	U	O		O		U	U
s	n	p	n	s	r	r	m
sa	ka	la	su	ra	-	su	ra
r	s	n	s	r	p	m	r
ri	Ri	-	ta	ma	ni	ki	va
g	m	r	s	n	p	m	p
-	na	Nee	-	ra	-	ji	tha
r	r	s	n	p	p	m	m
cha	ra	-	na	ya	ga	-	lu
r	m	p	s	S		s	-
Kau	-	va	nu	re		-	-
s	,	r	r		S	n	P
re	-	bh	ak	ta	-	ja	na
m	r	g	m	r	s	r	m
ma	no	-	-	ra	dha	pa	la
p	n	p	n	s	r	r	m
da	-	-	-	-	-	-	-
r	s	r	p	m	r	g	m
ya	ka	li	ki	ku	ma	-	-
r	s	n	p	m	p	r	r
ra	ka	ka	-	-	la	bha	ya
s	n	p	p	m	m	r	m
ni	-	va	-	ra	nu	kau	-
p	s	S	-	S	-	s	,
va	nu	re	-	-	-	re	-
s	n	p	n	s	r	r	m
che	-	sha	-	cha	la	ni	va
r	s	n	s	r	p	m	r
-	-	-	sa	Sri	-	vem	-
g	m	r	s	n	p	m	p
-	ka	te	-	-	-	-	sa
r	r	s	n	p	p	m	m
na	mo	-	-	na	mo	-	-
r	m	p	s	s	-	s	,
kau	-	va	nu	re	-	re	-
s	n	p	n	s	r	r	m
sa	ka	la	su	ra	-	su	ra

Ghana Raga panchakam

Katakam : Nata

Aro : S r g m p n s
Ava : s n p m r s

I	G M P N ; S ; S ;
II	m p n p n - s s n p p n - s n p n p - m m p n p - g m p m p n p m - g m p n p p - m p n p n s N S ; s ;
III	p n S r r S n n p r r s - n p n - s s n n p - m m r r s - p p m m r r s p m m p - n p p n - s s r r s s - p p s s n n - p p n n p p - m m p p m m r r s - s s n n p - p p n n s s r s - m m p p n n s s - s s m m r s - r r s s N S ; S;

II **Ragam : Gaula**

Aro: s r m p n s
Avo : s n p m r g m r s

1) R , r, S R , - S r s r – r s r – S s n p – m p n s R ; s ; //
R , r s R , S r s r – R r s R – p n s R – m p n s R p n S R ; S ; //

2) r m r r S n p – r p m R s n p – n s R – p m R –
n p m R – s n p m R – r s n p m R – m r s n p m R s ; s ; //

III **Arabhi**

Aro : s r m p d s
Ara : s n d p m g r s

1) R m g R – S r s n d – s r m g R – r p m g R
- d p m g R – R m p d P m g R – s r m g r s n d -
d r R s ; s ; //

2) R m g R – S s n d – s r m g R- r d p m g r -
s n d p m R – r m m p d p m g R – p d s n d
P m g R – d s r s n d p m g R – s n d – r s r –
d d s s r s n d – d s n d – p d s n d – R ; S; //

IV Ragam : Varali

Aro : s g r g m p d n s
Avo : s n d p m r g r s

1) g r S r – g g – g r s n – d d g g – g r s – s n s -
d n s – d n s – d d – g g – g m p d p – p m g – M g r s –
n d n s – D n s R S ; //

2) g r s r – g g – m p d p m – p d n d – N s r s -
n s r r s m – g g – g r s – g r s – r r s – n s r r s n -
d n s n d p – m p d m p – N d p m – g r s n S ; S ;

V Ragam : Sri

Aro : s r m p n s
Ava : s n p m r g r s

1) R g r S – N s r S – n s r g r s – n n s – n s n p m -
N s – N s – N – S ; S ; //

2) R ; g r R – r r g r – r s s n – S r g r r s n -
R p m R – n p m R – r g r – R r – s r s S s -
N n s – n n s – n n s – n s r s n P – R r g r s
S s r g n – N n s n p – M p n s r – m p n r s -
p n S s – n s r g r s n p – N n – S s – n n s -
s n p m p n S ; S ; R ; S; //

Jatiswaras without Swarapallavi Composed by T. S. Raghavan.

I Ragam : Nata **Aro: s r g m p n s**

Talam : Adi **Ava : s n p m R s**

	1_4	O	O
1)	S ; ; S N P P M P M R ; S N P N	G; M P S ; ; R	N P M G G M P N (S)
2)	s r s N , - n s n P – m p n s r s R s N – s r g m r – S n p n	S ; ; s n s N p m r – S	p M – g m p m n S – r g m p n (S)
3)	P ; ; m p n p m – g m p n P ; ; m p N ; ; n s S r – m R s n p – m p n s R- s n	p ; ; m p R ; ; s r , p m r – m p m	Np – m g m p n N ; ; p n r s – r g m p n (S_
4)	N ; ; p n s n p – m g m p s N n p p m – p s S – s n n p p r G m r s N , - n r s n p m, - p , S N P m – p , - S N p	N , - R s n s R – r s – s n – n p s n p m R, - s , M r S, - r	R s – s n p m p m p n s – R , r r g m p N, r , g M P n (S)

II Ragam : gawla **Aro: s r m p n s**

Talam : Adi **Avo: s n p m r g m r s**

	1	O	O
1)	S ; P N P M g M	R ; , S n	R , - s r m p n (S)
2)	s N- r s m p n – S n p m g m	r R – p M – n p	, r s n p m p n (S)
3)	S , - r g m r s – R, - n s r s n	p , n p m g m	R , - s n p n s
	R s – m r p m p – N p – m p n s r	S , - n p , m	R , - s r m p n (S)
4)	r s – m r – p m – n p – n n r s R, r	S n p m g m r s	R , - s r m p n (S)
	r s – m r – p m – n p – n n r s R , r	S n p m g m r s	R , - s r m p n (S)

III Ragam : Arabhi **Aro : S r m p d s**
Talam : Adi **Ava: S n d p m g r s**

1	O	O
1) D ; ; p d d p m g r s - r m	P ; ; d p	M g r – S r m p (D)
2) s r m g - r s n d - s r m p d p m	p d s n – d p m g	r s n – d s r m p (D)
3) D p – m p d – p d s n d p m g r s m p d s – r m g r – s n d p d s – r s	n d r s – m g r p , n d p – d P m	M g r – d s r m p g r – d s r m p (D)
4) p p m g – r r m g r s – s r m p d s	d s r – m g r s n	d p m g r s R
m g r – p m g r – d p m g r – s n d p	m g r – r s n d p	M g r – d s r m p(D)
5) m g r S-d p m P-s n d S – r	s n d p – m g r s	r m p d s r - ,
g r s n D, drsnd P, - m	d p m g R , r	p m g r – s r m p (D)

V Ragam : Sri **Aro: S r m p n s**
Talam : Adi **AVO: s n p m r g r s**

1	O	O
1) p , n p m – r g r S n s r	S , n s r g r	, s – n s r m p n (P)
2) P , - n p m p n – P , - n s n p m	P , - s r m p n	p , - r s n p m (P)
3) P N – m p n – r m p N – s r m p	N – n s r m p n	, - r s – s n – n p m (P)
4) p n n p m p – p s s n p n – p r r s	N s – r g r – s r s	n s n – p m p n s
R , - g r s n p – N s – s , r	S n p m – P N	s , n p m p n (P)
5) S ; ; r g r s n – p n s n p	N ; ; m p	n & n – p m r gr
S ; ; m r – p m – n p – s n – m p	R ; ; r g	r r s n p m p n
S – r g r s n p – N – s r s n p m	P – n s n p m r	r m p n s ;
r g r – s R s N ; - s r s – n	S N p ;	p s n – p N p m (P)

IV Ragam : Varali **Aro : s g r g m p d n s**

Talam: Adi **Ava: s n d p m g r s**

1		O	O
1)	S ; ; S N D P M R S ; R S N D N	g : g D g R g M	D p m g P ; D N (S)
2)	s r s N , - n s n D-n s r g r g r s N, - r s n D-n s r s n	S ; ; s n g r s n d – N	d p m – g m p d n d p m – g m p d n (S)
3)	P ; ; d n d p m – g m p d n P ; ; d n D ; ; s r R s n – DNS, g r s n d	S ; ; d n N ; ; n s r ; , r s n d p	s N – r s n d n N ; , g r s ; , g m p d n
4)	S ; ; g r – s N – d p m p d S ; ; g r – m g – p m – dp-nd S r g g r s – n s r r s n – d p d n r s n –snd-ndp-rssn-ndp	P ; ; n d Srg-nsr-dn G r s – r s n – sn Ndp – dpm – gr	p Mg r s n r S – pdn – mpdn D – g r r s – s n d S – srgm pdn (S)

Ragam : Nata **Aro : s r g m p n s: PatnanSubramanya**
Talam : Adi **Avo: s n p m r s**

1	O	O
	Pallavi	
P M – R ; s n s r s s n p	p n s r g m – s m	m r s – m s r g m
pa lu ma ru - - - nin - -	Ne - - ko - - ri - -	Yan na Na - - pai
P m g m – r g m r s – m g m p d n	S , s n p P	, m r s – s r g m
P a m - - ta - - - me – la - -	Je - - - se	- vu - - ra - - -
	Anupall	
N p p n – p p m g – m p m – rg m rs	M g m – p n p – s n	P – g m p d n s
G - - - la - - - lo - - - ve - -	La - - ya - - sri	- se - - - sha
N s r g – m r s – sr s s n p – d n	S r s – n p p	M r s – n s r g m
Cha – la ni – va – sa - - - - -	Sri – vew –	ka - - te - - sa
	Chittaswaram	
P m r s – n p m r s – m r s – s r s	N s – p p m r – r	G m r s m g m p
Sar – va - - - - low - - -	Ma – nan – ne	- la – ko - - ra
1) S , N , p ; M R S	R , N , S	; r g m p d n (sarva)
2) s n p M-g m p n – P m r s n p	D n s R – n s r	G M – p m p d n(sarva)
3) s n p – p m g m p – np m –r g m r s G m r s – n p d n (sarva)	M g m – p d n s r	
4) sp – n p n p m – g m p m – r s n p	R S – n s r g m	P d n s n – p d n
S r g M r s n – r S n – p d n s	R N – s p – n m	, p m – g m p d n (Sarva)

Ragam : Gaula | **Aro: S r m p n s**
Talam : Adi | **Ava: S n p m r g m r s**
Composer: Veena Kuppier

14	O	O

Pallavi

R g M – r s n s R – r r s s n p – n s r m r p p m g M – r r s
Che li mi ko - - ri rach chi - - yan- - - na - - - - de
R S – n s r s – r m m r – p m n p p m g m – r g m r r s n s – R S
Chita – mu - - - - - - - na - - - - - du bhag - - - - - - - - yamu

Anupallavi

P m n p – p m g m – r r m m p, - p p m – n n p – s n s n – p m M – r g m
Sa – la – li - - - ta - - gu na - - sri – lo - - - - - - - la - -
R m r m p n – p s n – m r r s – n r s s r s s – n n p p m p m – r g m r s
Sa – ra – sa - - - - - sri - - - - - veu - nu - - - - go - - pa - - - la

Chihaswaram

R r s s n s – r g m – r r p m –n p m g m – r s r – n s r s r m r – p m g m
R r m – r r p – m m n – p p s – n r s s, n p m – p m g , M – R s n s (che)

Charanam

S s n – n n p – p m g m r s – N ; S r – m g m r p m – g m r r s
Em – chi – chu da — ni sariga - - - - - - du – ra –

1) N ; ; S ; ; R ;	; M ; R	; P M R (Emchi)
2) N , s r s – ns r, - r s n s r	Mr- pmnp-sn	R s s n p n p r (Emchi)
3) p n p m – p m g m – r s r –	mpn-pns-ns	rs-mr srmp
nrsnp	s Sn – p Pm	r R s – rmpn (Emchi)
nnppm-snmpns-pns-rr		
4) S , - rrsns – rrm – rpm M	p m p n mprm	s r n s – rg M
mpn-mp-rmp –pns – np mpn	s r m –sr nsr	nrs – pnsmr (Emchi)
5) R ; ; - R ; - s n p m r s	R , R , r m	rpm n – p s n s
m r s – n s r s n p m – r g m r s n	s r m p n –r m	ns –m p n s R
s r m - n s r - pns-mpn-rmp-n	P	s-rmr-nrpr
	s – r m r – nr pr	(Emchi)

Ragam : Arabhi **Aro: S r m p d s**

Talam : Adi **Pallavi : Doraiswamy** **Avo: S n d p m g r s**

14	O	O
	Pallavi	
R mg R – sr S , n D D	P – mpd ssr	D ssr –mgr
Sa ra – si - - - ja – mm	Khiro - - - -	Ni - - - ku - -
d p mgr – s R snd – ssrr	M g r r – s s d r	R ; - S ;
sa ri - - - yev - - - - - - -	- - - va - - -	re - - - - -
	Anupallavi	
d d p – mpmgrr-mg r r s s	D s d – Rr – S	r r m g r – m m p
Pa – ra mat - - - mu - - -	dai – na – sri	- - - - su - - - -
r p m g r r – ddp P – snddp	Mp mgrr-mp	Ds - ds - S ;
Brah - - - man - - ya - - -	De - - - - ni	- - - - pai
Ddss R – srmgr – R snd	Dp – mp-drr	Dss – pdd-mp
Ma - - - ru - - - la - - -	Ko - - ni cha - -	- - - - - la
Rp mgr – mgr Rr – pdrpd	S – r m p d s d p	M g r s – d s r
Pa – ra - - va - - - su – dai	- yum - - -	Da - - ga - -
	Chittas waram	
Mgrr-pp mgrr-ddp pm	Mgr-R-snd	, s s r – srM
Gr – mmp – R mm p – snd – rsr	Mgr – dp – r p m	G r – m m p ;
M g r r S, - d R – S m – rp	Mddp – d s s	Nd – dRa – sr
Mgr R – srss – dRr – rm	P d s – dd p	M g r S – dsr (Sa)
	Charanam	
R S – D ; D D – P ;	Mp ds – sddp	Mp mgr – mpd
Na li nak – shi - - -	Nin - - - - - - -	Nem - - - - tho -
1) R S ; - D ; - P ; - M	G , - R, S	; r M p D
D, s – S, r – M, g – R s	, n D – P, m	G R, mdp (nali)
2) S n dd p p – m g r s – r p m g r s	S n d – rrs – mg	r-pmp D;
Mpds nd – r r s – mg R – rss	Drr Ss – dd	Pp –mgr-mpd (nal)
3) R ; ; r s n d p p – m g r s	R ; ; m g	R – p m d p – snd
Rmp Dd – mpd S s – d R r	S s r – S r s n	D R r – s s n d
S s r R – m g r – mg r Rs – s	R s n d – D p p	M – p d Rr – pd
S s – rmp Dd – RrSs-d	D p mgrs – mg	Rr – pd Rr-pd (nali)q
5) ddpp – mgrr-mgr-rssnd	Rrs – mgr-pp	Mgr - mgr sr
Mpdd pp – mgrs – rmmppd	Rr mgr – pm-d	Dp mp-dsnd
Dd ssr – ssrsnd – rssnd	Rsr-mgr-sr	Mgr-srsnd
Rrs – snd – snddp – mpd – mp	Ds dp - mgrs	Nd – rsr mpd (nali)

Ragam: Varali **Varanam** **Aro : S g r g m p d n s**
Talam : Athi (39th yanya) **Aro : s n d p m g r s**
Com: govindasamy Iyya

14	O	O
Pallavi		
P ; ; - p ; mp dd m	D p mgr – gmp	Dpm-grgrs
Tho - - ya – jak - - shi	- - ro – va -	Ni - - ki – di—
S, g r r s n – d r s – g r g m p	D , - N d p m	Gr – rggrsn
Nya - - - ya – man n a- tan	- - - - - - - - -	Ma - - - - -
Anupallavi		
D p m – grs – sndpm – grgmp	D Nd – pdmp	DpdnS-dn
To - - ya - - jath – ri ram – ga	Dai - - ya - -	Gim - - to - -
Srg – grs grr s n d p m – pd	N s r – ndp-mp	Dpm-grrsn
Ma - - - ta – la - - jik - - ki	- - - yun – na	Da - - ta - - ne
Chittaswaram		
S g r s n s – p m g r s – d p m g r	Nd-d N – dpm	G r g m P ;
D M G R g – m p D – M pd	Dn ns – s Nn	D p m – pdn S
D n s r – S , r – r g g r S, g	R s n – s r s n	D n n s – s N n
N d d p – m p d –d n n – S n d p	M g r – g m p d	N d p m – g r s n (tho)
Charanam		
N ; ; dn ddp – sn d p m	P ; ; dp	Mgr – gm p d
Nin – nu – la – ya - - -	Na - - ni	Na - - to – na ne
1) P, - D m g r – r g g r S , - G	R s n – d n S,	D g – r g m p d (ni)
2) Dn – dn dpm – DM G – rr	G gr –rs –ns	S rr G-grg
MpgRg –mpd M pdndn	Snd-pmg	G r – r G m p d (ni)
3) p d m g – d d m g r – g m p d m g r	Pmg-grr-gg	rr-sgrndn
Sgrs-dpmgr-gmpdnsg	R N – dnd pm	G , r g m p d (ni)
4) m p d N – dpm – grg – G M p	D n p d – p m g r	G g r r S ;
G r s n d p – m P d n S , d n	D, -G g r g	M p d – n d p m
G r g m P ; - d p m g r – g m p	D – m p d – rs –dn	S – Gg – gr K
G g r r s – n d p m – pdn S, r	N d p , d m g	R, G m p d (ni)
5) d n s ; n d p m g r – r g g r	S , d n s r g	R r s n – d p m p
D n S ; - d n D – G g r g m	M d N, d p m	G r g m p ;
D p m g r – g m p d – m p d n s – dn	S G g r R g	M g – g R ;
G g r r s – n d p m – pdn S ;	R – n d ; d	Mgr – gmpd (ni)

Ragam : Sri (22 mela)
Talam : Adi

Aro : S r m p n s
Ava : S n p m r g r s

14	O	O
R G g r s – s r s s – np mp	N s r G r – m p	M R – g r s n s
Em – du – kim – ta ——	Mo — di — je—	- Se - - ra - -
R m p N p m – rg R – m p n s r	S n – p d n P	M – R g r s n s
E - - mine - - ra – mu - - -	Ra - - na – pai	Vala - - -
	Anupallavai	
P , - npm – M , p m r – r g r s	N N p m – r g r	S N – s r m p n
Sum ta - - Ran - - - gu - -	Dai - - -	Na – sri - - -
S n p – Rr – g r s N p m - p n n	S r G r s – N	P m – r g r s n s
Su - - da – ra - - va - - ra - -	Nan - - - ne	Lu – ko - - ra
	Chittaswaram	
R G r s N , - r s n p m p n	S r g – S s – rm	P n p m – r g r s
R m p N p m – p n S – r g r s n	R N p m – p d n	P m – R g r s(Emdu)
	Charanam	
N S , p s – n P m – r g r s	N s r g – r s r m	P N s – n p m p
Neesa – te - - va - - run - -	Na - - - - - ri - -	- - da ra – lo -
1) N P ; ; M ; ; - R G R	S N ; ; P	N S, r m p (Nee)
2) n s r S n pd – n pm – rgrs	N p n S-r m p	N s r g – r s n p (Nee)
3) n p m r g – s r g – n s r s – n p n s	R g r s r – n s r	M p n – s r s n p(Nee)
4) sp – mp n p m – rgs R-snp	G R-nsr p m	N P – s n p m p
Nsr Gr – p m r G r – s n p n	S r g – S n p m	R g r s – r m p (Nee)

Ragam : Nata
Talam : Eka

Aro : S r g m p n s
Ava : s n p m r s
Composer : muthuswamy dikshithar

1_4	1_4
1) M P ; M – m g p m R, s Ma ha ga n a- pa thi	S S S ; S r G m Mana sa smara – mi
2) P N P, M mg pm R, s Ma – ha ga na p a- thi -	Mg pm R, s S sr G M M a – n a- sa – smara—ni
3) g m p n s n p m m g p m r s Ma – ha - - - ga – n apa – thi	G m p n s n p m Ssr GM Ma – na – sa - - - smara – mi
4) g m p n s r – m r s n p m R, s M a – ha - - - ga – na – pa – thi-	G m p r s n p m r s – s r G m Ma – na – sa - - - sma – ra - - mi
5) g m p – p n s – m r s n p m r r S Ma - - - ha - - ga – na – pa thi Mpn sn – np Pm srgm Vasshta vama de vathi vandita Samashti charanam	R r s – n n p – r r s – r s n p m g m Ma - - na - - sa - - sma – mi (Mahaganapathi)
1) g m p N p – p n s N s s Ma – ha - - de - - vasutam	; S S R – S N S ; Gu ru gu ha nu tam
2) sn p m g m p n S – N S S Ma – ha - - - de - - vasutam	; S S R – S N S ; Gu ru gu ha nu tam
S r G M – m r m r S ; p n Ma - - ra ko - - - ti – pra	S, n p , m m g p m R, s Ka - - sam – san - - tam -
Madyamakalam	
M P m p R s S r g m P Maha kavya Nata kadi Priyam	P m n p s n r s r r s N p M Mu – shika va hana mo do ka priyam (Mahaganapathi)

Ragam : Gaula
Talam : Adi

Aro : S r m p n s
Ava : s n p m r g m r s

1_4	O	O
	Pallavi	
1) S ; S R M M P ;	N P ; M	G M R S
Tya ga ra ja pa -	La pa sn	Mam – sni -
2) s r S – r s – R M M r m p	P n s – r s n p m	P m g m – R s
Jya – ga – ra – ja pa - -	La - - ya – sn -	Mam - - sni -
3) p m g m r s s r M r m P ;	R m p n s n p m	P m g m R s
Jya - - - ga – Ra - - Ja - - pa -	La – ya - - - sn -	Mam - - sri nit
S ; S N P S R S	R , M P n	N po r g m r s
Ya – nan – da kan – da	So - mas kanda	Vethividanga
Samashti chasanam		
1) R ; P p m M R G M	S R S ;	N S R M
Na – ga ra - - ja mani	Bhu – pha	Las – kru ta
2) sr sr pm – pm M R G M	P m g m R S	S r p m G M
Na - - - ga o Ra – - ja mani	Bhu - - sha	Lan - - kruta
S R M ; R N P ;	M G R – P	M – P ; p
Na ga ra – ja su tar	Dan – ga gau	- lan ga
P N S ; R ; R S	S R G M	S R SS S
Bho – ga di – prata	Sri - an ga	Ras – ti ta
R ; S S ; N P M	R ; G ;	M S R S
Bhu su ra di nu ta	Val – mi -	Ka lin – ga
R r s – n p N – s r n s – r g m	Rm r p m n p	P n r n S s
Sri gu ru gu n ap u j I t a vrnphatu ranga	Chrula jana nkksanb	Ni pu nam la ryag
S n p m p n s r g m r s n M p	R s n r S n	P – r g m R s
Bha – gi guta charana kara hruta kmu ranga	Yo gi vi di ta ja	Pa nata m ranga(Tyagaraja)

Ragam : Arabhi **Aro: S r m p d s**

Talam : Rupaka **Ava: s n d p m g r s**

Dikshitar

O	14	O	1
P ;	M p M m g r s	R ;	S r s S d r s
Sri -	Sa – ras - - wa -	Ti - -	Na – mos tu - -
R ;	; ; d s r m	P ;	M p d p m g r s
Te - -	- - va r ade -	Sri -	Sa – ras - - vva -
R ;	S r s S d r s	S r m g	R ; d d P
Ti -	Na – mos - - - tu -	Te - - -	- - pa – ra
P ;	P m g r s r m	P d s n	D d p p m g r s
De -	Va – te - - - -	Sri - - -	Sa – ras - - - wa -
R ;	S r s S d r s	D p m g	R ; m p d r
Ti - -	Na – mos - - te	Te - - -	- - pa – ra -
S n d d	P – m g r s r m	D r s	M g R p m g r
De - - -	Va – te - - - -	Sri pati	Gauri – pati guru
M p d r	S – d p m g r m	(Sri Saraswati)	
Gu ha vinu	Te vidi yu va te		
	Sanashticharanam		
R ;	S – D ; S	S R	S ; N D
Va -	Sa nath ra	Ya vi	Var ji ja
R S	R M mg R	R p m	P ds P ;
Vara	Mu ni bha -	Vi ta -	Mur – te -
Sn D -	D – s S R	R mg	R R R S
Va - - -	Sa – vad – ya	Ki la	Mir – ja ra
D R	S N D P	M p d	P Mg Rrs
Va ra	Vi ta ra na	Ba nu -	Kir – te da ra
D d r	S r – s r m g R	P m p	D s d p d d S
Hasayu	Tamu kam buru he	At luta	Charanam buruhe
R m g	R S – D s R	S n d p	, m g r s r m
Sam sa	Ra lit ya pa he	Sa ka la man	Tra kshara guhe
			(Sri Sarasvati)

Varali Ragam **Aro : s g r g m p d n s**

Khanda Eka Talam **Ava : s n d p m g r s**

(15 Aksharas) **Dikshitar**

1_5	1_5
1) P , d p m G R	S , g R,g g m pm gr
Lam – bo - - da	Ra - - - - - - ya
S, r s n D D,g R, g	R S , rn dp dm
Na - - - mas - - - -	Te – sri - - - - - -
2) P pm mpdn dppmgr	Sg rg mp pm gr
Lam – bo - - - - - - da	Ra - - - - - - ya
Sn d gg r mpm gr	Rs S dn srs ndpm grgm
Na - - mas - - - - -	Te - - sri - - - - (lown)
Samashti charanam	
P dm gr sr G	R sn dn sn S
Kum - - ba – pa - -	Ji ta - - - - ya
S gr gm pm pd	N S Sgr rg rs
I ba – va – da – va	Vara do - - - - ya -
Gr gm pm g g rs	Sn Sr N , s dn S
A – ba – ya – va – ra -	Pra – da - - - - ya
Sn dd nd p, d pm	Gg R sn sr S
Am - - - bu – ja - - - -	Sam nu ta - - - ya
Madyamakala	
Sg – rG m p d	Dm D nd N rs
Sambaswat ma ja ya	Yam – boo kata li pala
G p m Gr – s g r s	R n d P m g r g m
Sa ra – bhakshi ta – ya	Yara – gu hagva ja - - ya (Lam)

Ragam : Sri
Talam : Khanda Eka
(2 kalai choukam)

Aro : S r m p n s
Ava : s n p m r g r s

1_5	1_5
1) N ; ; P, n p m Rgr S ; Sri - - ka – ma – law ke	Ns Rgr sr sn P N S ; g r s Sri ve- - pa - - hi man la lite
2) N ; ; S , r snpm Rg rggrs ; Sri - - ka - - ma - - law – bo – ke R p m – r g R – s N – r s – n s r m p s Sri pati vinute si ta site sivasatite	Ns rggr sr – sn np Ns ; grs Sri va - - - p – himam lalite (Sri)
Samashti Charanam R ; p n p m – m r r g – rs – ns R ; Ra – ka - - chan – dra – mu – khi M r rm P – np – p n M pnrmp ; Ra – ma – - va - - nisaki - - -	 R s n p p G R g r s r N S ; Rak - - shi ta ko - - la mu khi P M r grR – rn – np pn S, r N S ; Ra - - - ja yo - - ga su thi
Madyamakala	
R R gr – S S r s – N p m	P n s r //
Sa kam bam sa to dari chandraka	La – dari //
R r r g – r s s r – s n n s – s n p m -	R g r s //
Sankari San – kara Guruguha bhak tava	San kari //
R rs sr – mp N sr – grsr	Ns pn //
E ka – shari bhava neswar – I sa	Prtya kari //
P dn – pn pm – rgr S -	R ns – rmps //
Sri kari suka kari sri maha	Triputasundari (Sri) / /

Nava ghana raga malika varnam of Veena Kuppaiyar

1 4	O	O
Pallavi .Ragam : Nata		
P p m – m m r s – s n r r s – s n p	S n s r s – m r s	P m r – S r g m
In - - tha - - ko - - pa - -	Me - - - la - -	Ra - - - - -
Pm – pnp – snpmgm – pdns	S snp – snp	Mrs – Srgm
Im – ti - - pai - - ni - - -	Sa - - - ni - -	Ni - - ku - - -
Anupallavi – Ragam ; gaula		
S rp pmgm – rrsn – pnsr	S N – srm – rm	Pn – mp NS
Chem – ta - - je - - ri - - -	Na - - - - nu	- - pam - - ta
P n s Rr – p m g m – r r s n p n	S r s Sn – pn	P – pm – gmrm
Me - - - - la - - - ra - - - sri	Ka - - la – has	- tee – swa – ra -
Chitaswaram -Ragam : varali		
P m – d p m G – g r sn – dpdn	S , - r r s – g r	G M – Pd mg
Grs – ggrg – m pdp nndp	Dns – ndp	Grgm p d p
Chitaswaram -Ragam : Arabhi		
M g r – s r m g r – pmg – rmpd	p-mgr-srmp	Dd pm – pds
Pds Rr – srmgr – Rsnd	P dr S – mpd	P – mgr srm (In)
Charanam Ragam : Sri		
P R – s r s n P – p n s n S	N s r g r s – n p	P m r g r s r m
Pan cha sa – ru – ni ba – - ri	Kor – - va – fa	La - - du ra - -
1) P ; ; N ; M ; P	R ; ; G	, R S R M (pancha)
Narayanan Gaula		
2) pndn – Snd – pdmp-gmrg	Rss – N n d p	N d n – S R m(pancha)
Riti Gaula		
3]N n d m – g r g m – d p m g r s n p	N S – n g r gm	Nndn – nnS
N s g r g m g s – g g m g r – ng r	N s n dm – M	Grs – ngrgm (pancha)
Bowli		
4].Pd – gpd gd – pgrg – rsnd	P D – s r g P	D pd – sndP
Dp – dg – pr – gp – gpdsnd – gr	, snd – r Sn	Dp – d P grg (pancha)
Kedaram		
5]S ; ; - sn Pm – Grsn	S ; ; - sn	Sr – sm gm pn
P S – s mgrs – mGr – srsm	P S n p m G	, m g m p n p s
S m g – g r s R , - s r s n p m g	, r s m g r s r	, r s n p s S
Pm – mg gr – smgm – pssngr	S s n – p m P	Mgr – smgm (pancha)

Ragam : Gaula (Janya of 15th Mela) **Aro : S r m p n s**
Talam : Adi **Ava: s n p m r g m r s**
Composer: Jnana sambandar

1_4	O	O
R P P M G M R S	S r s s r s n	P m p n s ;
Jam – ki ta ta ri ki ta	Ta ki ta ki ta tha ka	Ta ri ki ta tha
Sr ss rr mr – rs – mr – pm – np	Nnp Nnp	Pmr rpm
Thak kita kita taka tari kita talca	Taki ta thi kita	Tom thari kita tha
P n s N P p m g m R ;	S P N S	R ; S ;
Po di – pada vel - - van -	Gum – va di	Ve – ban
Vi nai ya ra to tha ma na	Me - - ja	Ya – ja ya
R R r Ppp Rrr Mmm	S R r S s n	P R R ;
To kumku tom kuku tom kuku tak kuku	Talangu that thari	Toha dit tham
S ; ; - S R S S ;	S r s rr ss	S r ss P pm
Tom - - tha ki ta tha	Tomkita kita thaka	Kita thaka Tom kita
P n p p n n p p S s n r r s s	R g m R S	S r r s N P
Tom ta ku ku ku ku tomta tomkita thari kita	Nam ta ka tom ta	Ta kardira ta thim
P R G M R S N S	S , R , N	; S R ;
Tha ka ja nu tha ka tha -	Tha dit tha	- ta dim
R , R , pm G M R ;	R , M , P	; N P ;
Chik kal me - - vi ya -	Tha – va the	- va sin -
S r s n P M p n r s R R	P N R s S	R ; ; ;
Ga - - - - ra va – la – va -	Va di ve – la	Va - - -
S R M r S s R S n P	P N s n p M	P R s R ;
Me du va gi ya pa tha pan ka ja	Ma yi le – ri ye	O – di va -
S s r G M R S R r s	S N P M	R S R ;
Tha tari ki ta tha ka di ki ta	Tha ka di mi	Ki ta diu
R P ; p m p m g m R ;	R ; ; p m	P ; ; ;
Ni nai – na – na - - - me	Kam - - da –	Nai - - -
P N p , M p m g m R ;	S r p m g m R	S ; ; ;
Ma n ava the yen - - - rum	Kan - - - - tha	Nai - - -
R M P n P – m P N s P	P N R r S	P R R ; ,
Aram da na turan dai t avam	Marau dai ni you	Pi ran dai - -
S r m R , p n s n p ; P	R S s – p n p	, p p m g m r s
Tha – ma tham chey –n ya mal – ach	Chin gara gam bi	Ra oy – ya – ramai
S r s R p m p n p m M p m	S r s r m r s	S r g m r s n s
Tha ta ka dit taka ta ku di ku dit ta ka	Ta ta ta jam – ta ri	Tokundari kta take
S s n p n s r S ; N n p	M p N p ;	P p m r g m
Tha ta ka ta ka dina tam – dif thaka	Ta ta dif ram	Tom taka taka tat
R ; ; ; P M P ;	R G M ;	M S R ;
Thom - - - - ta ka tham	Dik ke dim	Tha ka ta
S ; ; R – S ; ; P	N ; ; R	S ; ; ;
Tham - - dit tam ja	Din ta	Tham - -

Ragam : Arabi (29 th Mela) **Aro : S r m p d s**

Chatusra Laghu (4 Aksharas) **Avo: s n d p m g r s**

1_4	1_4
D r s n d d P Ta ri kita ta ka Tom	M g r s n d S Ta ka ta ri ki ta ta
Drs Rmg Rpm pdp Takita dikita Domkita takota	RMp ddpp mgrs rmp Tirukka zhukunram Vezhun malai
Dd pm pd S Ve – da – gi – ri	Drs Rmg rrsn Dsn Tomkita dikita kitataka namkita
Dks mgrs Rsn ddss Takumta takadina dikta kitataka	Dd rs R sn Chota muga nam sri
D d p p d p mg De-viyum ka – viri	R R sn D S Yum su ri – ya num
S n d d s r S Ja pan – gal chey ya	R p m g rs – mpds dp Ta – pan – gal chey - - - ya
P d d s sn D sr Uyarntha na - - yagar	Sr mg R rsD s s Uyarm - - tha Na - - yaki
S n d r S S A z ha giya maindau	R r s n D s r m g R Tarikita ta kita taka tom
S r mg r r d s r m r s Pa – ram – tha ner - - - riyil	Drsn dp Dis r r Ti – ru – niru Anin – tha
DDd sss rRr snD Talaugu Takumta kukunta kita tom	Dddd ssss rrrr mgrr Toka tari kitataka kitataka tarikita
DDd , r S ; Ta ta ta – fam ta	
Dd rs snd dp Po- ritta Sa-ma narai	PDp dpmg rsR Edirtu ka-zhu vi – nil
Srmg r r dpmg rs Amai - - - tha sam - - bandar	DRs sn dd S Ka - - vuth tuva me
R r mp dd sn Ta kun dari kita taka	S ndp mg rs Rmg rs Toka janu tari kita kita taka
R , R , S Ta dim ta	R , Rmg r r rsnd Dim ta tari kita taka dina
S ; S R Tam – ta dit	S ; S S Tam - tat ta

Ragam : Sri (22nd Janya) **Aro : s r m p n s**

Talam: Chatusra Eka **Avo: s n p m r g r s**

14	14
R ; ; G ; R S N	P ; ; N ; S r g r s
Ta - - tai – ta ta ka	Tai - - ta – ta kita taka
N ; ; N ; ; S N	P ; ; N ; ; S ;
Ta - - tai - - tai	Ta - - tat - - ta
R g g r R ; G r R s	S r g R S S N N P
Ta ri ki ta fam – taka tat tam	Tat tari ki ta ti ku ta ku
S N S ; P G R S	R ; ; ; R S S ;
Gum ta kum Nam – kut ta	Ri - - - nam - - -
R R G ; G R S ;	R rm M P Pnn PM
Tiru – var – ru - dau	Namtari kita tatari kita
P p p n pn p m pnsn S S	P pg R R Rgr SS
Ta ta ki ta ki ta ta ki ta ta ka ta ti	Ta ta ka Tomta Tomkuku Tom tom
S r s s – r s n n – p n p p r r S	S , r s n P – p d n p M
Takadimi dimitaka Ta – kita tadi	Ta – dik kudan diku – toku
R ; ; R – R G g r r s	S ; ; ; r m p n sn p m
Dan - - di kinnam tai - - -	Ta - - - kin – na – tom – taka
R ; ; r m p n – s n p m R	; ; R ; ; S ; ;
Tam - - takedina tarikitatath	- - dit - - tam - -

Ragam : Varali (39th mela) **Aro : S g r g m p d n s**

Talam : Chatusra Eka (4 Aksharas) **Avo: s n d p m g r s**

14	14
G G mp d p	M p d – n d p d m
Tat dim ta ka di mi	Ta di mi di mi ta ta ka
P M G G R S	P m g r g g r s
Ta ka dim dim ta ka	A nau tha mu ni fa na
D d g r r – g m p	S n d n P D
Sa va la sa ra A sa ra	Sa mu ta pa da
N n d p m g g r	P m g g r r s
Kin – ki ni janu jam	Ja nu tat jance jam
N s n d n r s	G m g p – g d p m
P ra na – la ya gati	Gam gana gana gana
S n d d d n s r	S , D , M
Sau – nutha Se – vi ta	Tam – tat – ta
S , r S S	G p m grsn srgr rssn
Tam – ta tam ta	Ta jam kita taka taka tari kita taka
P d n d d n r s	S s G r s n d n s r s n d p m
Padau jali vyag raga	To ka tai ta ri kita takatari kita taka
P d n s n d p m	G m p dndp pmg rrsn
Vy ag raga san k (k) ra	Tom ki ta kita taka tom – ta kita taka
S D N s r s	G g r g m p d p
Tris ra su la da ra	Nan – di – kes – vara
D m D n r s	RrG grsn srG grsn
Nada yo ga priya	Ta ka jan kitataka jamta kitataka
Dnss nrss nss S	Gg rr ss nn
Daku kuku kukudaka kum da tai	Ja nu jaya jaya janu
Dnsr Snd pdns Ndp	Mpd pmG Gpm gos
Ra – Vi – Cha – si lan - - kru	Ru - - pa ba yam – ka – ra
Gmpd ndpm gr S	Grgm gmpd
Da – ma – ru – ka – has tam	Tridi – ya sahasra
N d s n n r S	R g s r n r S
Di – hata na – da	Na te – sa kavet vam
S n g r S s n gr S	G r Gr Sr
Ta ka tat tam taka kota tam	Takka dikku taka
Srgr S srg rsN	S, S, S ,
Ki ta taka tam tom kita tari kita	Tat tat tam
Nsr sn – rsgr	S ; ; ;
Dam tari kita kita taka	Tam - -

Tanas in Ghana ragas

I Raga – Nata

1. g m p – np – n s s – g n p – np – s s m
pn – ps – s m s – smp – np – mmp
mm-gmp-gmp-np-Nss//

2. gmp – np – snrp – snpn – Mp -
gmp – npsn – pnp – dus – pdns –
rs – np – mrs – s – Pp – np – Se -
Ssrs – mrs – rgm – sm – rs – np –
mpdns – r S n s – S //

3. Ssmp – mrs – rgmp – dms – rgm –
Sm – rs – np – mp – dms – ssN –
S – ss – rs – n – SS //

4. m M pmp – smp – smp – nn – MMp –
Mp – NN – Mpnp – snp – Mps -
snp – Np – dup – pdn – srgm –
Smrc – npmpdnsrsm ss –
Mrs – rg – n ss//

5. Pssnp – mpnn – pmpn – pssn –
Pnpssm – pnpss – pn – MP –
Gmp – rgmp – mpnp – ssm –
Pupm – pnpssm sms – rs –
Mrs – pdns – rs – mrs – smp –
Dns – rs – nss – rs – N – SS –
Mrs – NS – S – pmmrs – rsN – SS//

Ragam : Gowlai II

1. R S – r r s r r s – n s – r r s – n s r –
   S r – s s r – s s n p – s n p p n p m p – r r s –
   R s N S S//
2. r r s – s r – s s r – s s n p – s n p – s n p m p – m m p –
   mm – rgm – mrs – rm – rm p – rm p – n p s n p –
   n p – r r s r s – N S S//
3. n s r M – r r m R s s r – s s s – s n p – m r s –
   r m p n p – s n p - p m p – N M p – p m p – m m –
   r g m – m R s – r m – r m p – r m p – n p – sm p –
   m p – r r s r s – N S S //
4. r r s – rr s – s r s s – s n p – p s s n p – p s n p – p s n p
   n s r m r p p m r r s – s r s s r s – s s n s – p m p n –
   s r p p m r – r p p m p m r – g m r s – ns –
   rmr – rmrs – nsrmrs-snpnp-rrs
   rsn SS//
5. r r m r – sr – s r s n p – s s n p – s s s n p – p n p
   - p m p – mysnp – up – mp - m
   rgmmrs – rmprrm – r m m p – rmp – np – mp
   np-snp-pssnp-psnssnp-mprrs -
   r s n SS //
6. r r m – r r s – s r – s s r – s s s – s p – p m p – s n p
   n s r r – s r p – p m r – p m p p r – Pm – p p – n p
   - p p m g – m m r – S r p m – rmp-pn – p pm -
   mpnmr – pmr – gm – r s r m – r r S – s r s s
   S n p – pm – pm r s – sn p – m p r r s – r s n SS//
7. S s n p – p n p n p m m – p m m r – g m r s
   N s r – snp-rsrp – P p p m – s s n p – r r s n m
   R m m p – p n p p m – m p m r – gm r s – n s n sn p
   R s n – SS //
8. n n P P m p m m r – mpnp-Pm – psnppm
   gm Mrrmmp – pnppm – m p m r – g m r s
   n s r p – m p g m – r g m – r s s r
   s r r s – r s n SS//
9. p p m – r m r – p p M – rgm – r s – n s r – s n p m p
   r r s r s – SS //
10. m r r – s n - p m p n – sr g – m r s n s – rSn
    p m p – n s r – n s r s n p – nr n n SS //

III Ragam : Arabhi

1. r S – snd – snddpd – dRrs – rnnss //.

2. d s s r s r – m g r m g r – r s s n – ddpd – drsr – s n SS //

3. r s s r s n – d r s n d – s n d s n d – d p d d – p M p
d d p m r m g r – r s r m – r m p – r m p – d p d – s s r
s r m g r m g r s – s n d d p d – d r r s – r s n SS//

4. d d p p m p – d m p d s – s r s r m g r s – n d r s n d s
n d d p – d d p – M p d – d p m g r – m g r r s – r m – r m p
- d s s r – d d r – d d p – d r r – s r – m g r – m g r r -
s n d d p – d d r r - r s n SS //

5. M M P m p d – m p d s s r – m p d d – m p – pdds
M p d – m p m g r – m m p m g r – m p m g r – m g r r s
R r m – r m p – m p d – m p d p s r – s r m g r – m m p -
m g r m p – m g r p p m g r – p m m g r – m g r r s
s n d d p – m g r – m p – m g r – P p – m g r – p m m g r
M g r r s – s n d d p – d d r r s – r s n SS//

IV Ragam Sri

1. ssr-srg – rgrrs-grs-sr-ssr-ssnnp
snp – pnp – m p r r s – r s n S S//

2. S S n –r g r R – g r s – s s G r s – srss
- S n s p – pp Mr – mmp – np – m
nsrg – rgrs – gRs – s r s – ss n p M p – n n s
n s r g – r s s n p – g r s – s r s – s p n p – m p n n SS – n n SS //

3. rgrssrm – M p M r p p n n p m – m p m r – r g r s – g o s s
rsssnp – M p – n n s – ssr
grssnp – Grs – S-ssn-pMr – r m m p -
m m p Pr – p m m r – p m r r – g r s – s r – s s n p –
m p n n s – sn – n SS //

4. P – p p Mr – m m p – p n p – m p – m p – n n s – n s r g r –
Grs – n s r – g r s – s r – s s n – s n p m – p m p – n n s
S n N – SS //

5. S-ss-nnp-mpnns-ssn SS - //

6. n s r S r – s s n p – m p n s r S r – s s n p n s r
- s s r s- s s n p – s r p n p n s – n n SS //

KAIVARA PRBANDHA

RAGA – NATA **TALA : RUPAKA**

O	1_4	O	1_4	O	1_4	O	1_4
PP	Ss	Ns	s s	s s	ssnp	s s	rssr
Dugudgu	Tham tham	Ta tha	Tham tham	Than ta	Tahnta ta	Ta ta	Ta ta dhi ki
m	pn P	M m	M m m m	M p	M m r s	S s	S s s s
Ta	Taku jham	Ja ga	- - - -	Jham	Tan takita	Yaki	Yatatrite
Mr	S s m s	S s	S r s	Sm	P s n	R	M m
Dhetam	- dhalam	Jajhem	Tai jhem	Tra	Them tai	Tam	Dham
Mr	S s n p	Sp	P p p p	P s	S s s s	M	P ;
Ta	Dhimikita	Tu tu	Dagna	Todiga	- - - -	Dam	Dhrem
Mr	Ssrg	Mr	ssnp	s s	ssss	pn	PP
Tu thu	ratuthuru	Jhem ta	Aita aiki	To di	Tathadhiga	Tana	Kujham
Pp	Nn ss	Nn	S s m	Ps	S S m	Ps	S s s m
Danga	- - - -	- -	Namgina	Kina	Nogima	Nam	Namgima
Pm	Mmrc	Ss	Mpmm	Mr	Sssm	Pm	Mmrs
Kinam	Taitha	Rita	Nitataya	- la	Kujan ta	Jhom	Jhanta